CASH AND CARE

Policy challenges in the welfare state

Edited by Caroline Glendinning and Peter A. Kemp

First published in Great Britain in September 2006 by

The Policy Press
University of Bristol
Fourth Floor
Beacon House
Queen's Road
Bristol BS8 1QU
UK

Tel +44 (0)117 331 4054
Fax +44 (0)117 331 4093
e-mail tpp-info@bristol.ac.uk
www.policypress.org.uk

British Library Cataloguing in Publication Data
A catalogue record for this book is available from the British Library.

Library of Congress Cataloging-in-Publication Data
A catalog record for this book has been requested.

ISBN-10 1 86134 856 8 paperback
ISBN-13 978 1 86134 856 2 paperback
ISBN-10 1 86134 857 6 hardcover
ISBN-13 978 1 86134 857 9 hardcover

Cover design by Qube Design Associates, Bristol.
Printed and bound in Great Britain by MPG Books Ltd, Bodmin.

Contents

List of figures and tables

Figures

Tables

Foreword

Professor Sally Baldwin

This book is dedicated to the memory of Professor Sally Baldwin, who was killed in an accident in Rome on 28 October 2003 at the age of 62, after a career at the University of York that spanned over 30 years.

The eldest daughter in a large West of Scotland family, Sally carried caring responsibilities at an early age as a result of her parents' illness and early death. After obtaining a first-class degree in English Language and Literature at the University of Glasgow, she worked briefly in Bruges and Edinburgh before moving to the University of York for postgraduate study. She took the Diploma in Social Administration with distinction in 1973 and was almost immediately appointed as the first research fellow in a group created at the University of York to evaluate the work of the Family Fund. This group later became the Social Policy Research Unit (SPRU).

Sally became Director of SPRU in 1987 and was made Professor in 1990. Under her leadership, the Unit doubled in size and established its reputation as a national centre of excellence for research on social security, disablement and policies for carers. Her own research encompassed all these fields and she was one of the first to articulate the links between social security policy and community care. Sally's doctoral research was a pioneering study of the financial costs to parents of a severely disabled child, published as *The costs of caring: Families with disabled children* (Routledge, 1985). Eventually this work contributed to the introduction of enhanced rates for disabled children in our current social security benefits and tax credits systems. This is a remarkable example of the impact of research evidence on policy and an important legacy of her work.

While Sally was Director, SPRU initiated a programme of research on the outcomes of social care, especially in relation to older people, disabled adults and their carers. This innovative work identified the outcomes that individuals themselves hoped to gain from care services, as well as the outcomes that professionals considered important. This emphasis on the needs, views and preferences of beneficiaries and recipients of service provision was arguably the defining interest and concern of her research. Long before it was fashionable to talk about 'joined-up' policy and practice, she argued that it was important to recognise that people's lives do not divide into neat segments distinguished by professional and organisational boundaries. She also undertook research on informal carers of people with mental health problems, a stream of research on deafness and ran a continual critical eye over community care policy.

After retiring as Director of SPRU in March 2002, Sally began to develop a new stream of research funded by the Economic and Social Research Council, which sought to undertake systematic reviews in social policy.

Beyond university life, Sally was a founding member of the Academy of Learned Societies for the Social Sciences, a trustee of the Family Fund, a member of the Executive of the Disability Alliance and Chair of the Association of Directors of Research Centres in the Social Sciences. She acted as advisor to many research funders, including the NHS R&D Programme. Locally, she served as a member of the York Community Health Council and was a Non-Executive Director of the York NHS Trust. In this role, as in others, she strove to translate research evidence into improved services. She was robust and determined in her advocacy of improved patient care, particularly in local cancer care provision and mental health.

Sally had very high academic standards and believed that rigorous, dispassionate research could and should improve social policy and practice. She was a most supportive colleague, very good at spotting and encouraging research talent, and many rising stars learned the trade under her calm and perceptive leadership. Sally really did make the connections between 'cash' and 'care'. These qualities are likely to be her most lasting achievement.

Jonathan Bradshaw
Department of Social Policy and Social Work, University of York

Acknowledgements

This edited collection originated in a conference held at the University of York in April 2005 to commemorate the contribution made to social policy research by Professor Sally Baldwin. The conference was made possible through financial support from the Department of Health and the Economic and Social Research Council (ESRC). Additional support was provided by the UK Social Policy Association. We are very grateful to Professor Waqar Ahmad (Middlesex University), Dr David Guy (ESRC) and Professor Gillian Parker (University of York) for helping to make the conference happen. Thanks are also due to Professor Saul Becker for his support. The support staff team in Social Policy Research Unit (SPRU) at the University of York helped to make the conference a great success.

Many people in SPRU assisted in preparing the typescript for this book and we are particularly indebted to them for their hard work in the face of challenging deadlines. Alison McKay and Sally Pulleyn prepared the typescript for publication; Ruth Dowling checked and chased missing references; and Lorna Foster scrutinised the final typescript with her customary expertise.

We are grateful to Philip de Bary and Emily Watt at The Policy Press for their patience, support and encouragement. Above all, we wish to thank all our contributors for their unfailing good nature and patience in responding to our increasingly urgent queries and requests.

Caroline Glendinning, University of York
Peter A. Kemp, University of Oxford
April 2006

Notes on contributors

Hilary Arksey is Senior Research Fellow in the Social Policy Research Unit (SPRU) at the University of York, UK. Her research interests are in the areas of informal care, employment and disability, and qualitative research methods. Hilary's recent publications include *Carers' aspirations and decisions around work and retirement*, which she co-authored, published by the Department for Work and Pensions in 2005.

Peter Beresford is Professor of Social Policy and Director of the Centre for Citizen Participation at Brunel University, UK. He is Chair of Shaping Our Lives, the national user-controlled organisation, and Visiting Fellow at the School for Social Work and Psychosocial Science at the University of East Anglia, UK.

Jef Breda is Professor of Sociology and Organisation Theory at the University of Antwerp, Belgium. His research concerns the changing institutional structure of social care provisions and the ambiguity of the social protection of older people in an ageing society.

Dries Claessens is a graduate in Social Work and Sociology. He is a lecturer on the Bachelor of Social Work programme at Hogeschool Antwerpen, Belgium. His theoretical and research interests are broadly situated in the interface between social theory and social work.

Sharon Collard is Research Fellow at the Personal Finance Research Centre, based at the University of Bristol, UK. Since joining the Centre in 1998, she has worked on a wide range of research projects, exploring topics such as the use of credit and other financial services by low-income consumers; the provision of money advice and debt counselling services; and financial capability. In a personal capacity, Sharon is on the Management Committee of Bristol Debt Advice Centre.

Naomi Finch is a Research Councils UK Academic Fellow in SPRU, University of York, UK. Her research has covered the areas of child poverty, family policy and comparative social policy. Her current research interests focus on pensioner poverty.

Joanna Geerts is Research Assistant in the Department of Sociology at the University of Antwerp, Belgium, where she is preparing a PhD thesis. Her research interests include the health status and care needs of the oldest old people, the interface between formal and informal care, and care policy and planning.

Caroline Glendinning is Professor of Social Policy and Assistant Director of SPRU at the University of York, UK, where she manages a Department of Health-funded research programme on Choice and Independence across the Lifecourse. She has a longstanding research interest in policy and practice at the interfaces between cash and care.

Pernille Hohnen has a PhD in Social Anthropology and works as Senior Researcher at The Danish National Institute of Social Research, Copenhagen, Denmark. Her research interests are within the field of economic anthropology and welfare; she has carried out several research projects concerning consumption, moral economy, and social and symbolic marginalisation. Her dissertation on economic, social and symbolic changes in post-communist Lithuania was published as *A market out of place? Remaking economic, social and symbolic boundaries in post-communist Lithuania* by Oxford University Press (2003).

Peter A. Kemp is Barnett Professor of Social Policy at the University of Oxford. He was previously Professor of Social Policy and Director of SPRU at the University of York, UK. Having spent many years studying housing policy, his research interests now include poverty, social security, carers and welfare to work.

Margareta Kreimer is Lecturer in the Department of Economics at the University of Graz, Austria. Her research interests include the theory and politics of employment markets; the impacts of economic, fiscal and social policies, particularly on women; and feminist economics.

Hilary Land is Emeritus Professor of Family Policy and, since 2002, Honorary Senior Research Fellow in the School of Policy Studies at the University of Bristol, UK. She is currently writing on care across the generations and, in particular, the contribution of grandmothers. She is a member of the Management Committee of the Women's Budget Group.

Jane Lewis is Professor of Social Policy at the London School of Economics and Political Science, and a Fellow of the British Academy. She has a longstanding research interest in gender, family change and family policies. Her recent books include *The end of marriage? Individualism and intimate relationships* (Edward Elgar, 2001) and *Should we worry about family change?* (University of Toronto Press, 2003).

Eithne McLaughlin is Professor of Social Policy at the Queen's University of Belfast. Her research interests include equality, disability and child poverty. She was Chair of the UK Social Policy Association 1999-2000 and a member of the Commission for Social Justice 1992-94. She is an Equality Commissioner for Northern Ireland.

Jane Millar is Professor of Social Policy and Director of the Centre for the Analysis of Social Policy at the University of Bath, UK. Her research interests are in family policy; social security and tax policy; poverty, inequality and social exclusion; and comparative social policy. Recent publications include the edited collection, *Understanding social security* (The Policy Press, 2003).

Jenny Morris is an independent researcher and policy analyst in the UK. Recent work includes being a consultant to the Prime Minister's Strategy Unit for the White Paper *Improving the life chances of disabled people*; work for the Disability Rights Commission on citizenship and disabled people and on the implications for social care of the Disability Equality Duty; a Knowledge Review for the Social Care Institute for Excellence on supporting disabled parents; and a Resource Guide for Local Safeguarding Children Boards on safeguarding disabled children.

Jan Pahl is Professor of Social Policy at the University of Kent, UK, and co-editor of the *Journal of Social Policy*. Her main research interest is the allocation of money within households, but she has also carried out research on domestic violence; on families caring for children with disabilities; and on various aspects of health and social care.

Karen Postle has a background in counselling and family and neighbour mediation. She teaches on the social work programmes at the University of East Anglia, UK, and works in a voluntary capacity as a neighbour mediator. Her research interests are in the areas of community care and social work education and practice.

Tess Ridge is Lecturer in Social Policy at the University of Bath, UK. Her research interests are childhood poverty and social exclusion, and children and family policy, especially support for children and families. She has considerable experience researching with children and families, and has recently completed a three-year ESRC Research Fellowship developing a child-centred approach to understanding how children fare within the policy process.

Peter Saunders has been Director of the Social Policy Research Centre at the University of New South Wales in Sydney, Australia, since 1987. He has conducted extensive research on poverty, inequality, household needs and living standards and has published widely on these topics. He has served as consultant to a range of international bodies including the Organisation for Economic Co-operation and Development, the International Monetary Fund, the Asian Development Bank and the Royal Commission on Social Policy in New Zealand.

David Schoenmaekers is a graduate in Sociology and Research Assistant with the Research Unit on Welfare and the Welfare State at the University of Antwerp, Belgium. In his research activities, he has evaluated the experimental phase of the Flanders Personal Assistance Budgets. Other research interests include the life conditions of older people and care use by children and youth.

Christine Skinner is Lecturer in the Department of Social Policy and Social Work at the University of York, UK. Her research interests focus on family policy generally and most recently on childcare and the work–life balance. Publications include 'Co-ordination points: a hidden factor in reconciling work and family life', an article in the *Journal of Social Policy* (2005).

Caroline Van Landeghem is a graduate in Pedagogy and Sociology. She has conducted research into the Flanders Personal Assistance Budgets (2003) and has worked as a coordinator with a disability organisation. She has a special interest in social services and is currently preparing a PhD thesis at the University of Antwerp, Belgium, on the sociology of organisations.

Kari Wærness is Professor of Sociology at the University of Bergen, Norway. Her research has covered the areas of social policy and family sociology, with particular emphasis on work and women, and on the relationship between unpaid care in the family and formally organised health and social services.

Part One
Introduction

ONE

Introduction

Peter A. Kemp and Caroline Glendinning

This book examines the twin issues of cash and care – and the relationships between them – in the contemporary welfare state. Traditionally, 'cash' has referred to earnings and the range of income maintenance measures such as social security benefits, pensions and tax credits that are provided through or on behalf of the welfare state. In contrast, 'care' has included both the care of non-disabled children and the range of practical, personal and social support needed by long-term sick, disabled and older people, whether provided by the statutory, voluntary, private or informal sector. 'Care' provided by the welfare state has typically been delivered in the form of services in kind.

However, this traditional distinction has begun to break down. For example, there has been a partial shift in both Britain and in other developed welfare societies towards providing payments or subsidies that enable people to purchase or otherwise fund their own support arrangements. The clearest examples of this are 'direct payments' (or personal budgets in some other countries), which allow disabled and older people to employ their own personal assistants. Similar cash payments or subsidies have been introduced to (partially) substitute or compensate for the care provided for children by their parents, usually their mothers. This latter example also illustrates the blurring of the cash and care divide in relation to income protection policies, with the shift from a 'passive' to an 'active' approach for people of working age. Thus, financial support for the childcare costs of low-income families, provided in Britain through tax credit arrangements, is part of a package of measures to encourage the movement from social security benefits into paid employment. Furthermore, instead of simply being entitled to social security benefits by virtue of unemployment, disability or caregiving responsibilities, people of working age who claim benefits are encouraged (and in some cases required) to undertake work-related activities ranging from attendance at work-focused interviews to participation in formal welfare-to-work programmes. These are all part of a shift from passive to active forms of welfare. Although these work-related activities are not care as defined above, they nonetheless reflect income maintenance activities provided through the welfare state that go beyond simple cash payments. Other income maintenance-related 'care' services include childcare, breakfast and after-school clubs and other activities that, while potentially important for child development, also enable parents (particularly mothers) to participate in the labour market.

The increasingly blurred boundaries between cash and care policies are responses to the fundamental social and economic changes that have taken place in recent decades (Esping-Andersen, 2002). These trends include the decline of the married male breadwinner family, in which the husband was the only or main breadwinner and the wife remained at home to take care of housework, childcare and any support required by disabled or older people (Lewis, 1992; Land, 1994). Instead, there has been a long-term rise in the labour market participation of women, including mothers, a trend not peculiar to Britain. There has also been an increase in the prevalence of cohabitation and of single-adult households. The latter in part reflects an increase in divorce and relationship breakdown and a marked growth in the number of lone-parent families. Meanwhile, an increase in repartnering has led to a growth in reconstituted families and hence considerably more complex and fragmented family structures than in the recent past. In addition, a long-term decrease in fertility rates, combined with increased longevity, mean that most developed societies are ageing, with increases not just in the number of people above state pension age, but also in the numbers of older and very old people with additional support needs, many of whom also live alone.

As well as these demographic trends, there have been important economic changes that have potential implications for both cash and care policies. A growth in service sector employment has provided new employment opportunities, especially for women and, more generally, for people with educational qualifications and 'soft skills'. Meanwhile, the long-term decline in manufacturing and the economic restructuring of the last two decades of the 20th century have been associated with a fall in employment rates among older men, especially those who have few qualifications or skills, and people in poor health. These developments are reflected in marked increases in the numbers and proportions of men and women who are economically inactive and recipients of Incapacity Benefits. An increasing proportion of the latter have mental health problems such as depression, anxiety and stress – what Overbye (2005) has referred to as the 'new disabilities' – in contrast to more obvious physical impairments. Moreover, although unemployment has fallen and employment has risen in Britain since the early 1990s, the number of workless households has remained relatively high.

Like many other advanced welfare states, the British government has introduced a raft of welfare to work initiatives and programmes, which are designed to reduce unemployment and economic inactivity. An important aim of such policies is to reduce the number of households in poverty or experiencing social exclusion. This strategy is consistent with the claim that 'work is the surest route out of poverty' (DSS, 1998, p 3). But while there is some empirical evidence for this assertion (see, for example, Jenkins and Rigg, 2001), work is not a guaranteed escape route, especially for those disabled people or people with substantial care commitments who are unable to take up paid employment. Consequently, social security benefits and other income transfers remain important tools to reduce the poverty rate. In this respect the New Labour government in Britain has repeatedly characterised its social security policy as 'work for those who can, security for those who cannot' (DSS, 1998, p iii).

The increasing emphasis on paid work is not just about tackling poverty; it is also part of a strategy to raise employment rates in the face of global economic competition (DWP, 2005b). Relevant measures in Britain include the various New Deal employment programmes, including those for lone parents, disabled people and partners of benefit claimants, and the extension of work-focused interviews to people claiming Carer's Allowance because they have very substantial caregiving responsibilities that impede their earning capacity. All these measures aim to encourage groups of people who were previously exempt from work-search requirements to consider taking steps towards moving into paid work. In other words, they aim to shift as many people as possible into the 'work for those who can' category (Hewitt, 1999). By increasing the size of the labour force, such measures are assumed to help contain wage inflation and are especially important to counteract changes in dependency ratios following the decline in the proportion of working-age people and the increasing number of people over state pension age.

However, the welfare-to-work strategy raises important questions about the work of caregiving, at both practical and theoretical levels. At a practical level, substitute care arrangements are necessary to enable parents (both lone and partnered) and those supporting disabled and older relatives to take up, and remain in, paid work. But, as numerous studies have shown, parents' perceptions of the quality, cost and availability of formal childcare services remain an important barrier to work. Moreover, policies for the care of frail older people, in Britain and many other countries, are based on assumptions about the continuing availability of significant volumes of unpaid informal or only quasi-formal care. These assumptions are not consistent with policies that aim to increase the proportions of women engaged in formal paid employment. It could be argued that informal care is a 'new social risk' (Bonoli, 2005a; Taylor-Gooby, 2005) that should be covered by the social security system. However, despite the elaboration of new theoretical approaches to the work of care, particularly the arguments for policies based on an 'ethics of care' (Sevenhuijsen, 2002), progress in developing policies that give proper value to care has been slow. One consequence of this has been the failure to tackle longstanding problems of gender equity and injustice, despite the significant increases in women's labour market participation.

The emphasis on paid employment as the means of maintaining economic competitiveness at a societal level, and as the main route out of poverty and social exclusion at an individual level, risks marginalising those who cannot work because of illness; who have exited the labour market because of age; or who prioritise looking after close relatives (children or older people) because of normative beliefs or a perceived lack of alternative options. The economic risks associated with disability and with the provision of support and care to relatives cut across 'traditional' forms of disadvantage caused by income, social class, gender and 'race'. Moreover, the social exclusion and reduced opportunities that are often associated with caregiving and disability are exacerbated by these traditional forms of disadvantage. While there has been much emphasis on 'work for those who can', less attention appears to have been given to the notion and reality of 'security for those who cannot' (Becker, 2003).

Another significant trend, begun during the neoconservatism of the 1970s and 1980s but not subsequently reversed, has been the introduction and growing penetration of market relationships into hitherto predominantly public sector welfare. Examples include the privatisation of former public services, the introduction of private financing and growth in user co-payments, the use of contracts as a dominant coordinating mechanism and quasi-markets more generally (Bartlett et al, 1998). These changes reflect critiques of the welfare state, not just from the right of the political spectrum but also from some parts of the left. The latter critiques include campaigning and evidence presented by new social movements concerned with the rights of women, minority ethnic groups and disabled people, groups who are traditionally heavy users of public services (Williams, 1999).

From more right-wing perspectives, the marketisation of the welfare state represents a response to the growth of individualism and rising consumer expectations about service delivery, which have led to calls for more user involvement and choice. One response to these critiques has been the substitution of cash payments, subsidies and vouchers for services in kind, on the assumption that the former options offer greater 'consumer' choice. However, such market-style options also depend upon the commodification of care and, as they have major implications for how care is supported, organised, delivered and paid for, also bring us back to considering the 'ethics of care'.

Some commentators have argued that consumer-style approaches to choice undermine the collective provision of welfare (Needham, 2003). However, for others increasing choice is a way of ensuring that the welfare state can survive, by making it more responsive to the needs and aspirations of those who use it. The clearest example of the latter perspective is evidence from disabled people using direct payments of the increased choice and control over their lives that such cash payments bring. But while direct payments and other types of vouchers and cash subsidies may increase choice and autonomy, they can also shift at least some 'transaction costs' associated with procuring, coordinating and reimbursing appropriate sources of support from the state to the individual. Cash payments also increase opportunities to introduce strict cash limits to both individual entitlements and collective welfare expenditure. Thus, payments to support the informal care of older people are usually well below the actual value of the work involved and require additional inputs of unpaid labour from informal carers; very low-paid and often unprotected labour from paid care workers; and/or the private purchase of additional services by older people and their families. Cash payment substitutes for care therefore have potentially negative implications for the social rights of both unpaid and low-paid carers, including their rights to social protection and pensions. Thus, while the increasing emphasis on independence, choice and user involvement may represent a step forward from the traditional producer-led public sector welfare state, they also create new tensions in relation to care work that are far from resolved.

This book explores these issues in depth. Part Two sets the scene by discussing new perspectives on care and justice and the role of evidence in policy making in relation to cash and care. Part Three reviews existing evidence and presents new evidence on traditional forms of disadvantage and exclusion associated with low incomes, disability and caring. Part Four examines new developments in childcare and informal care and their interrelationships with paid employment. Part Five examines the implications of these changes for both the concept and experiences of citizenship and independence. In Part Six, the concluding chapter points to the many unresolved issues and tensions that remain for welfare states in the future.

Part Two
New theoretical perspectives on care and policy

TWO

Care and gender: have the arguments for recognising care work now been won?[1]

Jane Lewis

Introduction

During the 1980s, an impressive volume of research on the nature of care and carers was published in the UK. Twenty years later the unpaid work of care that is performed in the family, still predominantly by women, has become a major issue on the policy agendas of western European and North American countries and the European Union (EU). However, the way the issue is now framed by politicians, policy makers and many influential male academics bears little relation to the concerns of the 1980s, which were care-centred (see Finch and Groves, 1983; Land, 1983; Baldwin, 1985; Lewis and Meredith, 1987; Ungerson, 1987). Since the late 1990s, the policy focus on care has mainly derived from concern about the labour market participation of women, with most attention paid to childcare. This debate is not care-centred, but rather focuses on how to 'reconcile' work and family responsibilities (the usual parlance at EU level); how to make workplaces more 'family friendly' (the usual term in the UK during the 1990s); or, since 2000 in the UK, how to improve the 'work–life balance'. When the DfEE Minister responsible, Margaret Hodge, opened the parliamentary debate on work–life balance in March 2000, she explained the change in terminology as reflecting a desire to include carers of older and disabled people and 'take the focus away from parenting' (House of Commons, *Hansard*, 9 March 2000, col 231), although this rationale has not been referred to subsequently. Indeed, work–life balance policies seem to be even more firmly led by labour market concerns, emphasising the role to be played by employers as much as or more than the state.

This chapter first explores the context of changes within the family, labour market and welfare state, within which care work has become a policy issue. Second, it reviews recent policy developments, particularly at the EU level, before returning to the issue of care work itself and, finally, addressing policies for care. The chapter argues that the fundamental insights of the literature of the 1980s (themselves derived from a close study of care) in respect of both gender divisions and inequalities, and the corresponding range of appropriate policies, remain crucial.

The context: family, labour market and welfare state change

The development of welfare states focused primarily on the relationship between capital and labour and this made the work–welfare relationship central. Social insurance, the core programme of the modern welfare state, was written into the labour contract, which covered the regularly employed, usually white, usually male worker. Academic literature has gradually recognised the importance of a parallel settlement at the level of the household, between men and women (Lewis, 1992; Orloff, 1993; Crouch, 1999; Esping-Andersen, 1999). The assumption was that men would take primary responsibility for earning and women for caring. Although this 'male breadwinner model' did make provision for care, it was at the price of female economic dependence. Thus, women and children were covered within social insurance programmes as dependants of the male breadwinner. This welfare model depended crucially on both full male employment and stable two-parent families.

The labour market changes of the last 25 years – more unemployment, flexibility and male exit, as well as greater female labour market participation – together with changes in family forms and a greater incidence of family breakdown, might therefore be expected to pose major challenges to modern welfare provision. These changes have been held by both academic commentators and policy makers to represent a process of individualisation (see especially Beck-Gernsheim, 2002), whereby family formation is more a matter of choice than need and adults have more economic autonomy as a result of their participation in the labour market. At the household level, family and labour market changes have eroded the normative assumptions associated with the male breadwinner model, so that the respective household contributions of men and women are a matter for negotiation rather than firm prescription (J. Lewis, 2001). Finally, and most recently, the assumptions underpinning policy at the EU and nation state levels have begun to shift from the traditional male breadwinner model towards an 'adult worker' model family. This is a major change that has significant implications for the pursuit of gender equality; it is now assumed that adult men and women will all be in the labour market, although to what extent remains largely unspecified in the case of women.

With the widespread entry of women into the labour market, the (much smaller) reduction in male labour force participation (mainly reflecting early retirement), the much greater need for two incomes (particularly because of rising house prices), and the even more dramatic and rapid pace of family change over the last quarter of a century, assumptions about the existence and desirability of the male breadwinner model family could no longer hold. Dual-earner families have become the norm in most western countries, although the number of hours women work outside the home varies hugely. Although it remains difficult to combine paid and unpaid work, especially in western Europe where a one-and-a-half-breadwinner model family has become the norm, it is still the case that women continue to do the vast majority of informal care work. In the US, where the vast majority of women work full time, there is, not surprisingly, much more outcry about family stress and 'the crisis of care' (Heyman, 2000). In addition, population ageing, a major challenge for all developed societies, has increased the volume of care needs.

The major changes in family formation and structure and in labour market participation have been accompanied by welfare state restructuring. The main feature of this has been a shift in emphasis from rights to responsibilities and from so-called 'passive' to 'active' welfare provision, so that claimants on the welfare system are 'encouraged' into work and work is 'made to pay' (Lødemel and Trickey, 2001). Gilbert (2002) has described these trends as a series of shifts from social support to social inclusion via employment: from measures of decommodification (that enable people to leave the labour market for due cause) to ways of securing commodification; and from unconditional benefits to benefits that are heavily conditional on work or training. These changes in the nature of welfare state provision have been driven by a variety of policy aims: tackling the problem of 'welfare dependence' (particularly in the English-speaking countries and especially among lone mothers); promoting social inclusion via the labour market (the more continental European approach, but also a focus of the UK Labour government); and, above all, promoting competition and growth – the dominant EU-level discourse (EC, 2000, 2003). The nature and impact of these changes in the Australian context are discussed in Chapter Six.

In respect of gender relations, the shift in ideas and practices in social welfare systems appears to be consistent with greater individualisation as reflected in greater female workforce participation and the increasing fluidity of family forms and intimate relationships. However, there is a danger that the new assumptions about the existence and desirability of what is now conceptualised as an 'adult worker' model family (J. Lewis, 2001) are outrunning social reality, for profound gender divisions remain in respect of both paid and unpaid work. Nowhere is there equality between men and women in the workforce, while time-use surveys show the small extent to which men have increased their contributions to the unpaid work of care and household labour (Gershuny, 2000). Rather, the promotion of 'active' welfare has focused on the employment side of the employment–care equation, while insufficient attention has been paid to the more complicated issues around care. This imbalance becomes more significant given that other dimensions of welfare state restructuring in the field of service provision have included the introduction of market principles and the conscious promotion of a mixed economy of provision, particularly in the UK. These developments have been justified largely in terms of promoting greater choice of supply – as Jenson and Sineau (2001) have argued, choice has become a central value in welfare state restructuring. However, there is little doubt that these service changes have resulted in more fragmentation and high turnover in services for older people and childcare, nowhere more so than in the UK. This in turn elicits the need for more rather than less informal care work (for example, to ensure continuity between different providers of care for older people and children alike).

It has therefore been argued that care is effectively a 'new social risk' (Bonoli, 2005b) that has arisen from the erosion of the male breadwinner model family and the restructuring of welfare states. The appearance on political agendas of policies about care is new and must be understood in the context of these profound changes in behaviour and in the assumptions underlying policies. However, these policies are not care-centred and are also contested.

Recent developments in policies about care at the EU and UK levels

Care lies at the interstices of relationships between the family, market and state; paid and unpaid work; and between formal and informal provision. However, it has never been the main focus of policy making.

Rather, care policies have been harnessed to other policy goals. Recently this has involved the promotion of policies designed to increase, above all, female employment (in the UK via tax credits and childcare services), which in turn reflects the broad structural changes in both labour markets and families and the desire to promote economic competition and growth. At the level of service change in any particular nation state, policies for care have again often been driven by other concerns.[2]

The dominant preoccupation in the recent development of care policies at both the UK and EU levels has been women's – particularly mothers' – labour market behaviour. Crompton (2002) has noted the difference between two major strands of literature on employment and the family: one – primarily feminist – emphasises changes in the normative assumptions underlying policies and in women's own attitudes; the other takes a much more instrumentalist approach and promotes female employment in the interests of increasing economic growth and competitiveness (see especially Esping-Andersen, 1999; Esping-Andersen et al, 2002). However, as Kaufman et al (2002) have observed, family policy debates are dominated by values and 'family rhetorics': 'family policy to a considerable extent is nothing less than the incorporation of social values into political institutions and social services' (Kaufman et al, 2002, p 346). Thus, the 'economy-first' strand of the academic literature on employment and the family may be seen as part and parcel of a shift in thinking about the 'proper' role of women; as citizen workers first and foremost.

Since the early 1990s, the European Commission has increasingly stressed the importance of the effective use of women's skills in a competitive, knowledge-based economy (EC and Council of the European Union, 2002) and has received academic backing for its position. Women have been seen as an untapped labour reserve. Reports to the Portuguese Presidency of the EU in 2000 (Ferrera et al, 2000) and the Belgian Presidency in 2001 (Esping-Andersen et al, 2001) both favoured higher female labour market participation as a means of increasing competitiveness and the tax base of continental European social insurance welfare states. This approach has meshed with arguments for gender equality in the workplace, which have historically been more strongly institutionalised at EU level than in member states. The approach has also been underpinned by research that has swung away from condemning the effects of maternal employment on young children towards endorsing institutional provision, at least for three- and four-year-olds (Gregg and Washbrook, 2003).

The EU Lisbon Council set a target of 57% female labour market participation in member states by 2005, rising to 60% by 2010 (Council of the European Union, 2000). The European Commission called for reforms of means-tested benefits so that each member of the household has an incentive to work (EC, 2002). Moreover, it is significant that recent EU-level employment policy documents have given more emphasis to the provision of formal childcare services than to policies enabling parents to care through, for example, parental leave programmes (the 1996 Parental Leave Directive was not highly specified and sought only to bring member states up to a minimum standard of provision). The provision of childcare has indeed been shown to have a more positive effect on rates of female labour market participation (Bradshaw et al, 1996; Gornick et al, 1997). In 2002 a benchmark for childcare was set by the Barcelona Council, whereby by 2010 at least 33% of children under the age of three and at least 90% of children between three and the mandatory school age should have access to childcare (EC, 2003).

It is also highly significant that in those EU member states with historically short part-time working on the part of women (the UK, Germany and the Netherlands) there have recently been major initiatives to develop childcare services. Such policies are in line with the desire to promote adult employment, because it is well known that services provide incentives to female employment. On the other hand, care leave, which is usually promoted by more conservative politicians, tends to promote female labour exit (Moss and Deven, 1999; Morgan and Zippel, 2003). Indeed, in Germany – the archetypal social insurance welfare state with strong male breadwinner family traditions – increased attention has been paid to family policies in general, over and above the longstanding preoccupation with social provision that preserves the labour market status of the (usually male) recipient (Bleses and Seeleib Kaiser, 2004). The promotion of 'family-friendly' policies and, since 2000, a better work–life balance have even entered the UK political agenda, where it has never previously been thought to be part of the role of government to intervene in the 'private' care arrangements of families.

The main preoccupation of the UK government has been to tackle social exclusion via increased labour market participation and the expansion of early years education in disadvantaged areas. This approach is viewed as serving two purposes: giving children in poor areas a better start in life by encouraging 'early learning'; and improving their material circumstances by helping their mothers (especially lone mothers) to move into employment (Lewis, 2003). The expansion of childcare has been a crucial underpinning to two targets set by the

UK government: to increase the percentage of lone mothers in employment to 70% by 2010 and to reduce child poverty by one quarter by 2004. These were set prior to and independently of the EU-level policy agenda, but are nevertheless congruent with it.

The way in which 'policy packages' are put together can have strong incentive and disincentive effects with respect to employment and care and, despite the shift towards an adult worker model family, often reflect an ambivalence about what the mothers of young children in particular 'ought' to do. Leitner (2003) has argued that only in Scandinavian countries does the policy mix enable 'optional familialism' – a mix of care leaves and childcare services that enables parents to choose between employment and care. But even here, policies are tilted towards providing leave until the child is three years old and after that towards the provision of childcare services, thus giving strong incentives to choose first of all care and then employment, especially on the part of women.

The instrumentalist arguments of those advocating a rapid move towards the adult worker model family have assumed the desirability of a 'defamilialisation strategy' whereby care work (for children and adult dependants) is commodified and put into the public, formal arena (Esping-Andersen et al, 2001, 2002). But policies that are based on the commodification of care work and thereby aim to increase female labour market participation are problematic. First, they do not tackle the problem of the inequalities arising from the gender divisions of paid and unpaid work in adult life. In other words they do not address the problem of how care work should be shared. This is important, because it is highly unlikely that all care can be commodified. Second, they do nothing to ensure that care work is valued: paid care work is usually low paid; and the value of unpaid care work has tended to be overlooked by policy makers.

Care is a universal human need (Nussbaum, 1999, 2003), so care work therefore warrants a central place in policy making. Arguably there has to be a real 'choice' to do it (Lewis and Giullari, 2005). However, it is politically difficult in modern 'active' welfare states to choose not to do paid work in favour of unpaid work, as well as vice versa. The remainder of the chapter will briefly outline some recent developments in policies for care and some alternative approaches; some of these developments are also examined in more detail in Part Four of this book.

Policies for care

Policies about care work are nested in very different policy logics at
the level of the nation state. Moreover, they have been characterised
by pendulum swings (see also Lister, 2002), particularly between cash
benefits and services, not least because care per se has not been the
main policy driver. Rather, care policies have been harnessed to other
policy goals, most recently that of increasing women's employment.

It is therefore necessary to consider the options for care–centred
policies. Currently new and radical proposals are entering the policy
agenda in some countries (the US, the UK and the Netherlands) that
see money as a solution to the problem of providing care. Alstott's
(2004) proposal for 'caretaker accounts' would permit a parent to spend
the money on their own education, pension or childcare. A similar
Dutch proposal would permit individuals to save money via tax
deductions and to use it to take time off to care or for sabbatical leave
or for pension contributions (Knijn, 2004). A dedicated sum for care,
allocated to the individual, would in theory permit people to choose
whether to provide care themselves or to buy it; and would have the
advantage from the state's point of view of shifting responsibility for
decisions about the nature of care provision to the individual.

However, there are major problems with such proposals, even if the
amount of money and the point in the lifecourse at which it was
allocated could be agreed. First, such a strategy is unlikely to offer a
genuine choice about care to all people. Women's freedom to choose
between employment and care work is restricted by the needs and
choices of others, mainly men. Care accounts would privatise the
issue to the individual account holder, who may not have the power
to exercise genuine choice. In the case of Alstott's proposals, it is highly
likely that women would use the money for childcare and men for
their own education or retirement – research into the household
division of resources has long shown that childcare, however it is
provided, is considered a female responsibility in the UK. Second,
compensation for care work – the value attached to it – is never likely
to be high. When care is commodified the jobs are some of the lowest
paid in western economies, which is why they also tend to be carried
out by women. If the amount of money provided in a care account is
unduly modest, then it is likely to perpetuate low pay in the formal
care sector, as well as providing an income for informal carers that
will not permit economic autonomy. Care accounts represent a highly
individualised solution; they appear to be as logical a policy response
to family and labour market changes in increasingly pluralist societies

as do the shifts in assumptions underpinning policies that favour an adult worker model.

Effective policies that recognise the human need for care over the lifecourse, and that also address the gender inequalities deriving from the unequal gendered division of paid and unpaid work, are central to women's welfare, both as carers and in very old age as the majority of people who need care. Both Nancy Fraser's (1997) philosophical analysis and Gornick and Meyers' (2003) empirical analysis of policies to reconcile parenthood and employment conclude by recommending a universal citizen worker/carer model. Similarly, a report (funded by the European Commission) from the European Foundation for the Improvement of Living and Working Conditions on flexibility and social protection has argued for the redistribution of working time over the entire working lifecourse, in order to address the asymmetry between men and women and promote a 'double flexibility agenda', involving the provision of time to care and the control of working time for men and for women (European Foundation, 2003). This constitutes a very different approach to that taken so far by the European Commission and the vast majority of member states in two crucial respects: first, it acknowledges the importance of care work in and for itself; and, second, it addresses the balance of paid and unpaid work in men's lives as well as women's.

Such an approach demands multiple policy measures. The Netherlands is the only country to have made the universal worker/ carer model family official policy via the Combination Scenario, which envisages part-time work and part-time care as the desired pattern for men and women.[3] However, implementation has proved difficult and, while part-time employment rates for men in the Netherlands are the highest among EU member states at 11%, those involved are usually not the fathers of young children (Knijn, 2001; Plantenga, 2001). The introduction of the 'daddy quota' in Scandinavian countries, whereby men are obliged to take part of the parental leave allocation (usually a month) or lose it altogether, was much more specifically aimed at changing the way care work is shared at the household level. But this has not been uncontroversial and the (right-wing) Danish government abandoned the policy in 2002 because it explicitly aimed to change behaviour in the private sphere of the family and was felt to place restrictions on men's choices (even though this 'use it or lose it' policy did not in fact compel men to care).

If the complexity of care needs and caregiving relationships are considered alongside the issue of gender equality, there can be no single policy solution. Those working with Schmid's (2000) idea of the need to facilitate the multiple labour market transitions that will become increasingly necessary with greater flexibilisation reach the same conclusion from an analysis that is based on paid rather than unpaid work (Gautier and Gazier, 2003). Thus, from the carer's point of view, the following dimensions are crucial to securing a genuine choice to engage in paid and/or unpaid work: time – working time and time to care; money – cash to buy care, cash for carers; and services – for child and elder care. Consequently a wide range of policies addressing all these dimensions at both the level of the household (and specifically encouraging men to care) and the level of collective provision are necessary to address the social risks arising from the erosion of the male breadwinner model which threaten the welfare of women throughout their adult lives.

Notes

[1] I would like to acknowledge the support of the Economic and Social Research Council grant 225-25-2001 in the preparation of this chapter.

[2] For example, social care reform in the UK can be seen to have been in large measure dictated by healthcare reform (Lewis and Glennerster, 1996).

[3] The European Foundation for the Improvement of Living and Working Conditions' survey on employment options for the future (European Foundation, 2000) showed that 71% of respondents (from all EU member states) wanted to work a 30- to 40-hour week, with convergence between male and female respondents towards a preference for long part-time working, which seems to provide support for this policy. However, these are preferences, and respondents probably assumed all other things – namely income – to be equal.

THREE

Research on care: what impact on policy and planning?

Kari Wærness

Introduction

During the 1970s, feminist researchers across the western world developed new research perspectives on the phenomenon of 'care'. This research interest was widely linked to the political objective of finding new ways to strengthen women's welfare and position in society. The topics, perspectives and influential academic disciplines in this field of feminist research varied between countries. Consequently there now exists a rich and fascinating multidisciplinary international body of research on care, which offers opportunities for researchers to learn much by reading studies from other countries.

Relationships between British and Nordic feminist research into care began to develop during the early 1980s. A British book, *A labour of love: Women, work and caring* (Finch and Groves, 1983), became very influential in Nordic research, while the influence of Nordic academics was apparent as British feminist researchers gradually widened their interests from informal to paid and professional care (Baldwin and Twigg, 1991). Today, the question of how research on care can have a greater impact on policy and planning is of urgent and international interest. This chapter discusses developments in research and policy on care, based on the recent experiences of the Nordic social democratic welfare regimes – welfare regimes that comparative research has concluded are especially women friendly. As research into care becomes a global enterprise, these developments should therefore be of particular interest to care researchers rooted in different and more problematic welfare policy contexts.

The chapter traces the development of research on care from a Nordic perspective. Despite the proclaimed 'woman-friendly' nature of the Nordic welfare states, this research has nevertheless had little impact on either rational economic approaches to the study of care or on approaches to the evaluation of care-related services. The chapter argues that theory and practice derived from the emerging feminist 'ethic of care' may provide the basis for fruitful new interdisciplinary and international approaches to the study and understanding of care. Moreover, these new approaches may also have the potential to engage with, and challenge, the mainstream economic and managerial discourses that continue to dominate research into care policy and service planning.

The Nordic context of research on care

It is 30 years since the first Nordic research on care work (*omsorgsarbeid*) from a feminist perspective was published (Wærness, 1975). The research formed a small part of the first Norwegian Level of Living Study, financed by the Social Democratic government. The care study generated much public discussion and was positively referred to in the final report of the Level of Living Study (NOU, 1976). Since then, many feminist or feminist-inspired studies on care have been carried out in the Nordic countries, most of them policy-oriented and focusing on public care services. However, despite the applied perspective of much of this research, its impact on policy and planning appears insignificant, if not wholly invisible. Instead, since the early 1990s so-called New Public Management approaches have increasingly provided the ideological underpinnings for rapid, comprehensive reforms in the public health and care services of all Nordic countries, despite the absence of a sound empirical evidence base. This is illustrated by the changes currently taking place in public home care services, which have been described as 'a struggle over the heart of the care work in Norwegian municipalities' (Rønning, 2004, p 6). Thus frontline care workers try to continue providing care services according to norms that both they and care recipients agree constitute good care, but these care practices very often contradict the criteria for good and efficient services as defined by the New Public Management ideology that is shaping the policies of service planners and managers.

The next section of the chapter will briefly describe two contemporary Nordic research discourses in the field of care. It will then describe how one of them, the feminist discourse, has developed over time and will propose arguments for more relevant theoretical work in this field. The chapter will then present some thoughts from a new emerging international field of research, that of the feminist ethics of care. Finally, it will be argued that it is important to strengthen dialogues between scholars from different academic disciplines, including economics, in order to develop an interdisciplinary social science of care that could have a significant impact on all levels of service policy and planning.

Nordic research on care from the 1990s – two parallel discourses with different impacts

Prior to the development of feminist research, the term 'care' (*omsorg*) was commonly used to describe a range of services provided by Nordic welfare states. Although there was extensive research into such services, this was undertaken from other, non-feminist, perspectives. These two traditions now exist in parallel.

Research on care for older people is a good illustration of the differences between these perspectives. Thus, dominant paradigms in gerontology have, since the 1990s, been heavily influenced by socioeconomic and market economic thinking; these paradigms have contributed to a definition of older people and their care as socioeconomic problems (Eliasson, 1996). Based on this construction, rational economic approaches aimed at increasing the efficiency of services are regarded as a high priority and are seen as important features of welfare services for older people. In contrast, feminist research perspectives have a predominant concern with the everyday world of care and a preoccupation with practical activities, skills, knowledge and ways of thinking – a focus that is at the bottom of public sector welfare service priorities and concerns. From a feminist perspective, questions about what 'care' really is and what it means to those who give and receive it are of critical importance. Feminist researchers have therefore criticised the perspectives underpinning service reform and planning for not being based on an adequate understanding of the distinctive nature of care and, therefore, for generating measures that are inappropriate for both care workers and those receiving care (Thorsen and Wærness, 1999). It is important to acknowledge that both conventional economic research and feminist research into service provision and delivery are normative, in the sense that both sets of researchers are concerned with both facts and what is good, desirable and possible. However, the normative perspective is most clearly expressed in many of the feminist-inspired studies, since it is in these studies that moral and human values as well as the researchers' own views are most often discussed.

Today, these two perspectives exist as parallel discourses in research on welfare services (Wærness, 1999). As rational and market-inspired New Public Management perspectives have come to dominate the health and welfare sectors, they have had an increasing impact on how these services are reorganised. Fundamental critiques from many different perspectives of this way of thinking seem so far not to have had any effect on public authorities' implementation of service reforms. In particular, knowledge derived from feminist-inspired research has had no impact on structural reforms in the organisation of care, even though such research has shown that some reforms based on New Public Management ideas fail to address the concrete, practical problems experienced by some care services (Dahl and Eriksen, 2005). Indeed, such reforms can even make the actual quality of care worse, despite appearances to the contrary (Slagsvold, 1995). Public debates on the reform of health and welfare services thus continue to be dominated by academic experts who mainly use a language of economic, technical and legal rationality – a language that in many ways is far from the pragmatic approach to the everyday experience of care that has been the central concern of Nordic feminist research.

Nordic feminist research on care – developments over time

The earliest English feminist research on care reflected two different discourses. One strand emphasised care as work while the other emphasised the emotional aspects of care (Abel and Nelson, 1990). Studies focusing on the work of care tended to interpret it as an oppressive practice (particularly for women), full of routine and alienating tasks. Studies emphasising the emotional dimensions of care considered it to be a meaningful activity that makes women 'better' people. These two perspectives might be described as 'the perspective of misery' and 'the perspective of dignity' respectively – a difference in approach that was also debated in early Norwegian feminist research. Both perspectives are also reflected in contemporary Nordic feminist research on care.

From the start, Nordic feminist research on care included both unpaid and paid care. Moreover, care was viewed in terms of both the work and feelings involved and included both the givers and the receivers of care. The first research seminar on the subject was arranged in 1978 by the then Research Council of Norway's Secretariat for Social Research on Women under the title 'Paid and Unpaid Care' (*Lønnet og ulønnet omsorg*). The topics discussed included: care work in the private and public sectors; children and care; women's self-organised help arrangements; care activities in families with small children; new roles for children, men and women; emotional fatigue in women working in welfare services; and the historical development of professional nursing. The seminar assumed that women had the main responsibility for care in both private life and public sector services. Further research into care was therefore justified 'in order to proceed in the work of extending social scientific knowledge in this area, based on a women's liberation perspective, and to give the authorities a broader basis with respect to planning and implementing a care organisation *that takes into consideration the needs of those giving and receiving care*' (NAVF, 1979, Foreword, emphasis added). Here, Norwegian feminist researchers appeared to be typical representatives of modernity in their optimism and faith in the importance of knowledge and of the women-friendliness of the Norwegian welfare state. Subsequently, newer definitions and distinctions in the field of care were gradually constructed and feminist researchers increasingly contributed to debates on welfare policy (Wærness, 1982). Indeed, feminist research on the 'social service state' and its importance for women became an important supplement to mainstream social policy research, which throughout the 1990s was otherwise mainly concerned with financial support, social security systems and the economic redistributive aspects of the welfare state. Over time, feminist research has increasingly focused on the public and paid care work of women (Dahl and Eriksen, 2005) and less research has been carried out on unpaid care in the family, with the exception of the focus on what has been called the 'new paternity' (Brandth and Kvande, 1997).

Throughout, a primary concern of feminist research has been the idea that care constitutes something 'good' – but a good that is threatened by male, scientific, bureaucratic and market economic rationalities, values and interests; and by the idea that care has traditionally been and still to a large extent is women's work. However, it is possible to see the beginnings of new developments in feminist research on care. Central among these has been an awareness of the risk that care can encroach on the freedom of the care receiver. Consequently, there is increasing interest in the creation and study of service arrangements that may be as good or better alternatives to more person-oriented and continuous care relations (Gough, 1996). There has also been interest in whether there is a 'masculine kind of care' that is different from the feminine kind (Brandth and Kvande, 1997).

Political-sociological and empirically rooted research on care has occupied a strong position in Nordic feminist research. However, Nordic feminist researchers have participated very little in the international development of political-normative theory on care. This does not mean that there are no important contributors in this area. Both the Swedish sociologist Rosmari Eliasson and to an even greater extent the Norwegian nurse, philosopher and historian Kari Martinsen have made important theoretical contributions to debates about the ethics of care, drawing on philosophy and on research into women's public sector care work in the past and present respectively (Eliasson, 1987; Eliasson-Lappalainen, 1999; Martinsen, 1989, 1993, 1996, 2000). However, this work has still not connected with international theoretical debates on care and gender, so their influence on thinking and writing about care in general, and in the Nordic countries in particular, has so far been more limited than that of leading North American feminist theorists. On the other hand, North American feminist theorists have paid far less attention to the specific dilemmas and problems faced by paid care workers in the welfare state. This is perhaps not surprising in view of the enormous differences between the Nordic and the North American welfare states.

This argument is not pursued further here. Instead, the discussion now shifts to the need to increase the impact of feminist research on policy and service planning. The concept of the 'rationality of caring' is proposed as a useful theoretical starting point for such research.

The 'rationality of caring' – a fruitful concept for research on public care

The concept of the 'rationality of caring' emerged through a grounded theory approach in an empirical study of public home help workers (Wærness, 1984) and was also inspired by Arlie Hochschild's notion of 'the sentient actor' (Hochschild, 1975). The concept was useful in making visible the rational action, reason and feelings that are all important elements in the provision of good-quality care in both private and public spheres. The concept was also important in showing how the rationality that dominates both planning and research on public sector care services overlooks important aspects of knowledge and potential courses of action involved in the provision of good care.

There is still little acknowledgement in public policy and planning that the instrumental rationality on which services are planned and organised is of limited usefulness when providing care for individuals. Knowledge that is important and useful to administrators and politicians is often of little help to first-line care workers. In contrast, solving specific problems in the everyday world of care work requires a way of thinking that is contextual and descriptive, rather than formal and abstract. The concept of the 'rationality of caring' suggests that personal knowledge and the ability and opportunity to understand the specifics of each situation where help is required are important prerequisites of good-quality care. This means that the human and moral dimensions of good care cannot necessarily be elicited in public sector care services where there is a great deal of (measurable) activity. These dimensions of good care also require quiet and space so that those requiring help are confident that their helpers can see them as individuals with specific needs – in other words, that people in a state of helplessness believe themselves to be in good hands. This means that each helper must not be too busy. To date, no economic studies of 'efficiency' in public sector services have taken into consideration this important aspect of care work. This is perhaps not surprising, since neoclassical economic theory has no room for concepts of intimacy, interdependence and nurturing; and concepts of value are restricted to atomistic, individual utility (Nelson, 2003).

Several empirical studies of public sector care services have confirmed that the concept of the 'rationality of caring' is helpful in reaching a critical understanding of the modernisation that Nordic care services have undergone in recent years (see, for instance, Gough, 1987; Szebehely, 1995; Christensen, 1998). As a 'sensitising concept' (Blumer, 1969, pp 147-8), the idea has proved useful in revealing the negative aspects of modernisation which do not easily relate to the 'rationality of caring'. This might help to explain why most of the research on public sector reform in this area ignores the results of feminist research on care (Wærness, 1999). For example, working from the feminist perspective, several researchers wrote a book entitled *Is care disappearing? The everyday world of care for the elderly in the late-modern welfare state* (*Blir omsorgen borte? Eldreomsorgens hverdag i den senmoderne velferdsstaten*) (Thorsen and Wærness, 1999). Its arguments aroused no special interest among planners and researchers working within the dominant planning discourse, despite the interest of professionals working in the field. The basis for the critique of the dominant perspective was as follows:

> Our critical view is not based on a kind of nostalgic understanding that care for the elderly was better 'before'. It is primarily based on the fact that we, as experienced researchers in this area, have found several examples of good care practices and relations between caregivers and those needing help in today's care services that we believe are about to be run over or disappear in the modernisation process in progress in this sector. We consider that planners and administrators do not pay enough consideration to

---

the distinctive character of care work when they propose changes and reforms in this sector. The fact that we can find home helps and nurses who provide good care is in spite, rather than because, of what the care organisation arranges. (Thorsen and Wærness, 1999, p 20)

Even economists analysing efficiency and productivity in the nursing and care sectors sometimes express reservations about the value of the efficiency measures they use. For example:

One may ask the question whether we are so far removed from data for real nursing and care services that the study has no value. We would nevertheless argue that the efficiency measures relate to variables and factors of great interest to the municipalities. (Edvardsen et al, 2000, p 10)

Despite these reservations about the validity of the measures that it used, this study still concluded that it was possible to identify more 'efficient' municipalities that could act as models for less efficient municipalities. The objections to such efficiency measures that are reflected in feminist research on care are not usually discussed in economic studies on efficiency in this sector, if indeed any reference is made to the fact that such research exists.

Feminist economists argue that feminist critiques of neoclassical economics are suppressed because they are threatening (Nelson, 2003). The relationship between feminist and economic scientific discourses on public care in Nordic countries seems to confirm this wider relationship between feminist analyses and mainstream economics.

The need for a new paradigm in research on care

However, Nordic philosophical and theoretical research on care has recently had a growing influence on professional and frontline care workers. For instance, a book about philosopher and nurse Kari Martinsen's theories about care has been published for use in basic nursing training (Alvsvåg and Gjengedal, 2000). Martinsen's work has created a distinctive stream of research on nursing, and her normative care theory is said to have had a great influence on nursing students and practitioners (Kirkevoll, 2000). Like the empirical feminist research on care, this theory is highly critical of the economic and technological rationalities that dominate contemporary policy and planning relating to public sector health and care services. Its influence on attitudes, through the professional education of care workers, means that those working in care services are likely to experience frustration at the gap between how they have learned that care should be provided and how it is actually practised in public sector services. Consequently care workers with appropriate opportunities may move to jobs where they do not have to provide direct care.

In recent years, the growing gap between the demand for public care services in Nordic countries and the supply of care has partly been filled by immigrant care workers. Thus a 'care crisis' has been avoided, as has any urgent need for a new approach to the planning of care services. When older people in a Norwegian nursing home tell journalists that 'the colour of the hands does not matter when it comes to providing good care', it could be assumed that the important basic elements in giving and receiving care and nursing reflect universal values. This may be true, even if important cultural differences also exist, such as the distinctive western ideals of care that Hochschild (1995) identifies.

However, this universalism implies that professional and unskilled care workers today may easily cross national borders in order to get jobs. In and of itself, this might seem a positive development in a globalising world, but it also has some negative distributional effects. For example, it is arguable that a 'care drain' from South to North is occurring – the transfer of care workers from poorer to richer countries. In terms of both money and needs for care services, countries in the South are poorer than countries in the North. Moreover, the redistribution of care workers from South to North may also contribute to the continued devaluation of care in the modern world, as care services in the North do not have to raise salaries and offer better working conditions to attract care workers from the North so long as jobs can be filled with new immigrant workers.

The problematic relationship between dominant economic and managerial discourses and alternative social and humanistic approaches in policy and research is a widespread contemporary issue on both the national and international agendas (Nussbaum, 1998). Nussbaum's description of the problems in development economics has many points of resemblance to the account in this chapter of the two Nordic discourses on care. However, a new area of study is emerging on the international academic agenda that is of great relevance to these issues. This area of study, with roots in a number of academic disciplines, has been termed the 'feminist ethics of care' (Sevenhuijsen, 2002). A feminist ethics of care is characterised by a relational ontology that is both descriptive and normative. It is encapsulated in the idea that individuals can only exist because they are members of various networks of care and responsibility, for good or for bad. The feminist ethics of care takes the idea of self-in-relationship as the starting point for considering obligations and responsibility. The moral subject in the discourse of care is enmeshed in a network of relations and (inter)dependencies in which s/he has to find balances between different forms of care – for the self, for others and for the relations between these. The feminist ethics of care implies a radically different relationship between morality and politics from political programmes that are based on constructions of individual rights holders as the 'basic units' of society. Because it starts from a relational ontology, the feminist ethics of care focuses primarily on the role of policies and politics in the safeguarding of responsibility and relationships in human practice and interaction. Social policies should, according to this ontology, be governed by responsiveness to the needs of those with whom they are concerned. Caring attitudes should not be confined to private interactions but should also count as a public virtue and should therefore enter into the considerations of policy makers. Instead of deriving responsibilities from rights (a top-down approach), the feminist ethics of care approach commences political reasoning from an understanding of interconnections and relationships and therefore from knowledge about daily practices of care and the responsibilities and dilemmas implied in these.

The feminist ethics of care does not argue that care is the only value or that it should always be given the highest priority in social planning and policy. The argument is rather that care, justice and freedom are different value domains that have to be balanced in all human activities (van Staveren, 2001). Theoretical writing about the feminist ethics of care so far seems very promising in its potential for bridging the gap between theoretical and empirical research, and in encouraging more theorists to engage with concrete problems in the real world of care in a way that practitioners and professionals in health and social services can also feel comfortable with. Theorists and empirical researchers in this field may thus be able to challenge the dominance of economic and managerial paradigms in the planning and organisation of public care services, although this will not be easy. They may also be able to influence the education of care workers so that they become more aware of how organisational structures can create problems in trying to combine the ideals of good care and the demands of economic efficiency.

In the longer term, the goal should be not just to challenge the dominance of economic discourse, but to develop genuine dialogue and collaboration in research between the two discourses that currently run in parallel and exert very unequal influences on service development and delivery. The fact that feminist economics is a growing area of study that is also closely related to the feminist ethics of care is one reason for optimism, even if the long-term relationship between feminist and mainstream economics is still uncertain. Feminist economics offers important insights into care in the modern world that are of value to feminist care researchers in other academic disciplines. In the words of the feminist economist Nancy Folbre:

> In order to solve the care problems we need to understand how markets work, but also how they don't work. At the same time, we need to recognise that institutional alternatives to markets – primarily the family and the state – are also susceptible to failure…. We need to develop an interdisciplinary social science that recognises the potentially unifying need to solve care problems, but acknowledges the distributional conflict that can unfold in efforts to offload care costs. (Folbre, 2004b, p 13)

FOUR

'Pseudo-democracy and spurious precision': knowledge dilemmas in the new welfare state

Eithne McLaughlin

Introduction

Since the 1970s, consultation with service users has become an accepted feature of both policy making and professional practice. This reflects the impact of grassroots social movements on ways of thinking about welfare in Britain (Williams, 1999). The first part of this chapter locates this growth in consultation practice in a broader social and political context – the crisis of legitimacy in public services and the welfare state (Needham, 2003), and the crisis in the legitimacy of expert knowledge that characterises social life in the age of modernity. The chapter then reviews the nature of policy making, noting the limitations of the rationalistic What Works agenda and similar academic models of the policy-making process. The third part of the chapter summarises two main approaches to the generation of knowledge about the social world. Finally, the chapter illustrates the strengths of interpretivist social research by summarising some of its key contributions to the understanding of health, illness and disability. The social model of disability and the critique of rehabilitation that it has generated are presented as examples of the way that social research is more likely to influence overall policy trajectories than the design of specific policies (Graham, 2002).

The changing context of knowledge: the welfare state meets modernity

A key characteristic of what social historians describe as the late modern period is that a more educated, quizzical and cynical public and media question the truthfulness, evidential status and credibility of all forms of knowledge (La Tour, 1993). Claims to know the 'truth' about the social world and the status of experts were profoundly shaken by two developments. First, the women's, disability and environmental movements, collectively known as the 'new social movements' (Young, 1990), developed radical critiques of the professional paternalism that had underpinned so much of the post-war welfare state. These critiques developed into broader debates about scientific truthfulness and the relationship of science and expert knowledge to public policy making and the public interest (Beck, 1992). Second, the neoliberalism of Thatcherism and Reaganism prioritised the individual and the consumer and extolled the virtues of small government. Together, these developments created a crisis of legitimacy in the traditional European welfare state (Commission on Social Justice, 1994; NESC, 2005).

The new social movements shared egalitarian philosophies in which experiential knowledge is accorded higher or equal value to that acquired by formal study (La Tour, 1993). By the turn of the twenty-first century this influence, together with neoliberal consumerism, had led to the emergence in the health field, for example, of that contradictory beast the 'lay expert' (Prior, 2003; Lohan and Coleman, 2005). Validated by both egalitarian and neoliberal consumerist discourses, service users have come to insist on having a say in how public services are designed, delivered and monitored.

Throughout the 1980s and 1990s, neoliberalism embedded New Public Management approaches into the governance of public services. New Labour followed with its ethos of 'marketplace democracy' (Fung and Wright, 2001); and the new social movements continued to resist professional paternalism through the discourse and practices of the service user movement. All these factors contributed to the development of participative forms of policy making and new forms of public service governance. Participation and public consultation rapidly became a 'one size fits all' solution to all manner of ills (see also Chapter Sixteen).

It is now largely accepted that public service provider organisations and individual professional staff need to demonstrate increased responsiveness and flexibility and to perform within higher standards of quality assurance if the public are to trust them with their 'tax dollars' and/or their lives. Increased responsiveness and flexibility have been institutionalised through a variety of mechanisms, including public participation and public consultation in policy making. For example, the new 'positive equality' duties in relation to 'race', gender and disability in Britain require consultation with the 'representatives' of disadvantaged social groups as routine elements in equality-proofing processes.

Alongside the development of a more democratised welfare state, greater public scepticism about science and expert knowledge has meant that the knowledge base of many professional practices in social work, health and social care has been questioned. This has been evident around issues as diverse as the removal, retention and use of human organs and tissue; vaccination; embryology; adoption, fostering and child protection policies; and 'community care'. Overall, these challenges constitute a major redefinition and repositioning of social and public services and the welfare professions vis-à-vis the 'public'.

However, much of the work of welfare professionals and service providers in liberal welfare states involves rationing (limiting access to services that are free or subsidised at the point of use) or social policing (the surveillance and regulation of citizens' behaviour). The implications of these roles for the acceptance – or lack of acceptance – by welfare institutions and professionals of experiential knowledge, and for their relationships with service users and other civil society representatives, have been insufficiently theorised to date. Rather than articulating the tensions in these potentially conflicting roles, policy makers and welfare professionals have striven instead to be seen to be influenced by the experiential knowledge of users and 'the public', while at the same time controlling and limiting the impact of this on decision making and in governance systems.

User participation and influence in the governance of public services remains limited and controlled by the professional and/or managerial staff. 'Tick box' participation practices may be used to lend legitimacy to the policy processes in these services, while providing only the most superficial involvement in and influence over policy making. The positive equality duties referred to above mean that policy makers and service providers are now often required to confirm that they have consulted with 'representative' service users and other representatives of civil society before bringing proposals to senior management teams or boards. However, the views of those consulted do not need to have had any impact on the content of those proposals. Limiting and controlling public participation in and influences on policy making may be achieved by a range of practices. These include manipulating the timing of consultations (consulting late in the decision-making process means that earlier decisions are unlikely to be revised in response to new inputs at a late stage); drawing tight boundaries around the range of issues being consulted upon; accepting the responses to public consultation only in certain limited formats;

and giving different values and weights to contributions to consultation processes in terms of their credibility, truthfulness and status as 'evidence'. Thus, manipulation of the timing, methods, content and technologies of participation and public consultation can lead to 'pseudo-democratisation' of policy making and public service governance. Participative policy making may thus become the tokenistic incorporation of potentially dissenting and troublesome voices (Morrison and Newman, 2001).

Notwithstanding the problems of superficiality, these pseudo-democratic developments are generally accepted to be an advance both on New Public Management practices (Kelly and Muers, 2002) and on traditional paternalism and representative democracy. New Public Management placed insufficient value on engagement with service users and other stakeholders and failed to develop an adequate response to the power deficit between user and provider that arises under conditions of non-commercial service provision (NESC, 2005).

More recent prescriptions for the rejuvenation and re-legitimation of the welfare state and public services may be summarised as involving greater democratisation and accountability of public institutions and of public service staff to citizens; the development of new forms of citizenry; the decentralisation of power to lower levels of governance; the adoption of more participative policy making; and an emphasis on 'evidence-based' policy making. These last two elements are important but potentially contradictory elements in New Labour's response to the crisis of legitimacy. On the one hand, participative policy making places new expectations and requirements on policy makers to utilise and integrate a plurality of knowledge into policy making. On the other hand, welfare professionals and policy makers are enjoined to adopt 'evidence-based' and research-informed practice. New forms of professional regulation have also developed indirectly under the guise of 'clinical governance'. However, 'evidence' is as socially and politically constructed as any other human activity. There is little to indicate a significant development of epistemological pluralism; nor have policy makers, practitioners and professional educators been quick to abandon traditional hierarchies of the 'truthfulness', credibility and legitimacy of different forms of knowledge. The epistemological pluralism demanded by the participation and democratisation agendas does not sit comfortably with the pragmatism and traditional scientific certainties of 'evidence-based' policy and practice. The contribution of social research knowledge to the creation of 'evidence' is discussed further below; the chapter next considers the role of evidence in policy making.

The relationship of evidence to policy making

Since 1997 there has been a surge of interest in the theory and practice of 'evidence-based' policy making in the UK (Hargreaves, 1996; Davies et al, 2000, 2002; Hammersley, 2001; Young et al, 2002; Fox, 2003; Walter et al, 2003; Boaz and Pawson, 2005). The government's position was set out in a speech by David Blunkett in 2000:

> We need to be able to rely on social science and social scientists to tell us what works and why, and what types of policy initiatives are likely to be most effective. (Blunkett, 2000)

Blunkett's statement reflects the enlightenment ideals that government and policy making are, should be and can be rational, 'scientific' and benignly 'disinterested'. Within central government there is some recognition that what constitutes good or reliable evidence about the social world is not necessarily only that which mimics 'hard' science. Thus, the Cabinet Office (1999, 2000) recognised the need for a range of evidence, especially when dealing with complex social issues such as social exclusion. However, despite the Cabinet Office's advocacy of epistemological pluralism, and some recognition of the problems of equity, power and privilege in its proposals for creating public value (Kelly and Muers, 2002), a strong preference for quantitative 'scientific' social research remains evident among policy makers, and may even have been strengthened through the Exchequer's endorsement of US-style quantitative evaluations of pilot social programmes. Ambivalence about the evidential legitimacy of qualitative social research, public consultation and other 'soft' inputs can still readily be identified in government research commissioning and utilisation (see also Boaz and Pawson, 2005).

In practice, policy making involves the interplay of individual and institution; structure and agency; disagreements and power playing, with much of the latter involving consensus and alliance-building around the legitimacy and admissibility of different types of knowledge as evidence. As Coote noted in the *Guardian*:

> Policy and practice in the field of social change is an art form. Policy and practice do not follow linear pathways or respond readily to the appliance of science.... Ministers talk about evidence but routinely play fast and loose [with it] when it suits their political purposes. (Coote, 2004)

Indeed, the role of evidence in policy making under New Labour has not been as rational and apolitical as the 'evidence-based' policy agenda purports. For example, Pawson and Tilley's (1997) 'critical realist' approach has been recommended to health service practitioners and managers (see also Boaz and Pawson, 2005). Pawson's approach focuses on how power and status affect the way knowledge is accepted and/ or utilised.

A Foucauldian appreciation of knowledge as the product of systems of power involves an awareness of the contested nature of evidence. Such sensitivity is crucial to the development and practice of meaningful participative policy making and deliberative democracy. Some recognition of this exists in central government. However, a scientific, rationalistic and supposedly apolitical discourse of policy making continues to threaten these other aspirations because it curtails epistemological pluralism. Thus, in the UK, issues of public consultation and participation in policy making have been largely defined as problems of information management within public administration (Morrison and Newman, 2001) – in other words, the processes of accepting and utilising knowledge-as-evidence have been depoliticised. Depoliticisation has arguably masked the inequalities and systems of power that determine the acceptance of only some knowledge as evidence. As Morrison and Newman (2001) point out, the alternative is to view public consultation and participation in policy making as a process of mediation and negotiation through which different groups come to a consensual accommodation as to what should be done. In a consensual, problem-solving approach to policy making, dialogue between expert and lay participants would not be closed down by recourse to 'trump cards' of 'science', technique, measurement and method (see also Lister, 2004).

The rationalistic model of the policy process assumes that good-quality, unambiguous evidence is weighed up within a logical, sequential and disinterested process of decision making by benign bureaucrats. However, the contention that decision making is logical and sequential and directly influenced by evidence has been discredited for some time (see, for example, Weiss and Bucuvalas, 1980; Pawson and Tilley, 1997; Graham, 2002; Young et al, 2002):

> The whole bureaucracy of [policy making] opens up, with
> its long corridors, waiting benches, responsible, semi-
> responsible, and incomprehensible shoulder shruggers and
> poseurs. There are front entrances, side entrances, secret
> exits, tips, and counter information; how one gets access

to knowledge; how it should be [constructed]; how it is twisted to fit, turned inside out and finally neatly presented so that it does not say what it really means and signifies what people should rather keep to themselves. All of that could be more easily ignored if only one were not dealing with very real and personal hazards. (Beck, 1992, pp 216-7)

A lack of commitment to consensual decision making, problem solving and negotiation remains characteristic of policy making in the UK. That 'policies emerge in a more random and unscientific manner than the rhetoric of evidence based policy making and clinical governance suggest' (Coote, 2004) and that the policy process is not logical and sequential are not new insights. The incremental model of policy making articulated by Lindblom (1979) in the 1970s, for instance, theorised the policy process as a long-term project with no definite beginning or end. Lindblom used the analogy of water slowly permeating through, over, under or around limestone bedrock to describe the effects of evidence (and other influences) on policy making. Thus, policies form in a fluid and diffuse way over time. From time to time these processes may result in clearly recognisable policy change at specific times; or there may be barely perceptible, incremental change over long periods. Lindblom's approach reflected the influence of social theories of critical realism and phenomenology, with their rejection of the enlightenment philosophical tradition. Rationality, utilisation of knowledge and evidence-based decision making may all occur within policy-making processes, but Lindblom and others rightly caution against assumptions that these are the dominant or only factors determining why some policies come about and others do not (see Hudson and Lowe, 2004, for an overview of different models of the policy-making process).

Moreover, changes in policy-making processes can make it even less appropriate to assume the orderly deployment of appropriate scientific evidence:

Though planned and directed from the centre, almost all the social programmes introduced by New Labour have sought to 'empower' people locally to decide for themselves how to implement them. That brings into play individuals and groups who have plenty of local knowledge but who are not inclined to follow orders from the top, nor [are] familiar with research methods.... Once they are in control,

how can they be encouraged to base their decisions on
formal evidence – especially if it bears little relation to
what common sense tells them? (Coote, 2004)

Coote's question assumes the place of 'scientific' or expert knowledge
to be at the top of a hierarchy of knowledge and evidence with
experiential and lay knowledge at the bottom. Meaningful practice of
participative policy making and deliberative democracy, however,
requires a pluralist starting position on epistemological issues and the
abandonment of such fixed knowledge hierarchies. The absence of
knowledge pluralism and consensual decision making in the cultures
and practices of welfare governance in the UK means there is a gap
between discourses of participation and democratisation in the arena
of representative politics and practices of policy making on the ground.
   The critique of naive understandings of the place of evidence within
social and public policy making was reflected in the 2005 launch of
the journal *Evidence & Policy*. However, the differential status of and
credibility given to diverse forms of knowledge remain relatively little-
discussed components of the relationship between evidence and policy
making in the UK. This may be because so much of the relationship
is implicit and unarticulated by those involved. The resolution of
conflicting evidence(s) and reconciliation of conflicting influences
on decision making largely proceeds behind closed doors.

The limits of knowledge about the social world

Debate as to how knowledge about the social world is best produced
and which types of knowledge are closest to the truth – epistemological
issues – have a long history and a vast literature. The pluralist
epistemological position advocated above accepts that all forms of
knowledge about the social world have limitations of some kind. It
also assumes that what is important in the utilisation of knowledge
for the public interest is not these limitations per se, but, rather, that
the limitations and their consequences are properly acknowledged in
the application of that knowledge to decision making. Social scientific
knowledge has the potential to contribute both to the way social
problems are constructed and to the formulation of responses to these
'social problems'. It is both these capacities which enable social science
to prompt paradigmatic shifts in policy trajectories (Graham, 2002)
from time to time. The primary contribution of social research lies in
such paradigmatic shifts, rather than contributing to policy design
and policy learning in a manner equivalent to that of engineering in

the physical world. An example is the shift from passive to active paradigms in the provision of financial assistance to unemployed people in the UK, a development stimulated more by qualitative than quantitative research on labour supply and unemployment (for example McLaughlin et al, 1989; see also Chapter Six on similar developments in Australia). Another example is the influence of the social model of disability on policy and practice; this is discussed further below.

There are a large number of competing vocabularies with which to describe differences in method and approach within the social sciences. Positivist social science (Hyde et al, 2004) or naturalism (Dixon et al, 2005) seeks to 'read across' to the social world the established standards and practices of natural science (Medwar, 1984). According to this approach, knowledge is true if it is falsifiable, testable, has predictive value and is replicable. These constitute the key characteristics of quantitative social research. Quantitative social research is favoured by policy makers in the US and the UK and transnational bodies. The limitations of this kind of approach are rarely discussed in policy arenas. These limitations are in part inherent and in part a result of the way that, in a rush to embrace 'hard science', some social scientists and their champions in the policy world have invested the results of positivist quantitative research with spurious precision – that is, with degrees of certainty that exceed those justified by probability theory and standards of falsifiability, replicability and so on. They have also too often ignored the inherent unity of theory and method – the recognition that all theories are underdetermined by fact and all measurement is theory-dependent (Gordon, 2000). Thus what we are prepared to accept as evidence and what we are capable of knowing depend on the beliefs we already hold; these are reflected in our choice of measures, definitions and so on. The closed nature of the positivist, hypothesis-testing social research approach means that it is difficult for research in that tradition to generate genuinely new understandings of social phenomena, but easy to generate multiple confirmations and apparently ever more sophisticated measurements of the knowledge we already accept as 'true'. The result is a spurious precision and inaccessible technicalisation in social research.

The alternative to spurious precision and empiricist naivety of the positivist approach is the qualitative or interpretivist tradition of *Verstehen* or hermeneutics (Dixon et al, 2005). In this approach the focus is on the subjective meanings, concepts and values people have and the uses they make of them. The human subject is placed centrally in the analysis as a self-interpreting, intentional animal (Taylor, 1971). This approach has been especially important in contributing critiques of dominant common sense and taken-for-granted understandings of social phenomena, and thereby to shifts in policy paradigms and trajectories.

The limitations of this latter approach centre on two main problems. The first relates to the limited scale and nature of the generalisation that is appropriate from small numbers and samples generated on a non-random basis. The second limitation stems from the problem of egocentrism. A double dose of egocentrism is present – that of the researcher and that of the research subject. The qualitative researcher and analyst needs to be conscious and wary of the egotistical tendency to universalise inappropriately from the self.

Despite these limitations, interpretivist social research has contributed very significantly to advancing understandings of health, disability and care. The strength of interpretivist research is the way it can generate entirely new conceptual frameworks and the paradigm shifts identified by Kuhn (1962) as so fundamental to progress in knowledge-building over time. Probably the most significant paradigm shift contributed by interpretivist social research in the field of health studies has been the social model of disability and the critiques of care and rehabilitation which derive from it (see Chapters Sixteen and Seventeen). A further contribution has been the enhanced understanding of the surveillance and governance functions of welfare systems and practices. These can be understood as part of longer-term processes of modernisation and the emergence of complex societies (Foucault, 1973; Wright and Treacher, 1982).

A further contribution has been the making visible of and theorising about the experiences of everyday life. Both continuity and social change result from the micro-level social actions of individuals, as well as from macro-level structures and processes. Thus, individuals actively construct meaning from experience, social interactions and cultural products. Lay understandings of illness, disease, well-being, care and disability interact with, and in democratic societies will eventually shape and limit, expert and professional practice and knowledge. An example of this process occurred between 2000 and 2002 in the UK, when the disjunction between lay and professional attitudes towards the treatment and use of cadavers prompted public enquiries into post-mortem and other pathology practices.

The broadest social scientific contribution to the study of health and care has been the socialisation of biological and physical phenomena. The concept of 'embodiment' reflects the recognition that the physical world, physical sensations and biological events are socially and culturally constructed so that we cannot know what we feel, touch or sense without the intermediary influence of culture and society.

The social model of and response to disability

A concrete example of the socialisation of the biological lies in the contrast between the biomedical and the social models of disability. The biomedical model of disability assumes that disability is the functional consequence of a physical impairment or illness in an individual. Consequently the response of public services and those who work in them should be to cure or curtail the effects of the physical problem or help the individual to come to terms with post-treatment limitations on their quality of life, lifestyle and opportunities.

In contrast, the social model understands disability to be the result of the problematic ways that social institutions and modern cultures respond to the presence of physical and mental impairments among a minority of the population. It is the response to the impairment which is understood to be disabling and abnormal rather than, or as well as, the impairment itself. The environmental and contingent nature of disability is thus emphasised, as is the normality of physical impairment in human populations (McLaughlin and Byrne, 2005). The implication is that public services and the people who work in them should act to promote more positive responses to impairment on the part of their institutions, services and society generally, as well as within their own personal practice. Understanding disability as largely resulting from negativity towards and exclusion of people with impairments also underscores the importance of the interactions that occur between patients, clients and staff in public services and social institutions. The social model of disability challenges medical and care professionals to review their practice and assess its consistency with the rights, dignity, freedoms and social inclusion of those they 'treat'. Chapter Seventeen contains a more detailed account of the development and impact of the social model of disability on policy in the UK.

The social model of disability has also prompted a critique of rehabilitation services (see Seymour, 1989; Priestley, 2003). In contrast to the taken-for-granted knowledge base of the rehabilitation sciences, the social critique of rehabilitation has demonstrated that the extent to which rehabilitation is 'successful' does not depend primarily or only on individual 'patient' characteristics. Rather, it depends on the severity and nature of the acquired condition (for example whether it carries social stigma); the prior social statuses (for example age, gender and lifecourse position) of the individual; and the resources or constraints provided by their social networks and the social institutions with which they come into contact.

The critique of rehabilitation has also shown how the emphasis in the rehabilitation sciences on the psychological traits of 'patients' has constituted a form of oppression because it reinforces the negative portrayal of disability as an individual tragedy, with the associated depiction of the 'good' patient as one who heroically triumphs over personal adversity while being guided by kindly and benign professional advice and counsel (Seymour, 1989; Oliver, 1997; Priestley, 2003).

At the same time, social research based on the social model of disability has also facilitated the expression and communication of the very real pain, difficulties and personal challenges that acquired impairment, chronic ill-health and other aspects of disability may all involve (Wendell, 1996). These accounts remind us not to minimise or ignore the very real difficulties involved in being disabled in a society that extols physical perfection; engages in healthism (Leder, 1990; Hyde et al, 2004; Lohan and Coleman, 2005); and demands continuously high economic productivity. Equally, nor should appreciation of the strength, resilience and coping of some people with impairments lead to pathologising those individuals who for one reason or another have less resilience or capability to cope with the difficulties, exclusions and oppressions that society places on people with impairments.

Conclusions

The unresolved tension at the heart of the democratised welfare state is that participative policy making and democratised governance seek to give credibility to non-expert knowledge and the views of the lay public, but leave obscure how much credibility and influence such knowledge is allowed, compared to that contributed by 'science', expert and professional opinion, pragmatic influences and other constraints on policy making. The failure to acknowledge, still less address, this tension means that a pseudo-democracy of public consultation has joined with the apoliticism of the 'evidence-based' agenda and the spurious precision of positivist social research. Participative policy making and public consultation sit ill at ease with the rigidly hierarchical systems of accountability and decision making structured into the parliamentary system in the UK (Faris and McLaughlin, 2004). The result is a heady brew of hidden agendas, mismanaged expectations and misunderstandings. Lack of clarity around the issues explored in this chapter runs the risk of bringing public consultation and participative policy making into disrepute as the organisations of civil society experience consultation fatigue, phoney sincerity and a lack of regard for the truth (Frankfurt, 2005). Far from being a benign opportunity, it is even possible that participative policy making and governance arrangements may simply impose a new set of burdens on service users and citizens (Contandriopoulos, 2004), without providing the gains that should result from their voices being heard and listened to.

Whether these dilemmas and the incomplete welfare state response to modernity can be moved forward so as to prevent well-intentioned developments in governance becoming precisely the opposite is a challenge to which researchers, practitioners and the public can and should all contribute. Doing so requires commitment to the utilisation of high-quality but accessible knowledge and a willingness to learn from those at the receiving end of social policies, welfare and public services (see also Lister, 2004).

Part Three
Traditional forms of disadvantage:
new perspectives

FIVE

The costs of caring for a disabled child

Jan Pahl

The aim of this chapter is to draw together 20 years of research in Britain on the costs of caring for a child with a disability and to reflect upon the impact of that research on policy in the UK, in particular policy related to financial support. The hope is that the chapter will not only present new perspectives on a very traditional form of disadvantage, but will also offer researchers ideas about how they can ensure that the results of their work make an impact on policy. However, before outlining the research, it may be useful to review briefly some of the work that has been done on the link between research and policy.

The impact of research on policy

The process by which research makes an impact on policy is notoriously intangible. Researchers may cherish the hope that their work will be seized upon by policy makers and incorporated into the next ministerial speech. Official statements may even foster the same theory. Thus, the general aim of the Department of Health's programme of health and personal social services research was described in 1990 as:

> ... to provide objective information for Ministers as a basis
> for developments in health policy, improvements in public
> health, and increasing efficiency and effectiveness in health
> and personal services. (DH, 1990, p xiv)

The same approach informs the idea of *evidence-based policy,* and the view that the introduction, or the continuation, of a social policy should be based upon clear evidence that the policy works. As David Blunkett, then Secretary of State for Education and Employment, said in a speech in 2000:

> Social science research evidence is central to development
> and evaluation of policy. We need to be able to rely on
> social science and social scientists to tell us what works
> and why, and what types of policy initiatives are likely to
> be most effective. (Blunkett, 2000)

The evidence-based policy movement originated in evidence-based
medicine and in a model of research in which the randomised
controlled trial was the only acceptable source of evidence. However,
from this start it has spread into the social sciences and into all areas of
the welfare state, despite cynical references to 'policy-based evidence'
(Marmot, 2004; Stevens, 2004).

In practice, things are often far less clear than many advocates of the
evidence-based approach admit. Those who have interviewed policy
makers have discovered that they often find it hard to identify any
research that has had an impact on their thinking. Weiss concluded
that those who are responsible for policy making:

> ... have great difficulty in disentangling the lessons they
> have learned from research from their whole configuration
> of knowledge. They do not catalogue research separately;
> they do not remember sources and citations. With the best
> will in the world all that they can usually say is that in the
> course of their work they hear about a great deal of research
> and they are sure it affects what they think and do. (Weiss,
> 1986, p 219)

There have been many attempts to identify the different ways in which
the policy process handles the input of knowledge. One typology
distinguished between the:

- *knowledge-driven model*, in which it is assumed that research leads
  policy;
- *problem-solving model*, in which research follows policy;
- *interactive model*, which posits complex and ongoing relationships
  between policy makers and researchers;
- *political/tactical model*, which sees policy as the outcome of a political
  process, and the research agenda as politically driven;
- *enlightenment model*, which sees research as illuminating the landscape
  for policy makers, while standing at some distance (Young et al,
  2002, p 216).

Thomas (1985) distinguished between the:

- *insider model*, where the researcher knows and works with the government machine, either at national or local level;
- *gadfly model*, where the researcher seeks to challenge the government machine;
- *limestone model*, where research results are simply left to find their own way through the fissures in the system.

Researchers may choose rationally between these models, but it seems more likely that they simply adopt the styles which best suit their temperament. In this chapter I shall draw on Thomas's set of models as a way of distinguishing the different routes by which research on children with disabilities has made an impact on policy.

However, there is a fundamental process that persistently cuts the ground from under the feet of social scientists, which was pointed out by Booth in an overview of work on the links between research and policy (Booth, 1988). In so far as the findings and insights of social science research are judged to be of interest and use, they tend to be absorbed into the language of everyday discourse and in a short while can become appropriated as 'what everyone knows'. Thus, yesterday's research may have influenced today's policy, without the policy makers being aware of its influence.

In considering whether research has influenced policy we must start by recognising the many influences brought to bear on policy makers. Research plays only a minor role in a play in which the main parts are surely taken by the ideologies of the government of the day, the priorities of dominant interest groups, the current financial constraints, the media scandals which shape public opinion and so on. We turn now to a field of study where, over the past 20 years, researchers have certainly been active in their attempts to shape policy: how successful have they been?

The costs to families of having a child with a disability

The first large-scale study in the UK to examine whether severe disablement in children affects their families' income and expenditure patterns was carried out by Baldwin (1985). It was funded by the Department of Health and Social Security and the methods used were rigorous. Families for the study were selected from the list of over 40,000 families who had applied for help from the Family Fund, the

York-based organisation established in 1973 to give help to families
with a severely disabled child. It was recognised that they might not
be representative of all severely disabled children, but this constituted
by far the most comprehensive available sampling frame. The sample
was stratified by region, social class and age of the disabled child.
These families were then matched as closely as possible with families
who had taken part in the most recent Family Expenditure Survey
(FES). The resulting samples comprised 469 families with a severely
disabled child and 682 control families from the FES. A slightly
modified version of the FES questionnaire was then administered
between January and July 1978 to all the families in the Family Fund
sample. Data on the incomes and expenditure patterns of these
households were compared with similar data from the FES control
group of families. There were also in-depth interviews with 48 families
(Baldwin, 1985).

The results were unequivocal. The *families with a disabled child were
likely to have lower incomes*, on average, than the control families, even
when benefits intended to help with the costs of disablement were
included in their incomes. Differences in women's employment rates
were particularly marked, so that women with a disabled child were
less likely to have jobs and, when they did, tended to work fewer
hours and earn less. At the same time, the *families with a disabled child
had additional costs*, both in terms of everyday living costs and in terms
of larger items bought less frequently. The conclusion was clear:

> The financial costs of caring for severely disabled children
> at home are considerably greater than the existing level of
> support from cash benefits, services in kind and the Family
> Fund. The case for improving financial support is strong.
> (Baldwin, 1985, p 167)

The study ended by setting out policy recommendations. These
included:

- reducing the qualifying age for Mobility Allowance to two. This
  benefit was intended to help with the higher transport costs of
  people unable to walk because of physical disability. At the time
  the higher rate was only available for children over the age of three
  and the lower rate for children over the age of five;
- changing the criteria for Attendance Allowance by abolishing the
  six-month qualifying period, making the benefit payable from birth
  in the case of severe impairments, and allowing parents to claim

the allowance when the child is in hospital. This benefit was paid to people in need of substantial care and at the time was available only to children over two years of age;
* setting up a system of interest-free loans, perhaps administered by the Family Fund;
* extending the Invalid Care Allowance (ICA) to married women. At the time this benefit, which went to people caring for someone who was receiving the Attendance Allowance, was only available to men and single women.

More generally a strong case was made for improving the general level of financial support, through a new benefit which might help with extra expenses, make up for lower parental earnings, and compensate 'the disabled child and other family members for the restrictions and stresses of severe disablement' (Baldwin, 1985, p 171).

The impact on policy

So what was the impact of this research? Despite the rigour of the Baldwin study, there was a demand for a more comprehensive national survey. A researcher at the conference in York in 2005, where this chapter was first presented, reported that Baldwin had worked with the civil servants responsible for designing the questionnaire for the 1985 survey by the Office of Population Censuses and Surveys (OPCS), which was the first national survey to provide comprehensive evidence of the financial situation of families with disabled children (Smyth and Robus, 1989).

The impact on policy is harder to document. '*Post hoc, ergo propter hoc*' is not a strong argument, but it is often all we have. It seems likely that the introduction in 1988 of a disabled child premium attached to Income Support was a result of the studies by Baldwin and by the OPCS. Income Support is a means-tested benefit, so the premium only went to the poorest families.

However, some new non-means-tested benefits were also introduced at this time. The Mobility Allowance and the Attendance Allowance were replaced in 1992 by the Disability Living Allowance (DLA). It has been argued that the new benefit was introduced 'following evidence that disabled people faced extra costs of living' (McKay and Rowlingson, 1999, p 107; see also Berthoud et al, 1993). Baldwin's work was a key part of this evidence.

The DLA has a mobility component, payable at a higher rate to those aged three and over, and a lower rate to those aged five and over.

Thus, the change in the age of eligibility that Baldwin recommended was not implemented. The DLA also has a care component, payable at higher, middle and lower rates, with limitations on children under the age of 16 qualifying for the lower rate. The other rates can be claimed from the time the child is three months old, but he or she has to have care or supervision requirements that are 'substantially in excess of the normal requirements for a child of the same age' (CPAG, 2004, p 150). This does represent a lower age than was the case at the time of Baldwin's study.

Baldwin's suggestion for a system of interest-free loans has still not been fully implemented. The introduction of the Social Fund in 1988 might be seen as a response to this recommendation, but it is more likely to have been a way of reducing demand for the previous scheme of Exceptional Needs Payments. The sums available have always been cash-limited. Social Fund loans are interest free, but have to be paid back: in 2003, 28% of budgeting loans and 20% of crisis loans went to disabled people (Finch and Kemp, 2004).

However, loans from the Social Fund are only available to families living on Income Support or Income-based Jobseeker's Allowance, and the Family Fund remains the main source of grants for a wider range of families. Bradshaw has analysed the process by which, in 1973, resources were suddenly allocated via the Family Fund to severely disabled children, a group which had attracted practically no attention before that time (Bradshaw, 1980). The reason for its introduction seems to have been the pressure on policy makers from the media attention given to the effects of thalidomide.

The continuing need for larger cash sums is shown by the fact that many families with disabled children only manage by taking out loans from banks and other lenders, often at high rates of interest. A study of 98 families from the Family Fund database showed that, on average, families spent £60.37 per week on paying off credit facilities, that is on debt repayments (Woolley, 2004). This situation confirms the continuing importance of Baldwin's recommendation.

One clear change was the extension of the ICA to married women in 1986, the year after Baldwin's book was published. Britain is relatively unusual in having a benefit that compensates carers for loss of earnings (Glendinning and McLaughlin, 1993; McKay and Rowlingson, 1999; Ungerson, 2000). The ICA was introduced in 1975, but it was denied to married women until a European Court case in 1986, initiated by the Equal Opportunities Commission (EOC), successfully argued that the ICA contravened the European Commission Directive on equal treatment of men and women in the social security system. This is an example of the ways in which membership of the European Union has influenced policy in the UK and of the power of pressure groups such as the EOC.

However, writing in 1994, Baldwin described the ICA as a 'contentious, complex and unsatisfactory response to the situation of carers', offering only symbolic recognition of the work of caring and its importance to society (Baldwin, 1994, p 187). The situation has not changed much today. In 2003 the ICA became the Carer's Allowance, which goes to those who are caring for 35 hours per week or more, and is effectively means-tested, being denied to anyone earning £79 per week or more. At a current rate of £44.35 per week this benefit values caring a long way below the national minimum wage level. A study in 1992 showed that, even with the ICA, the incomes of individual carers and of the households in which they lived were substantially below incomes for the general population (McLaughlin, 1992).

Continuity and change in help for children with disabilities

A number of recent studies help us to see whether the situation has changed for disabled children and their families over the past 20 years (Beresford, 1995; Dobson and Middleton, 1998; Dobson et al, 2001; Woolley, 2004; Preston, 2005). All of these studies concluded that families with disabled children continued to spend more on their children than comparable families without a disabled child, and to earn less because of the demands of caring, as well as because of the lack of suitable substitute care. At the same time the benefits available did not compensate for the costs of disability. It was estimated that benefits for disabled children would have to be increased by between 20% and 50%, depending on the child's age and type of impairment, to meet the costs of the minimum essential budgets (Dobson and Middleton, 1998).

Many families with disabled children did not even claim the benefits to which they were entitled (Preston, 2005). The reasons for this included reluctance to be on benefits, lack of information about benefits and difficulties in getting hold of forms and filling them in. This situation may reflect increases in the stigma attached to claiming benefits and in the complexity of the benefits system as a whole. It can be compared with the situation in the early 1980s when 95% of families with severely disabled children were receiving the Attendance

Allowance, as found in the studies carried out by Baldwin (1985) and by Pahl and Quine (Pahl and Quine, 1987; Quine and Pahl, 1989).

The insecurity of life on benefits is striking. Preston reported that families were often perplexed when their child's DLA award changed, while their child's needs and their costs had not. She concluded:

> Far from providing financial security for families, the current system renders families with disabled children extremely vulnerable to high levels of poverty and social exclusion. The provision of long-term financial support is essential if 'security for those who cannot work' is to become a reality. (Preston, 2005, p 81)

Preston's recommendations focused on increasing the take-up of benefits, by publicising what is available, providing better information and making it easier to claim. At the same time she argued for increases in benefit levels both for the children and for those who care for them. Finally she pointed out that, since parents of disabled children are less likely to be in paid work, they are also less likely to receive the Child Tax Credit and help with childcare, and many feel marginalised by the welfare-to-work strategy of the current government (Preston, 2005, p 83).

However, recent research suggests that a real change may be taking place in the financial situation of families with a disabled child. Reports on Households Below Average Income (HBAI) are produced every year by the Department for Work and Pensions, using data from the Family Resources Survey. Evidence from these surveys makes it possible to see how households with a disabled child are faring, by comparison with households without a disabled child.

Table 5.1 presents the risk of being in a low-income group, by various household characteristics, using low-income thresholds of 50%, 60% or 70% of the median income. It shows that families containing a disabled child have for years been more likely to be in poverty than other families. Thus, in 2002/03, 31% of families with a disabled child had incomes below 60% of the median income, compared with 19% of families without a disabled child.

However, between 2002/03 and 2003/04 there was a sharp drop in the risk of poverty among households with disabled children at all thresholds: those living below 60% of the median income dropped from 31% to 22%. In the poorest group, that is those living at or below 50% of the median income, families with a disabled child were actually less likely to be in poverty than families without a disabled

Table 5.1: Risk of being in a low-income group for households with children (%)[a]

	Below 50% median income		Below 60% median income		Below 70% median income	
	Disabled child	No disabled child	Disabled child	No disabled child	Disabled child	No disabled child
1999/2000	12	10	29	22	45	34
2000/01	12	11	26	21	40	32
2001/02	10	10	25	20	42	32
2002/03	15	9	31	19	44	30
2003/04	9	11	22	20	39	31

Note: [a] Disposable income calculated before housing costs
Source: DWP (2005a)

child. These findings could be a sampling error, so it will be important to look at data for the following years. However, it seems likely that they represent the impact of the disability and severe disability elements in Child Tax Credit, which benefit all DLA recipients, and are considerably more generous than the disability elements in the previous Working Families Tax Credit or in Income Support.

Personal communications from individuals at the conference in York where this chapter was first presented suggest that a number of factors have played a part in influencing policy in this area. A representative of a leading charity in the learning disability field said that research results had been used to support arguments for increasing financial support for children with learning disabilities. This underlines the point that voluntary organisations and think-tanks can offer a route by which research results can be fed into debates and so make an impact on policy. Leading researchers attending the conference reported that meetings with ministers or interested civil servants had led to some policy changes, underlining the importance of personal contact in spreading new ideas and knowledge.

One problem seems to be that disabled children are often invisible in policy debates. As *disabled* individuals they tend to be overshadowed by disabled adults and by policy initiatives about getting this group into paid work. As disabled *children* they tend to be overshadowed by concern for children generally and by policies related to child poverty and childcare. Children were not even included in the OPCS disability studies of 1969 and 1996, although they were represented in the 1986 survey, perhaps as a result of Baldwin's contacts with the relevant civil servants. Children were excluded from the first five Health Surveys for England, although those aged two and over were included from 1996, and there was a special section on children of all ages in 2002.

To whom should benefits be paid?

Another important question concerns the payment of benefits. To whom within the household should benefits intended for children be paid? Baldwin suggested in her conclusion to her 1985 book that one effect of having a disabled child was to alter the financial relations of husbands and wives, so that they cooperated more in planning and decision making, while the men made a larger proportion of their earnings available for general family expenses than would normally have been the case. She went on to say that financial arrangements within households were 'a relatively uncharted area' of family life (Baldwin, 1985, p 142).

Over the past 20 years there has been a growing body of research on the control and allocation of money within the household (see, for example, Pahl, 1980, 1989, 1995, 2005; Goode et al, 1998; Molloy and Snape, 1999; Snape et al, 1999; Laurie and Gershuny, 2000). This research has mapped the ways in which couples organise their finances, examined the correlates of particular financial arrangements and documented the implications of different systems of money management for individuals within households. The results have opened what used to be called the 'black box' of the household and have shown that households cannot be regarded as unproblematic financial units. Couples manage their finances in a great variety of different ways, and the route by which money enters the household has implications for what goes on within it. Thus, for example, power in decision making within the household reflects the amount of money which each individual has contributed: the higher the proportion of household income a person has contributed, the greater their power in decision making is (Pahl, 1995).

This research has shown that whether income is received by a man or a woman can shape the ways in which the money is spent. Money in a mother's pay packet, or in a benefit labelled as being for the family, is more likely to be spent on the children and on collective goods than money that enters the household through the father's pay packet (Pahl, 1989; Goode et al, 1998; Molloy and Snape, 1999; Snape et al, 1999). These findings have important implications for tax and social security policy, as well as for our understanding of social and economic processes within households.

So what evidence is there of the impact of all this research on policy related to the receipt of benefits? First, it can be argued that the continuation of Child Benefit owes something to research on the allocation of money within the family. This is a universal benefit, paid to the mother of a child under 16 years of age, or under 19 if the child is still in full-time education. Despite threats to abolish it or means-test it, Child Benefit continues as a non-means-tested, universal benefit paid to all mothers (CPAG, 2004). The various campaigns that have been waged in its defence have all made use of results from research on the intra-household economy and on the importance of paying money directly to mothers (see, for example, Walsh and Lister, 1985; Hawkins, 1991).

Second, policies about who should actually receive particular social security benefits have also been shaped by research in this field. A baseline from which to measure change comes from a comment by some of the leading experts in the field of social security. Writing in 1984 about proposals to pay benefits for children to mothers rather than fathers, they said:

> The forced redistribution of considerable amounts of money from husband to wife might be resented by many people, including the authors of this book, who consider that the distribution between husband and wife is a matter for them rather than for the government. (Dilnot et al, 1984, p 112)

Ironically, the (male) authors did not seem to notice that paying benefits to husbands, rather than to wives or couples, could also be seen as an intrusion by the government into family life!

Since then we have moved to a situation in which it is recognised that deciding who should be the recipient of a particular benefit is an important issue and one which is very much a matter for the government. Indeed some of the more recent research on this topic was funded by the Department of Social Security (DSS) specifically to examine different ways of paying benefits (Goode et al, 1998; Molloy and Snape, 1999; Snape et al, 1999).

The importance of protecting the interests of children against men's personal spending was emphasised in the study by Goode et al (1998), which was funded by the Joseph Rowntree Foundation. At the time one policy option was to split benefit payments for families, so that each recipient received their own individual entitlement. The researchers interviewed 31 couples and concluded that:

> Most expressed a desire to preserve the identity of benefit
> income as money for the family. Men and women feared
> that if this were replaced by a principle of individual
> ownership, men might exercise this entitlement to the
> detriment of the family as a whole. (Goode et al, 1998,
> p xiii)

Snape, Molloy and Kumar were funded by the DSS to examine whether
different methods of administering benefits affect perceptions of
entitlement held by either partner. The research involved interviews
with 33 couples, all of whom were claiming either Income Support
or Jobseeker's Allowance (IS/JSA). The results showed that, in general,
respondents did not want to change to individualised benefits. Despite
the potential for boosting self-esteem and providing an independent
income for each partner, benefit splitting was expected to pose problems
that would run counter to an ethos of sharing and encourage a sense
of personal entitlement to the income (Snape et al, 1999, p 9). The
study concluded by advocating greater flexibility in methods of
administering benefits, to reflect the different needs, priorities and
circumstances of people on benefits.

We now have a situation in which couples have to claim IS/JSA,
and the associated disability premium, as a couple, but can choose
which one of them is actually the recipient. Child Tax Credit has to
be claimed by the couple, as a couple, but the payments go to whoever
is deemed to be the main carer, usually the mother (CPAG, 2004,
p 1297). Working Tax Credit, although it is claimed by the couple, is
actually paid to the employee, with their wages. The Carer's Allowance
is paid to the carer, while the DLA for a child is claimed by an adult
with whom the child is living.

In general, then, the current rules for the payment of benefits appear
to reflect the findings of research and the work of researchers. It is
recognised that paying benefits to the man, as 'head of the household'
or 'main earner', as was the case 20 years ago, may not be appropriate.
Research has shown that who receives the benefit affects how the
money received is defined within the household. Much of the relevant
research has been funded by the DSS, and as such can be regarded as
insider research. But the increased understanding of this topic reflects
the fact that the findings from over 20 years of research about the
intra-household economy have seeped into the public domain, as if
through *limestone*, to become part of the taken-for-granted knowledge
that 'everyone knows'.

Conclusion

What can we conclude about the impact of research on policy? Certainly over the past 20 years there have been real changes in social security benefits for disabled children, in terms of the reasons for which they are paid, the amounts paid and the person to whom they are paid.

It is clear that research is only one of many influences on policy. Research may have supported the case for more generous benefits for families with disabled children, but it was media publicity which prompted the setting up of the Family Fund. The EOC was responsible for taking the relevant case to the European Court, which led to changes in the rules around the ICA. Personal contacts between researchers and civil servants and ministers led to changes in policy, as well as to the carrying out of particular studies to provide evidence which could inform policy decisions. In all of these instances research could be seen as providing a bedrock of information on which government departments, the media, voluntary organisations and think-tanks could build.

The story of 20 years of research on the costs of caring for a child with a disability has many lessons for researchers who want their work to influence policy. It suggests that there are a number of different strategies that researchers can adopt. These include:

- working with individuals and groups in central and local government to change policy and practice: the 'insider' model;
- working with voluntary organisations, pressure groups and think-tanks to supply evidence for campaigns: the 'gadfly' model;
- working with the media to change the ways in which people think about particular issues: the 'limestone' model;
- working with professionals and service users to change training programmes and practice guides;
- working with social and intellectual networks to develop ideas and strategies for change;
- writing books, articles and reports to inform and support all the above activities.

Perhaps the overall conclusion is that researchers must not only produce good research, but must also be inventive, versatile and skilful disseminators if they want their work to influence policy. There is no one route to the creation of an evidence base for policy and practice, nor to the growth of an evidence-informed society.

Acknowledgements

This chapter was first presented at the conference held at the University of York in 2005 in memory of Professor Sally Baldwin. My thanks and appreciation go to all those who contributed to the discussion at the time, and especially to Professor Jonathan Bradshaw for drawing to my attention the data from the surveys of Households Below Average Income and for commenting very helpfully on an earlier draft of this chapter.

SIX

Disability, poverty and living standards: reviewing Australian evidence and policies[1]

Peter Saunders

Introduction

The Australian economy has experienced over 13 consecutive years of strong economic growth, following extensive deregulation of its financial, product and labour markets. Throughout this period, the Commonwealth government has tightened its targeting of income transfers and relied increasingly on competitive tendering between government and non-government agencies to deliver its social programmes, leading the world in many of its reform initiatives. The fact that the Australian welfare system has traditionally relied on an extensive array of non-government agencies has made the task of privatising welfare more manageable than some other countries have found. However, the counterpart to this is that many of Australia's welfare structures and institutions are more fragile than elsewhere, and questions are being raised about their ability to withstand current pressures. As the middle class is required to pay for services while being income-tested out of social transfers, support for the welfare state is declining, placing pressure on government to implement further programme cuts and/or user charges that reinforce the problem.

Australia's pro-market reform strategy emerged under the Hawke–Keating Labour governments of the 1980s, when the initial changes were introduced as part of an Accord between the government and the trades unions that delivered wage restraint in exchange for employment generation and a boost in the social wage. Since its election to office in 1996, the Howard government has combined an even more radical free market approach with a conservative social agenda built on notions of personal responsibility and mutual obligation. Market deregulation has been accompanied by increased real wages, but high productivity growth has meant that growth in output has not translated into employment, and unemployment remains stuck above 5%. Welfare receipt among the working-age population increased from around 11% in 1965 to over 19% in 1997 (Whiteford, 2000). Although welfare receipt has declined since then to below 16% by 2002, government policy remains focused on getting those on welfare into work.

Against this background, this chapter examines the circumstances of households that contain disabled members in the context of proposed reforms to the main income support programme for disabled people, the Disability Support Pension (DSP). After briefly reviewing the Australian policy context in the next section, the chapter compares the economic circumstances of those who have a disability or long-term health condition with those who do not. It then reviews community attitudes to mutual obligation for unemployed people and disabled people (a major theme in the welfare reform debate). The final section summarises the main conclusions of the chapter.

The policy context

The welfare system has been a central focus of policy reform in Australia over the last two decades. This is partly because of its growing size and cost, but also because of its perceived failings. Chief among the latter is the combination of high effective marginal tax rates and the growing complexity that has been a direct consequence of the targeting policies pursued by successive governments. While political rhetoric has stressed the need to address these seemingly intractable problems, policy makers have accepted that this cannot be achieved without a substantial increase in funding or a significant reduction in benefits, neither of which attract anything like the necessary degree of public support. Attention has instead focused on increasing employment among the welfare-dependent population, principally by requiring them to undertake activities thought likely to lead to this outcome.

Addressing the growing problem of welfare dependency was the key task given to the Reference Group on Welfare Reform (RGWR) established in 1999 to develop a new welfare reform blueprint (RGWR, 2000). The central tenet of the RGWR approach was that 'the nation's social support system must be judged by its capacity to help people participate economically and socially, as well as by the adequacy of its income support arrangements' (RGWR, 2000, p 3). This was to be achieved through a new participation support system involving a simpler structure that encouraged participation through mutual obligation (the idea that those who receive a benefit paid for by taxpayers should be expected to 'give something back', in the words of Prime Minister John Howard), underpinned by a network of social obligations involving government, business, communities and individuals, and by individualised service delivery, supported by a social partnership approach also involving government, as well as the community and commercial sectors.

In practice, the reforms introduced since 2000 have tightened mutual obligation requirements on those receiving unemployment benefit in order to increase participation in employment, with some improvements in services, but has failed to grapple with the problems of complexity or disincentives.[2] Virtually no effort has been made to explore the ideas of social partnerships and social obligations, except as part of the political rhetoric accompanying the reform process.

Attention has focused on reforming the unemployment benefit system in ways that link eligibility to mutual obligation activities designed to facilitate the welfare-to-work transition. These measures are to be extended to lone parents and disabled people, following measures announced in the 2005 Budget (see below). The general principle underlying mutual obligation receives a high level of public support, as long as its requirements are reasonable and take account of the circumstances of those who must comply with them (Eardley et al, 2001). There is also evidence that welfare recipients who have made a successful transition into employment also support it, many indicating that it had helped them to find a job by increasing their motivation and promoting contact with other people and with the labour market (Saunders et al, 2004).

The number of people receiving the DSP increased more than fivefold between 1972 and 2004, from 138,800 to 696,700, or by 5.2% a year on average – well above the increase in both the disabled population and the total working-age population.[3] DSP numbers accelerated after the introduction of the Disability Reform Package in 1991, since when the numbers have more than doubled and annual growth has been closer to 6% (Department of FaCS, 2004). Relatively few of those who receive DSP are in employment or participating in an employment support programme. The Australian Council of Social Service (ACOSS) has indicated that only 9% of recipients have a part-time job and 6% participate in an employment programme (ACOSS, 2005a). Both figures are well below those prevailing in many other Organisation for Economic Co-operation and Development (OECD) countries (OECD, 2003a).

These trends have been viewed with alarm by a government

concerned not only with their budgetary consequences, but also with the harmful psychological and motivational impacts, and the adverse 'role model' effects of joblessness on children. The Secretary to the Treasury has captured these concerns in the following remarks:

> There are now more people on DSP than there are in receipt of Newstart Allowance – unemployment payments … when one in nine Australians aged between 50 and 64 is on the DSP, I think we can safely conclude that we have something other than a safety net. Indeed, we have to consider whether we haven't created a set of opportunities and incentives to institutionalise voluntary early retirement. (Henry, 2003, p 10)

These concerns have led the government to tighten eligibility for DSP in reforms announced in the 2005 Budget, following an unsuccessful attempt to introduce them in 2002, when the legislation was rejected by the Senate. Since then, the federal election of October 2004 resulted in the government gaining control of the Senate, paving the way for the reforms to be enacted.[4] The key feature of the reforms is a reduction in the capacity-to-work requirement from 30 to 15 hours a week that will make many applicants for DSP no longer eligible, forcing them instead onto the lower Newstart Allowance (NSA), the main benefit for unemployed people.[5] In justifying the changes, the minister responsible argued that:

> The community feels it is a fair principle that people are asked to work in keeping with their abilities and capacity. This very simple sentiment … is the basis of the changes in the Government's Welfare to Work package. The biggest change, in a practical sense, is that we ask people who can work part time to work part time. This group of people … will be asked to actively look for work and meet mutual obligation activities, such as the highly successful Work for the Dole. (Dutton, 2005, pp 5-6)

The fair-minded language conceals a darker reality in which those on DSP will not be 'asked' to look for work but required to, if they are to remain eligible for benefit. The minister's confidence in the public's acceptance of the changes can also be challenged (see below), as can the claim that the Work for the Dole scheme has been 'highly successful'.[6] Although the requirements will only apply to new applicants (including existing recipients who go off payment and then return), they will divert those deemed eligible to work for between 15 and 30 hours a week from DSP onto NSA, which is paid at a lower rate and indexed to prices not earnings.[7] In addition, NSA is subject to a harsher income test than DSP and a far more demanding set of mutual obligation requirements. There are also a number of programmes that support job search and employment participation that are tied to receipt of NSA.

One of the most striking aspects of this debate is the lack of attention given to the adequacy of payments for disabled people. This reflects the absence of research on the relationship between poverty and other living standards indicators and disability status that can be traced back to the 1970s when the Poverty Commission reported (Commission of Inquiry into Poverty, 1975). This can be explained in part by the emphasis given to meeting needs through services rather than income support, although both are important. Attempts to examine the adequacy issue have also been thwarted by lack of data, including on how needs vary with disability status (the equivalence scale issue). It is, however, possible to overcome some of these problems with new data on the incidence of financial stress or hardship (both synonyms for poverty, a word not used by the current government) and these are used in the remainder of the chapter to estimate the impact of disability.

Comparing living standards

Reflecting its emphasis on the income targeting of benefits and heavy reliance on income taxation as a revenue source, Australian research on living standards has focused on comparing the disposable incomes of different groups and monitoring how these have changed over time (Bradbury et al, 1990).[8] Poverty research in Australia has also been dominated by the use of income-based measures. The Poverty Commission has been described as a 'landmark in the long pursuit of justice for disabled Australians' in part because it 'insisted on a relatively broad view that included deprivation of items other than income, such as public services ... highlighted the special costs faced by disabled people, and pointed out repeatedly how these reduced employment chances' (Gleeson, 1998, p 323). The Commission estimated that the poverty rate among the 'sick and disabled' was more than twice the national rate of 10.2% in 1972/73. By 1996, disability poverty had increased to 26.7%, although the national rate increased even faster, to 16.7%, implying that the relative picture for disabled people had improved (even more markedly after taking account of housing costs) (King, 1998, table 4.2).

Although poverty studies provide a valuable benchmark for assessing the income risks facing different groups in the population, the failure to allow for the costs of disability in the equivalence adjustment and the reliance on cash income as an indicator of the standard of living are major weaknesses.[9] Increasing recognition of the role played by factors other than income have raised more general challenges for the income poverty approach, as Lister (2004) and Saunders (2005) have argued. There are sound reasons to be concerned about the relevance of income poverty in a world where economic well-being and autonomy are increasingly conditioned by such factors as wealth holdings, time pressures, caring responsibilities, access to services, and the freedom to make choices and realise one's potential as captured in Sen's notion of capability (Sen, 1999).

Recent theoretical and empirical developments in the international poverty literature have specific relevance for disabled people, who have not been well served by the standard income poverty approach. The great benefit of identifying disadvantage in terms of observed deprivation, or as processes or actions that produce exclusion, or as a failure of capabilities, is that it directs attention to the *demonstrated* outcomes associated with particular characteristics or conditions, rather than focusing on how inadequate income (or access to resources more generally) is *presumed* to create poverty by restricting the ability to meet basic needs. Direct observation of living conditions also avoids the need to make an equivalence adjustment, since the ability to meet actual needs from available resources is evident from the observed levels of deprivation or functioning.

But Australia is currently a long way from implementing these kinds of measures to support policy. In 2004, the Senate Community Affairs References Committee (CARC) undertook an inquiry into poverty and its *Report on poverty and financial hardship* documented evidence of widespread poverty, which it considered to be 'unacceptable and unsustainable' (CARC, 2004, p xv). However, the inquiry was seen as overtly political and the Committee was unable to achieve a bipartisan approach, splitting along party lines. The government dismissed the report's recommendations (which included the setting and monitoring of poverty reduction targets) on the grounds that poverty targets have no real benefit and would involve extra bureaucracy when 'practical programmes' are what is needed.[10]

Lack of data is another obstacle. There is no Australian counterpart to the British Poverty and Social Exclusion (PSE) survey, nor have there been any systematic attempts to plot the national profile of deprivation, despite a successful pilot survey of the approach in the mid-1990s (Travers and Robertson, 1996). Some information has been collected in a series of recent surveys, including in the latest Household Expenditure Survey (HES), the new longitudinal survey the Household Income and Labour Dynamics in Australia (HILDA) and the General Social Survey (GSS) introduced for the first time in 2002.

Data from the first of these sources (HES) can be used to classify aspects of the living standards of households according to their disability status. In addition to including a series of questions on hardship and financial stress (described and analysed by Bray, 2001, and McColl et al, 2001), the 1998/99 HES asked respondents to indicate whether or not they (or other household members, including children) had a disability or suffered from a long-term health condition.[11] In using the HES data, the aim is not to produce a definitive account of how economic and social circumstances relate to the presence of a disability, but to provide an overview of the association between the presence of disability in a household and a variety of indicators of its standard of living. The results compare the value of each indicator between households that contain no individuals with a reported disability or long-term health condition (hereafter 'disability' for short), households with at least one adult with a reported disability, and households with no disabled adults but at least one disabled child. Households containing an adult aged 65 or over have been excluded. Household income has been adjusted to reflect differences in household need using the 'modified' OECD equivalence scale that assigns a value of 1.0 to the first adult, 0.5 to each subsequent adult and 0.3 to each child.

Income levels and poverty

Table 6.1 compares the after-tax (disposable) incomes of households by their disability status, as defined above. The median income of disability households is 14.9% lower than that for non-disability households, the gap being greater where there are disabled adults than where there are only disabled children. The mean income relativities are slightly larger than those based on the median, although the patterns are the same. These relative income differences increase considerably after the equivalence adjustment. The median income of households with a disabled adult is over 23% below that of households with no disability, and the gap for households with a disabled child is even larger, at 36%.

The income differences shown in Table 6.1 are reflected in the

Cash and care

Table 6.1: Mean household income, by disability status (A$, 1998/99)

Household type	% of all households	Median income Unadjusted	Adjusted[a]	Mean income Unadjusted	Adjusted[a]
No disabled member[b]	55.1	752	464	824	495
At least one disabled adult	42.3	626	354	713	404
No disabled adults but at least one disabled child	2.6	678	297	759	337
All disabled	44.9	640	340	729	391
All households	100.0	696	408	782	449

Notes:
[a] Incomes have been adjusted using the modified OECD equivalence scale.
[b] Disability includes a long-term health condition (see text).

Source: Household Expenditure Survey, 1998/99, confidentialised unit record file.

patterns of income poverty shown in Table 6.2, which are based on poverty lines set at different percentages of median (adjusted) income. The use of a range of poverty lines allows the sensitivity of the results to be assessed. On the basis of the 50% line, disability is associated with a two percentage-point increase in the risk of poverty where it affects an adult, and a five percentage-point increase where it affects children. These differences virtually disappear at the 40% benchmark, but are substantially larger at the 60% of median income poverty line. The findings are consistent with the view that the welfare system provides a comprehensive but modest income safety net that protects

Table 6.2: Patterns of income poverty, by disability status (%)

Household type	Poverty rate 40% median income	50% median income	60% median income
No disabled member	4.5	7.4	12.1
At least one disabled adult	5.0	9.4	22.6
No disabled adults but at least one disabled child	5.6	12.3	24.9
All disabled	5.0	9.5	22.8
All households	4.8	8.4	16.9

Source: Household Expenditure Survey, 1998/99, confidentialised unit record file.

most people from extreme income poverty, but income from other sources (primarily earnings) have an increasing impact as the poverty line is shifted up the income distribution.[12]

Table 6.3 examines the employment patterns of households classified by their disability status. Joblessness is about two-and-a-half times higher among disabled households than among households generally. Household employment rates are lower where there is a disabled adult, particularly the incidence of full-time employment. In contrast, where there is a disabled child, although the incidence of employment is again lower, the incidence of full-time employment is higher than for other households. This is consistent with these households needing one adult to remain at home to care for the child, leaving only a single breadwinner who is more likely to work full time.

Hardship, deprivation and exclusion

As noted earlier, the indicators examined below are relatively new in Australia and cannot be claimed to provide as clear a picture of the profile of deprivation and social exclusion as the more sophisticated indicators common in the UK and Europe. But they overlap to some degree with data generated in the PSE survey (Gordon et al, 2000) and have been used to examine the extent of financial hardship and deprivation in Australia (Bray, 2001; Saunders, 2003) and to compare the deprivation profiles of Australia and Britain (Saunders and Adelman, 2004).

The indicators used to explore how deprivation and exclusion are associated with disability are shown in Table 6.4.[13] The 14 indicators

Table 6.3: Jobless households, by disability status (%)

Household type	Jobless households	One employed person	One person employed full time
No disabled member	10.3	38.7	52.6
At least one disabled adult	25.6	31.2	38.6
No disabled adults but at least one disabled child	23.0	34.6	58.5
All disabled	25.4	31.4	39.8
All households	17.1	35.4	46.9

Source: Household Expenditure Survey, 1998/99, confidentialised unit record file.

(H_1 to H_{14}) have been combined into five separate exploratory dimensions of hardship:

- *financial hardship* – based on experiencing at least five of the indicators;
- *restricted social participation* – based on experiencing at least two of the indicators H_1 to H_6;
- *severe financial stress* – based on experiencing any one of the indicators H_7, H_8, H_{10} and H_{11};
- *expressed need* – based on experiencing at least one of the indicators H_9, H_{12} and H_{13}; and
- *lack of support* – the inability to raise money in an emergency, based on indicator H_{14}.

Although these definitions embody arbitrary decisions about how many conditions constitute each domain of hardship, the fact that we are primarily interested in comparing the indicators by disability status makes this less of an issue than might otherwise be the case. Having said this, it needs to be emphasised that the results are exploratory and should thus be treated with a degree of caution.

Table 6.4: Indicators of hardship and financial stress

Hardship indicator	Definition
H_1	Cannot afford a week's holiday away from home each year
H_2	Cannot afford a night out once a fortnight
H_3	Cannot afford to have friends/family over for a meal once a month
H_4	Cannot afford a special meal once a week
H_5	Cannot afford brand new clothes (usually buy second-hand)
H_6	Cannot afford leisure or hobby activities
In the last year due to shortage of money:	
H_7	Could not pay gas, electricity or telephone on time
H_8	Could not pay car registration or insurance on time
H_9	Pawned or sold something
H_{10}	Went without meals
H_{11}	Was unable to heat the home
H_{12}	Sought assistance from a welfare or community agency
H_{13}	Sought financial help from friends or family
H_{14}	Could not raise $2000 in a week if had to

Source: Household Expenditure Survey, User Guide, 1998/99; ABS (2000).

Table 6.5: Incidence of different indicators of hardship, by disability status (%)

Household type	Financial hard-ship	Restricted partici-pation	Severe financial stress	Expressed need	Lack of support
No disabled member	7.8	16.8	16.0	11.0	15.4
At least one disabled adult	18.1	28.4	27.4	19.0	25.7
No disabled adults but at least one disabled child	26.5	37.5	37.4	25.5	32.6
All disabled	19.7	31.3	29.0	20.3	27.7
All households	13.2	23.3	21.8	15.2	20.9

Source: Household Expenditure Survey, 1998/99, confidentialised unit record file.

The incidence of each of the five indicators of hardship among households categorised by their disability status is shown in Table 6.5. These results indicate that the presence of disability has greater negative consequences than was implied in the earlier comparisons of income levels (Table 6.1) or poverty rates (Table 6.2). In overall terms, the comparisons are more similar to those based on the 60% of median income poverty line than the 50% benchmark. Having a disabled household member is associated with a substantial increase in the incidence of financial hardship, a higher probability of experiencing severe financial stress and is more likely to result in having to sell or pawn things, or seek help from others. Disability also leads to less social participation, and disabled people are more likely to report not having access to external financial support if it is needed. Households with a disabled member are thus not only more deprived, but are also at greater risk of becoming so in times of crisis.

Attitudes to mutual obligation

The earlier policy discussion identified mutual obligation as a major theme in the current government's welfare reform agenda. Table 6.6 presents a range of the results on support for imposing mutual obligation requirements (MOR) on three groups of unemployed people – those aged under 25, those aged 50 and over and those who are disabled. They are derived from the Coping With Economic and Social Change (CESC) survey conducted by the Social Policy Research Centre at the University of New South Wales in 1999 (see Saunders, 2002, for details). The results differentiate between the views of all respondents (shown in the left-hand columns for each group) and those of respondents who share the characteristics of each group, in terms of their age and disability status (shown in the right-hand columns).[14]

For the CESC sample as a whole, there is a high level of support for applying almost all forms of MOR to young unemployed people, with almost half agreeing that young unemployed people should be required to move to another town in order to find work. In contrast, support for MOR for those aged 50 and over is much lower, with only three requirements receiving majority support: look for work; engage in training/retraining; and undertake useful community work. Support is lower again when it comes to applying MOR to unemployed disabled people, where the level of support among the population is below 50% in all but one case (training/retraining) and is often below one-quarter (Table 6.6).[15]

The results shown in columns two, four and six of Table 6.6 compare the MOR responses of those who share the characteristics of unemployed people to whom mutual obligation would apply. What is striking about these results is that there is no strong tendency for those who share characteristics to be more sympathetic than the

Table 6.6: Attitudes to mutual obligation, by recipient and respondent characteristics (%)

Require-ment	Young unemployed (under 25)		Older unemployed (50+)		Unemployed and disabled	
	All respondents	Under-25s only	All respondents	50+ only	All respondents	Disabled only
Look for work	92.8	94.6	53.7	48.5	33.5	19.3
Complete a dole diary	79.9	80.0	40.9	35.2	25.7	14.6
Work for the Dole scheme	82.5	80.3	38.2	35.7	24.6	16.3
Training/retraining	81.8	86.3	61.5	51.3	51.8	33.1
Useful community work	78.4	77.9	62.8	57.8	46.3	30.4
Accept any job	64.9	56.5	32.8	62.2	18.1	14.7
Move to another town	49.1	49.9	9.4	9.5	5.3	3.5
Change their appearance	71.2	72.8	33.8	71.6	25.4	18.2
Improve reading and writing skills	83.9	82.9	41.1	62.4	45.4	32.1

Source: CESC survey (see main text)

population at large when it comes to the treatment of unemployed people. Thus, support for applying MOR to young unemployed people is slightly *higher* among those who are themselves under 25 than among the general population. The level of support for applying MOR to those aged over 50 is lower among the over-50 group, although the differences are generally rather small. In relation to disabled people, the already low level of general support for MOR declines even further among those who are disabled themselves, but the level of support for mutual obligation is generally below 20% and nowhere exceeds one-third.

The main policy challenge for disability income support is how to introduce work-oriented mutual obligation (or activation) requirements on those who receive DSP to assist those who can, with support, get into work without penalising those who cannot. This involves confronting the kinds of dilemmas that Overbye (2005, p 168) has described in the Scandinavian context: knowing when to stop so that those who are unable to get a job do not end up 'with a self-image as secondary citizens'. Deciding who should be subjected to activation programmes also raises acute trade-offs between responsibilities and rights, and between cost-effectiveness and equity, as Thornton and Corden (2005) have emphasised. Programmes that target only those who are most likely to benefit run the risk of further alienating others, while making participation compulsory would require a sophisticated process for identifying those too ill to work and/or a complex and potentially very damaging system of penalties for those unwilling to be involved.

Conclusions

The above discussion indicates that the presence of disability is associated with low levels of income and high exposure to income poverty; and it is difficult to imagine that this association does not reflect causality. Disability also reduces the ability to participate in employment for many, unless support is provided to enable disabled people to find and keep a job. The evidence on living conditions paints an even bleaker picture of the impact of disability, revealing larger gaps between the circumstances of disabled and non-disabled people.

Notwithstanding this, considerable attention has been placed on the design and impact of the income support system for disabled people, because of the rapid growth in numbers, but also because this is the gateway to other assistance. The recently announced DSP reforms are designed to encourage more recipients into part-time work, but their success will depend critically on the kinds of enabling measures that accompany the more stringent eligibility requirements (not to mention the availability of suitable jobs). In order to be successful, the reforms will need to be accompanied by measures designed to assist disabled people to overcome the very serious barriers (including employer discrimination and a lack of appropriate counselling services) that currently prevent them from joining the labour force – an outcome that many of them already aspire to (Morris and Abello, 2004).

Employment support will be particularly critical if increased employment participation among those receiving DSP is going to achieve anything beyond improving the budget bottom line. While there are uncertainties surrounding their longer-term impact, the short-run consequences of the reforms are more predictable. They will reduce the incomes of the many DSP recipients who are already reliant on a poverty-level income and produce increased pressures to comply with new MOR. This will only add to the financial and other pressures already known to exist among this vulnerable group.

Notes

[1] I would like to thank Karen Fisher and Alan Morris for comments on a draft of this chapter, and Peter Siminski, Kelly Sutherland and Roger Patulny for providing statistical and other support. The usual caveats apply.

[2] The government's initial response to the RGWR report set out an agenda for implementing its main recommendations, but produced few actual reforms (Commonwealth of Australia, 2002).

[3] The factors contributing to the increase in numbers receiving DSP have been examined by Cai (2003) and Cai and Gregory (2003, 2004). These studies indicate that increases in the inflow rate have contributed more to growing numbers than declines in the outflow rate, but also that unemployment has been a major factor (in combination with policy changes) in explaining the growth in numbers, although most of the growth remains unexplained.

[4] Following the 2004 election, those sections of the Department of Family and Community Services (FaCS) that dealt with programmes and benefits for working-age people were moved into the Department of Employment and Workplace Relations (DEWR), in an attempt to overcome the departmental (and ministerial) rivalries on which earlier reforms had foundered. This has also shifted the balance of bureaucratic power away from

the more socially liberal mindset within FaCS to the more hard-nosed economic mindset of DEWR.

[5] ACOSS (2005b) estimates that up to 60,000 DSP recipients will be affected by these changes.

[6] A recent evaluation of the Work for the Dole (WfD) programme concludes that 'there appear to be quite large significant adverse effects of participation in WfD' (Borland and Tseng, 2005, p 23), mainly as a result of the reduced job search activity among those who are required to participate in the programme.

[7] In August 2005, the single adult (over 21 years of age) rate of NSA was A$199.65 a week, 16.2% below the corresponding DSP rate of A$238.15.

[8] Several studies have estimated the impact of the social wage by imputing as income the cost to government of providing national education, health and welfare services, although this has been done at a high level of aggregation, focusing on the impact on the relative positions of households defined by size, type, age or source of income (Harding, 1996; ABS, 2001).

[9] In Britain, Zaidi and Burchardt (2003) estimate that if the special needs of disabled people are taken into account, the disability poverty rate increases from around 50% above that for non-disabled people to almost three times higher (cited in Hills, 2004, table 2.3).

[10] The Senate inquiry recommended that a new disability allowance be introduced to meet the additional costs associated with disability, that payments to carers be reviewed and improved, and that a range of measures be introduced to increase employment and education among disabled people. These recommendations have had no impact.

[11] The disability conditions referred to in the question are: sight problems not corrected by glasses or contact lenses; hearing problems; speech problems; blackouts, fits or loss of consciousness; slowness at learning or understanding; limited use of arms or fingers; difficulty gripping things; limited use of legs or feet; any condition that restricts physical activity or physical work (for example a back problem); and a disfigurement or deformity. Long-term health conditions include the following (each experienced for at least six months): shortness of breath, or difficulty breathing; chronic or recurring pain; a nervous or emotional condition; any mental illness that requires help or supervision; long-term effects as a result of a head injury, stroke or other brain damage; a

long-term condition that requires treatment or medication; and any other long-term condition such as arthritis, asthma, heart disease, Alzheimer's disease, dementia and so on.

[12] Other information not presented indicates that disabled households have a much higher propensity (27.2%) to have income from government benefits as their principal source of income than households unaffected by disability (10.2%). This means that the level of benefits relative to the poverty line is a more critical issue for disabled people.

[13] The HES questions on which this information is based first asked respondents if they had undertaken each activity, and then for those who had not, whether or not this was due to a shortage of money (or lack of affordability).

[14] Small numbers prevent a breakdown of the views of respondents by personal characteristics and whether or not they themselves were unemployed at the time of the survey.

[15] These results thus suggest that the public has a less sanguine view of mutual obligation than Minister Dutton implies in the remarks attributed to him earlier.

SEVEN

Consumers without money: consumption patterns and citizenship among low-income families in Scandinavian welfare societies

Pernille Hohnen

> To be an individual does not necessarily mean to be free.
> The form of individuality on offer in late modern or post-
> modern society, and indeed most common in this kind of
> society – privatised individuality – means, essentially,
> unfreedom. (Bauman, 1999, p 63)

Introduction

How does it feel to be poor[1] in a society otherwise dominated by
affluence? What kind of participation and what kind of choices are
available to poor consumers? And, more generally, what are the
consequences of the increased emphasis on consumption and
consumerism for social marginalisation and the distribution of social
welfare in Scandinavian societies?

This chapter examines the creation of new forms of poverty and
social vulnerability in contemporary Scandinavian welfare states by
analysing the relationship between access to consumption on the one
hand and the experience of welfare and social integration on the
other. The analysis builds on empirical results from a primarily
qualitative, comparative research project on social vulnerability and
consumption carried out in Denmark, Sweden and Norway.[2]

Understanding the social dimension of consumption becomes
particularly significant in the light of the increased individualisation
and marketisation of the Scandinavian welfare states epitomised by a
change in political regulation as well as by a shift in political rhetoric
(from 'citizen' to 'consumer'). In contemporary Scandinavian society,

the norms and social control inherent in the evolving national discourse on 'consumption' influence a broad set of everyday experiences, choices and access to social participation (Bourdieu, 1984; Edgell and Hetherington, 1996). The aim is therefore to study what Bourdieu (1999) has called *la petite misère* (the little misery), focusing on those groups of the population who are subject to the rhetoric of affluence and to material welfare among other social groups, but who themselves are unable to take part in consumerism. We use the concept of *social vulnerability* to indicate the *relatively* deprived situation of these families (Hjort, 2002, 2004).

Consumption studies and social inequality

The field of consumption studies is extensive, and researchers have analysed consumption from a variety of perspectives. However, researchers have recently criticised consumption studies for overestimating the symbolic and expressive side of consumerism (Löfgren, 1996; Warde, 1996; Carrier and Heyman, 1997; Hjort, 2004). For example, Warde writes:

> ... much recent theoretical discussion of consumption has assumed that now survival is assured, the means of physical and social reproduction guaranteed, the practices of consumption have become more diverse in their purposes, more expressive in their intent. (Warde, 1996, p 303)

Carrier and Heyman (1997) have argued that much of this research gives priority to a cultural perspective, where consumption is understood as communication, search for pleasure, an expression of social identities and status, or promoting new forms and content of the self. One implication of this is that the analysis of the functional value of consumption is ignored (see also Hjort, 2004). Another implication is a lack of concern with poor consumers, because the preoccupation with symbolism and culture seems to invoke the assumption that consumers are first and foremost 'middle class' (Chin, 2001, p 11).

Following up this criticism, Lodziak (2002) has launched an attack on what he calls 'the myth of consumerism', which, in his view, characterises much theorising within the field. Consumption studies, he claims, may be characterised by a set of ideologically based assumptions:

During the past ten years or so, within the academic fields
of the sociology of culture and Cultural Studies, a theoretical
consensus has emerged with respect to the study of
consumption. This consensus portrays the realm of
consumption as an arena of choice and individual freedom,
it focuses on the meaningful nature of consumption – its
symbolic value rather than its material use value – and it
emphasises the significance of consumption formation,
maintenance and expression of self-identity and lifestyle.
(Lodziak, 2002, p 1)

Lodziak's criticism includes the following points of concern: that
uneven access to 'the market' and the influence of commercial interests
on consumption strategies are not regarded as significant in determining
consumption patterns; that the meaning of consumption is a priori
considered to be cultural or symbolic in contrast to economic and
material; that generalisations of 'consumer' behaviour are often based
on experience of small groups of consumers; and, finally, that
consumption is about 'freedom of choice' and that consumerism
therefore promotes individual freedom.

Several of Lodziak's points of criticism are directly relevant to the
present study, including the emphasis on the 'role of the market', since
consumption patterns among poor consumers are highly influenced
by the availability of shops and banks as well as by access to mainstream
'technologies of consumption', for example debit or credit cards. The
'market' is not neutral, and the commodities available are not just a
product of consumer wants. Furthermore, Lodziak suggests that to
the majority of people – even in western 'affluent' societies –
consumption is primarily about fulfilling 'needs'. He then proposes to
deconstruct what he calls ideologically based theorising by
reintroducing a distinction between 'basic needs' and 'wants' and to
give priority analytically to the study of 'basic needs'.

The importance of 'basic needs' in terms of poor people's
consumption has been emphasised elsewhere (Bourdieu, 1984; Douglas
and Isherwood, 1996; Kempson, 1996; Hjort, 2004). Even though
consumption in poor families is generally directed towards meeting
basic needs, this focus does not necessarily result in lack of concern
with 'wants'. By suggesting to change the focus from 'wants' and back
to 'basic needs', Lodziak therefore throws out the baby with the bath
water. Criticising the obsession with 'wants' implicitly found in most
consumerist theory – consumerism defined roughly as theories about
'unnecessary consumption' or 'basic needs in a superfluous form' –

Lodziak at the same time fails to grasp that the most significant aspect of contemporary consumption for most social groups in modern society is the dilemmas and choices associated with having to cope with *both* limited financial resources and the fulfilling of basic needs, *and* the (for many) imaginary access to free choices of the meanings, pleasures and identities of 'superfluous' consumption. Furthermore, the experiences of low-income families in Sweden and Denmark suggest that, in a society of affluence, 'wants' may easily become 'needs'. Therefore it seems to be the inability to combine the consumption of 'basic needs' and 'wants' as well as limitations in operating in both fields that epitomises social exclusion in a contemporary consumerist society. Consequently, to understand social vulnerability and new forms of poverty, we need analytical tools that can shed light on the uneven distribution of 'freedom of choice'.

Theorising 'freedom of choice'

Bauman (1998, 1999) focuses on two sets of 'constraints', which together set the frame in which individual freedom of choice operates:

> One set is determined by the *agenda of choice*: the range of alternatives which are actually on offer. All choice means 'choosing among', and seldom is the set of items to be chosen from a matter for the chooser to decide. (Bauman, 1999, p 72; emphasis in original)

This framework implies that 'freedom of choice' in a sociological perspective has to be analysed not in terms of abstract possibilities of choice, but rather in terms of available alternatives. He calls the other set of constraints a *code of choosing*, by which he means:

> ... the rules that tell the individual on what ground the preference should be given to some items rather than others and when to consider the choice as proper and when as inappropriate. (Bauman, 1999, p 72)

In short, 'freedom of choice' must be related to *actual alternatives*, as well as to *that which is considered legitimate*. *Actual alternatives* depend on the money that is at one's disposal and the actual 'market services', for example, variety of shops, banks and 'consumption technologies'. The *code of choosing* is based on normative discourses on consumption as well as on 'poverty' in surrounding society. A code of choosing, therefore, consists of several sometimes opposing discourses and rationalities epitomising ethically, economically and socially 'correct consumption'. Consumption strategies must often reconcile the demands on the political and ethical responsibilities of consumers on the one hand, and the often contrasting dominant market rhetoric of 'affluence', 'lifestyle', 'identity' and more generally 'pleasures' of consumption on the other. Furthermore, poor citizens' consumption patterns are not only regulated by discourses of consumption, but also by discourses of poverty dictating the right way to spend your money sensibly (Zelizer, 1997).

Methods

The empirical data on which this chapter is based consists of 51 semi-structured interviews with Scandinavian families with small children and very limited financial resources, and 24 semi-structured interviews with Scandinavian middle-class families. This chapter focuses on the Danish interviews with families living in Avedøre Stationsand draws occasionally on the Swedish data from Lindängen (Malmö). Despite differences between Sweden and Denmark, the focus here is on the basic similarities in an attempt to identify common characteristics of new forms of social vulnerability in the Scandinavian welfare states. Although I shall also occasionally refer to the contrasting experiences of the middle-class families, this is not the focus of the present analysis.

Experiences of consumption in low-income families

Strategies of consumption in low-income families

One of the main characteristics of consumption patterns among the interviewed low-income families in Denmark and Sweden was their thoroughly planned consumption:

> 'Before I go shopping I make a list – I always do. Once a month I buy what we need for the whole month, meat, pasta etc. Once a week I supplement this with purchases like milk and bread.' (S3[3], lone mother, employed, one child)

Most of the interviewed families would make a list of the items that they had to buy when they went shopping. Although there might be some deviation from the list, they clearly attempted to buy only what they needed. Furthermore, many had strategies for how they used their money each month, for instance by calculating the amount of money available for each week and counting the number of 'meals' placed in their freezer. The consumption of these families was predetermined in the sense that they 'counted' the amount of money for material things they needed, such as children's shoes or a winter coat. Most families knew precisely how much money was at their disposal as well as what kind of purchase the money was to be used for. The careful planning was not surprisingly aimed at fulfilling basic needs such as food, clothing and rent:

> 'I don't usually buy anything on impulse....' (S24, father, social welfare recipient, five children)

In addition, the families also had a clear conceptualisation of their 'range' of shops and an elaborate knowledge of prices and special offers at several of the low-price supermarkets in the neighbourhood. Most householders kept themselves up to date with regard to prices and special offers by carefully scrutinising the local advertising pamphlets that each household received regularly:

> Interviewer: 'Where do you buy clothing?'
> Interviewee: 'You know, in Føtex, Bilka.... [low-price supermarkets].' (D4[4], lone mother, employed, one child)

The interviewed middle-class families seemed to consider their consumption in a fundamentally different manner. Although they too planned their consumption and made long shopping lists, they regarded both possible places to do the shopping and money much more flexibly. As they were generally short of time rather than money, they tended to plan their shopping in terms of what they considered most practical rather than in terms of what would save them money. Furthermore, they did not operate with a limited list of shops, but presented their consumption as related to a sudden impulse and short-term decision making:

> Interviewer: 'Where do you buy clothing?'
> Interviewee: 'Everywhere! Simply everywhere, where the girls pass by!' (D24, middle-class father, employed, two children)

Access to the market: shops and services

Apart from money at one's disposal, access to the market is determined by the availability of shops and services. In several different ways, limited access to the market seemed to be of crucial concern for the families interviewed. In the Danish case, such limits were most apparent as all the families live in a neighbourhood where the variety of shops is limited. But even in several of the Swedish interviews, the question of access to low-price shops was a main concern:

> 'The possibilities for shopping are just so bad. If you have children, you can't do your shopping here ... you can't get nappies, you can't get children's food ... or rather you cannot count on getting what you need. I find it tedious to have to take the train to do my shopping.' (D15, lone mother, social welfare recipient, four children)

> 'This place is like a dried-out patch of land ... nothing grows here. There should have been a larger supermarket ... we don't have a bank either....' (D17, father, social welfare recipient, three children)

Frustration and ambiguity characterised opinions about the services that the market offers to families in these 'poor' neighbourhoods. Most people found the range of shops unsatisfying and the lack of a number of shops and shopping possibilities incomprehensible. The Danish respondents especially did not understand decisions about the allocation of shopping centres and supermarkets, and they felt ignored by decision makers, shopkeepers and public authorities. Furthermore, their opinions also reflect their dependency on a specific kind of shop (low-price supermarkets), which further narrowed their 'range of choice' in the neighbourhood. They could not make use of a small grocery shop, for example, because they considered it too expensive. If the one locally available low-price supermarket (Netto) was out of minced meat, then they simply had to buy something else for dinner, a situation that many families found intolerable. In contrast, although middle-class families in the neighbourhood also found local shopping possibilities unsatisfactory, they were far less dependent on local shops, because they usually owned a car. When the topic was raised, they generally just shrugged their shoulders.

Strategies of control

'I don't place money in an envelope, but I divide it so that I know what I have for each week.' (S14, lone mother, employed, one child)

'Sometimes I make a list, but sometimes, when I only need a few things, I only bring 100 kroner with me and I hurry out of the shop in order not to spend too much money.' (D4, lone mother, employed, one child)

Interviewer: 'Do you have a national debit card?'
Interviewee: 'No, I don't want one. If I had one I would spend too much money.' (D12, lone mother, social welfare recipient, five children)

Interviewer: 'Do you have a national debit card?'
Interviewee: 'I would rather have cash. Then I know how much I have and know when it is spent.' (D4, lone mother, employed, one child)

Most interviews reflect the considerable effort of these families to control their consumption. One of the most frequent strategies among the Danish families was not getting the national debit card (*Dankort*[5]) that is very common among the rest of the population, but only bringing or withdrawing the amount of money they had set aside for that particular week – or for that particular item. Respondents talked about being able to 'feel' the money and 'feel' when it is gone – to have it in their hands, to 'grasp it quite literally'. This implies a wish to keep the money tangible, visible and controllable in contrast to the 'airy' and symbolic forms of money connected to debit and credit cards. Ironically, with no bank in the neighbourhood, the opposition to cards also limited access to the consumption of necessities. A few interviewees complained about having to take the train in order to go to a bank to cash or change money.

In short, the constrained market access that these families experience seems related to both a lack of commercial and local planning (for example, the placing of low-price supermarkets), and to household strategies of resisting the more 'symbolic' means of payment, common among middle-class consumers. The poor consumers are therefore caught in a dilemma, because easing their own access to consumption (for example by getting a debit card) would also transfer the physical banknotes into a symbolic form of value that restricts their control of spending. The same kind of dilemma over access to the market and control of spending was revealed by the use of cellphones. Many families have chosen to buy a telephone card for a fixed amount of money to ensure control of spending. This choice, however, also limits access to some of the mobile services, as well as special offers. In addition, the families' responses to advertising pamphlets also reflect the same dilemma concerning market access and market restrictions:

> 'I would have preferred to have a sign saying "no commercials" on my front door. But I can't because I have to know about special offers. For example, yesterday there was a "birthday" offer at Kvickly ... two kilos of chicken legs for 15 kroner. That's cheap! So I hurried down and bought three packages.' (D7, lone mother, employed, one child)

Other interviews also reflect ambiguity in connection with advertising pamphlets, because these, along with television commercials, expose possibilities of consumption that low-income families cannot afford.

The battle between 'needs' and 'wants' – coping with ambiguous moral discourses

Focusing on the 'codes of choosing', reflected in the interviews, considerable ambiguity is evident in the rationalities and moralities of 'legitimate choices'. In particular, consumption for children seems to be an area of ambiguity and of great concern for many parents with limited financial resources:

> 'I would like to give them [my children] something different a little more.... Sometimes, when I look in the cupboard I think it's a bit bare.... I would really like to give them a little more ... but it isn't possible ... sometimes I feel sorry for them.... I think that they ought to have some of the things that other children get....' (D9, mother, social welfare recipient, two children)

> 'I would so much like things to work out a bit better. There are so many things which children would like to have, but which I just can't give them, such as branded

goods, designer clothes and so on.' (D11, lone mother, social welfare recipient, two children)

To increase the consumption level of their children and to keep up to the standards of their social environment seems to be of particular significance. The ability to fulfil the needs and wants of their children is the parents' most significant measure of social vulnerability.[6] In addition, parents tend to sacrifice their own wishes so that they can provide their children with more than just necessities. On this point, the consumption patterns of Scandinavian families seem to resemble consumption patterns among Belgian low-income families (Kochuyt, 2004). Kochuyt finds that parents in low-income families to a large extent compromise their own needs in order to be able to raise their children's consumption level above the level of basic needs. He suggests that parents, in an attempt to compensate the children for the family's disadvantageous financial situation, create 'artificial affluence' for their children and 'artificial poverty' for themselves. This pattern of uneven intra-household consumption was prevalent in the Swedish as well as in the Danish material:

> 'I almost never buy clothing for myself.' (S14, lone mother, employed, one child)

> 'I never go to the dentist – it is too expensive.' (S13, lone mother, employed, one child)

> 'It is more difficult to spend money on myself than it is to spend DKK 400, 500 or 600 on my children. I say to myself: "No, you can wait. The children need this and that" ... I end up forgetting myself.' (D3, lone mother, employed, two children)

Especially among mothers, there seems to be a tendency to get something nice for their children, instead of buying clothing for themselves. Viewed from a welfare perspective, these mothers seem to go very far when it comes to sacrificing their own needs (for example, buying medicine, going to the dentist, buying clothing) in order to secure 'affluence' for their children.[7]

Caught between 'unreasonable' and 'unwise'

The level and range of choice concerning consumption for children seem crucial for estimating the experience of social welfare among parents. However, it is also within the field of consumption for children that parents face the most difficult dilemmas over priorities. Generally, parents do not find it adequate to be able to provide their children with 'basic needs' but want their children to have what other children have.

The most significant area of consumption for children is entertainment and social activities. Although some parents would like to buy more clothing and so on, most wished to be able to give their children experiences and fun. Parents found access to entertainment and participation in social activities important both in order to let the children experience the fun side of life, and in order for them to obtain what the parents regard as socially important competencies:

> 'It may be unwise if, at the end of the month, I say to my children: "Let's eat at McDonald's or go to the cinema". These are reasonable activities, but for me they are unwise.... But there must be room for this ... so that my children can say: "Today I had fun!"' (D9, mother, social welfare recipient, two children)

> 'I would really like to be able to give my children swimming lessons. He just throws himself around in the water and calls it swimming....' (S16, mother, social welfare recipient, three children)

> 'I would like to go on vacation and things like that ... I really would like to fly somewhere with my younger child. But I don't have the money. It will have to wait.... It is because I would like the younger child to try flying....' (D13, lone mother, employed, two children)

The above statements suggest that parents go through a great deal of trouble in order to give their children experiences, and that they consider such experiences important dimensions of life in today's society. It seems that entertainment and leisure time activities have indeed become battlegrounds of social inclusion as well as signifiers of social identities in a consumerist society (Bauman, 1998). The empirical data suggest that parents struggle to create space for such activities within their limited finances, and that they do so by compromising their own consumption. This emphasises the significance that parents (and children) attribute to children's 'entertainment consumption'. The changing boundaries between necessity and 'luxury', which are crucial here, have been conceptualised by Hjort as a development of 'social necessities' in consumerist Scandinavian society (Hjort, 2004).

Making the right kind of choice

As we have seen, the consumption patterns of poor families in general are governed by the aim of meeting basic family needs. Almost all the families stated this aim as their primary economic goal. They also usually managed to meet this goal – at least for their children. However, many told about diversions from this norm, and almost all at times found it extremely difficult to convince themselves, and, in particular, their children, about the *legitimacy* of this *rationale*:

> 'I wish I didn't always have to say no [to the children] ... that I just sometimes didn't have to save....' (S14, lone mother, employed, one child)

> 'I would like my children to have what they need or what we need ... and sometimes a bit more ... sometimes you need niceties!' (S15, woman, who stays at home, three children)

Sometimes parents find it necessary to allow their children what they, the parents, think is important and significant – despite their not being able to afford it. Several parents struggle to explain the ambivalence of their clearly spoken priority of basic needs on the one hand, and the fact that they also find that their children have the right to 'more' than just necessities on the other:

> 'We can save, K and I. We don't need expensive clothing or restaurant meals. But what about the children? If they get to know that the other children have been in Tivoli.... That is we can't do it, because we need the money we have, but we did it anyway ... we needed the money ... but I couldn't bear to say "No, we can't afford it". So we have just been to Tivoli and spent a lot of money and now

what shall we eat?' (D1, mother, social welfare recipient, two children)

This last quote clearly reflects the conflicting moral discourses to which the family is subject. On the one hand, they adhere to the rationality of 'sensible' spending, which means focusing on the fulfilling of basic needs. On the other hand, they are subject to other moral discourses, mainly the conviction that children ought to have what other children have and experience that which appears available to them. In short, there are times when parents feel obliged to compromise the overall priority of needs in order to provide the children with experiences that are considered 'normal' in society. The same kind of dilemma is reflected in an earlier quote (D9), where a mother suggested that going to McDonald's or to the cinema were *reasonable* activities, although to her they were at the same time *unwise*.

Finally, this last quote reflects the overall different character of concerns with consumption in poor families as compared with the middle-class families. The poor families' concerns were often of a moral character, and their actions associated with negative consciousness and shame. Such moral concerns about their own consumption patterns were largely absent from the middle-class families. The 'code of choosing', in other words, seems to be fundamentally different for the poor families, not only because their code is, to a larger extent, morally invested, but also – and more seriously for the experience of social exclusion – because the contradictory moralities create a situation where no legitimate choice is available at all.

Conclusion: the significance of uneven access to consumption

The Scandinavian welfare state debate has increasingly focused on 'consumers' and consumer choices in contrast to the former focus on 'citizens'. This rhetorical shift is related to increased marketisation and individualisation, as well as to the development of new forms of political government in the Scandinavian welfare states (Østerud et al, 2003; Togeby et al, 2003). Politicians as well as sociologists speak of a shift from a political system involving the population and the state as the main actors towards a system of consumerism and post-modernity, where the main agents are individual consumers and the market and, to a much smaller extent and in a different manner than before, the national state (Bauman, 1998, 1999; Bourdieu, 1999). Apart from viewing consumers as important social and political agents this new system places a considerable political responsibility on consumers' shoulders. Moreover, the concept of 'political consumption' not only indicates increased demands for social 'responsibleness' but it also highlights the field of consumption as culturally, socially and *morally* important.

Sestoft (2002), in a very interesting analysis of the development of new forms of regulation within the field of consumption in Denmark, suggests that:

> The political consumer (in this way) becomes a new political subject of power in the national state because the government transfers political rights to the consumer and the consumer receives rights and duties from the governmental system. (Sestoft, 2002, p 82, author's translation)

Viewing consumption in this way allows us to see it as part of a much more general change of the boundaries between 'politics' and 'market' and individual citizens resulting in the transferring of former political problems to the market and to the individual citizen. Sestoft analyses this transfer of responsibility as a 'technology of the self' drawing on Foucault's notion of governmentality (Foucault, 1988, 1991; Rose, 1990). Using written material from Denmark, she suggests that the field of consumption has become simultaneously politicised and morally and culturally invested, and that consumers increasingly 'automatically' evaluate their own consumption patterns in terms of social and ethical values. Guidelines and campaigns 'publicly financed but directed against 'governing' individual consumption, now substitute for direct rule' (Sestoft, 2002, p 82). Sestoft points not only to a change in forms of governing, but also to changes in the cultural values that consumption expresses. Thus, she argues that the development of 'expert guidelines' in Denmark (for example, in health, the environment, human rights and social responsibility) especially points to a series of normative values concerning 'correct consumption'.

Both the individualisation of social responsibility and the 'moralisation' of the field of consumption are crucial considerations for looking at changing processes of social vulnerability. However, although discourse analysis may be a starting point, we need to examine differences in actual experiences when analysing the effects of changing discourses. In other words, although we may agree that we live in a society dominated by consumption or even by consumerism, we still need to know in what way this alters the processes of social differentiation and marginalisation and to what extent this change leads to shared experiences and equal social rights. The empirical research results in this chapter indicate some areas where the roles and experiences of 'consumership' may be unevenly distributed as well as indicating some new areas of concern.

First, there is the field of equal access to the market, where Caplovitz (1963) suggested 'the poor pay more'. Although the analysis uses a limited number of interviews, our findings indicate that access to 'the market' is constrained for 'poor' consumers, not only by a limited range of shops, but also because the new 'technologies of consumption' based on money in symbolic and 'fluid' forms seem incompatible with poor people's consumption patterns.

Second, although both the poor families and the middle-class families were exposed to discourses of 'correct consumption', the consumption patterns of the poor were characterised both by different purchasing patterns, and more crucial emotional and moral concerns. Thus, although at a discursive level 'technologies of the self' and new forms of 'responsibleness' may be a shared condition in contemporary society, research on experiences with consumption indicates a different and more ambiguous set of disciplining rules and norms directed against the most vulnerable consumers. Experiences of having to choose, yet finding each choice somehow illegitimate, prevailed among the 'vulnerable' families, and this inability to 'make the right choice' formed a critical dimension of their experience of social vulnerability.

Third, an important aspect of new forms of social vulnerability is the relative position of being 'fixed' and 'bound' in a society otherwise dominated by people and images emphasising the 'mobile' and 'flexible'. Part of the above discussion about money as being either 'tangible' or 'symbolic' may indicate these new forms of social distinction.

We may conclude, therefore, that the change from 'citizenship' to 'consumership' that we are witnessing in the Scandinavian countries as well as elsewhere creates new forms of social distinction and new demands on social policy. However, the traditional emphasis on welfare redistribution and social equality that has hitherto characterised the Scandinavian welfare system may be difficult to maintain, not only because it is difficult to finance, but also because the increased individualisation and marketisation of political government, epitomised by the public promotion of 'freedom of choice', transfers the problem of social distribution to the sphere of individual responsibility.

Notes
[1] In this chapter, poverty and consumption are viewed as mutually constitutive in modern society. I am aware that poverty in other contexts refers to a specific income level, often specified as below half or 60% of the median income. However, the aim here is to explore the range of non-economic processes that constitute new ways of social exclusion and vulnerability. As a consequence, the experience of poverty is understood to be related to a broader set of processes that together act as boundaries for participation in society.

[2] This is a common project between The Danish National Institute of Social Research, Copenhagen, The National Institute for Consumer Research (SIFO), Oslo, and The University of Social Work, Lund. The project is financed by the Nordic Council of Ministers (The Welfare Research Programme).

[3] Swedish interview and number.

[4] Danish interview and number.

[5] It should be mentioned, however, that many of these families might not have been provided with a debit card from their bank, even if they wanted one, and this might have influenced their opinion on cards.

[6] Children were not interviewed and their viewpoints are not included in the analysis.

[7] The interviews do not provide us with similar examples of fathers' sacrifices; however, as the majority of the interviewed parents were women, this does not necessarily indicate that fathers' priorities are different.

EIGHT

Affordable credit for low-income households

Sharon Collard

Since the early 1990s the UK has seen a rapid growth in the availability and marketing of consumer credit products, particularly to the lowest-risk, highest-profit customers. In addition, intense competition in the financial services market has made credit available to a relatively wide customer base, including people with poor credit records or a history of bad debt. Consequently, use of credit has increased dramatically and the majority of UK households now have access to, and make use of, mainstream consumer credit facilities such as credit and store cards, unsecured personal loans and hire purchase (Kempson, 2002).

Despite this expansion, access to high street credit is still severely constrained for people on low and insecure incomes. As a consequence, many of them borrow from lenders operating at the lower end of the sub-prime credit market[1] where annual percentage rates (APRs) typically range from 100% to 400% (Rowlingson, 1994; Kempson, 1996; Speak and Graham, 2000; Whyley et al, 2000; Whyley and Brooker, 2004).[2]

The higher cost and less favourable conditions attached to loans from some of these sources can add considerably to the financial problems of people who are already vulnerable. It is estimated, for example, that low-income consumers pay on average around £130 a month in interest payments on consumer credit, equivalent to 11% of their income (National Consumer Council and Policis, 2005). Those with the most restricted access to credit may be forced to borrow from unregulated, illegal moneylenders, where charges can be astronomical and consumer protection is non-existent (Herbert and Kempson, 1996; Speak and Graham, 2000; Whyley et al, 2000).

This chapter examines the provision of credit to people on low incomes from the perspective of both the borrower and the lender.[3] It then goes on to explore the size and nature of the potential market for more affordable credit and considers the options for delivering affordable credit to those who most need it.

The main credit sources available to low-income households

While many people on low incomes have some choice between different types of credit, on the whole their options are restricted to sources that are high cost and have other associated disadvantages. The main attraction of these types of credit is that they are straightforward to access. Most importantly, they do not require credit checks.

Mail order catalogues are the most widely used form of credit among low-income households, particularly among low-income families with children and people unable to work because of long-term ill-health or disability (Kempson, 2002). *Home credit companies* (also known as licensed moneylenders, doorstep lenders or weekly collected credit companies) are the main commercial providers of small-value personal loans in Britain. Other forms of commercial credit that are aimed at people on low to middle incomes include pawnbroking, sale and buy-back and rental purchase. Payday loans tend to be used by people who are slightly better off. See Box 8.1 for further information about these credit sources.

The biggest non-commercial provider of loans to people on low incomes is the government-run *Social Fund Budgeting Loan scheme*. Budgeting Loans are interest free and are intended to meet the lump-sum needs which people on qualifying social security benefits may be unable to cover out of their income, such as furniture, carpets and white goods. They are, however, only available to people who have been in receipt of Income Support or Income-based Jobseeker's Allowance for at least 26 weeks. Moreover, because the scheme is cash-limited, applying for a budgeting loan is something of a lottery and a significant proportion of applications are turned down every year.

Credit unions are another potential source of low-cost credit for people on low incomes.[4] At present, however, many people on low incomes do not have a credit union in their vicinity. The link between saving and borrowing can also be a drawback for people on low incomes, in particular the fact that members usually have to establish a regular pattern of saving before they can take out a loan. Some credit unions have therefore experimented with 'instant access' loans.

Since the late 1990s several *community-based loan schemes* have been established in the UK, which offer lower-cost personal and business loans without the need to save. These are not-for-profit organisations

Box 8.1: Main commercial credit sources available to low-income households

Mail order catalogues often provide goods through a network of agents working on commission who either buy for themselves or for a number of customers. Goods bought in this way and repaid over 20 or 40 weeks are, technically, interest free. If repayments are spread over more than 40 weeks, interest is charged at 28.8% or more (Jones, 2002). The mark-up on goods is also high. **Home credit companies** offer small-value, short-term unsecured loans that are usually repaid weekly in cash. Traditionally, repayments are collected from customers' homes by a network of agents. Typical APRs range from 100% to 400% depending on the lender and the size and term of the loan. **Pawnbrokers** also offer small cash loans, which are secured on property, usually jewellery. Typical APRs range from 70% to 200% based on a loan of £100 over six months (Collard and Kempson, 2003). **Sale and buy-back shops,** such as Cash Convertors and Cash Generator, buy second-hand goods and give the customer the option of buying back the goods at a higher price within an agreed period of time. These transactions are not currently covered by the 1974 Consumer Credit Act, and companies do not have to advertise their APRs. **Rental purchase outlets** such as BrightHouse allow customers to spread the cost of furniture, white goods and other household items by paying regular instalments to the shop. Although the advertised APR is usually 29.9%, there is evidence that customers are strongly encouraged to take out 'optional' insurances and service cover, which significantly increase the costs of borrowing (Jones, 2002). Like mail order, the mark-up on goods is high. **Payday loans** are offered by a growing number of cheque cashers, pawnbrokers and home credit companies. The customer writes one or more personal cheques to the lender and receives the amount of the cheque, less a fee. The lender then waits for up to 30 days before presenting the cheque or cheques. Fees can range from £6 to £14 for a £100 cheque held for 30 days and between £2 and £7.50 for a £50 cheque retained for 14 days (Dominy and Kempson, 2003).

run in partnership with a commercial bank. Again, they tend to be locally based, serving small geographic areas (CDFA, 2004).

Credit use by people on low incomes

A survey of people living in the poorest fifth of UK households **(see Collard and Kempson, 2005)** shows that four types of commercial credit predominated among the sources they had used in the last 12 months: home credit, mail order catalogues, credit cards and other personal loans (such as from a bank or finance house). Use of these sources of credit was eclipsed, however, by borrowing from the Social Fund and from family and friends (Table 8.1).

There are some important differences between the sources of credit used depending on the financial circumstances of the household. Those with a full-time wage in their household had more often used mainstream credit – credit cards,[5] personal loans and store cards. In contrast, use of home credit was low and hardly anyone had used rental purchase. Borrowing from friends and family was particularly common among this group of householders.

The pattern of use was quite different among people living in households without a full-time wage, that is, those dependent on social security benefits or with only part-time or occasional earnings. Among this group, home collected credit and mail order catalogues were the sources of commercial credit most often used. Use of rental purchase companies was also mainly concentrated in this group. Even so, 6% had credit cards and 4% had personal loans. Previous research has indicated that these commitments generally remain from a period of full-time employment (see, for example, Kempson and Whyley, 1999).

Table 8.1: Sources of commercial credit used in the last 12 months by people living in the poorest fifth of UK households (%)

	All[a]	On benefits or only part-time or occasional earnings	Full-time earnings
Home credit	6	8	1
Mail order	8	9	5
Credit card	7	6	8
Personal loan (eg bank)	5	4	7
Store card	3	2	6
Car loan	1	1	2
Rental purchase	1	2	*
Hire purchase	1	1	2
Payday loan	1	1	1
Pawnbroker	1	*	1
Credit union loan	4	5	2
Loan from family or friend	13	11	20
Social Fund loan or grant	20	25	2

Notes: [a] All people living in the poorest fifth of UK households; * = less than 1%.
Source: Policis, cited in Collard and Kempson (2005)

But by far the most common source of borrowing was the Social Fund, used by a quarter of these householders in the past 12 months. Compared with households that had a full-time wage, borrowing from friends and family was much less prevalent (Table 8.1).

The survey also indicates that three-quarters (75%) of people living in the poorest households say that they have a need to borrow money – at least from time to time. This percentage was the same whether they had a full-time wage or not. At the same time, it was clear that the need to borrow small sums of money was greatest among those without a full-time earner in their household. Faced with the prospect of raising £200-£300 in the event of a crisis, six in ten people (61%) living in households with no full-time earner said this would be very difficult or impossible without borrowing, compared with less than three in ten (28%) who had a full-time wage coming into the home.

There were also significant differences in the level of credit impairment between people in households with and without a full-time wage. This was captured in a number of ways in the survey, including adverse credit records (such as County Court Judgements or bankruptcy); a history of missed credit payments in the past 12 months; and refused credit applications. In each case the incidence was a good deal higher among people who did not have a full-time wage coming into their household.

Taken together, this analysis suggests that the need for more affordable credit is greatest among people who live in households without a full-time wage – those living on social security benefits, or who have only part-time or occasional earnings. Previous research has likewise found that users of high-cost credit tend to be people living on low incomes over the long term, who are likely to rent their home, and who have dependent children living at home. A significant number of them borrow to make ends meet or to pay bills as a result of ongoing income inadequacy. But a high proportion also borrow from high-cost lenders to pay for Christmas and birthdays, and to buy branded clothes and consumer electronics for their children, to prevent them being stigmatised at school (Kempson et al, 1994; Kempson, 1996; Kempson and Whyley, 1999; Whyley and Brooker, 2004).

Lending to low-income borrowers

Lending to people on low incomes differs from mainstream lending in several key respects. The risk of low-income borrowers defaulting on loan repayments is generally higher, as their circumstances are much more likely to change. Moreover, they prefer to repay their loans weekly in cash, with payments collected from their home. Both these factors increase the costs of lending. The amounts borrowed tend to be relatively small and for short periods. As the costs of lending are largely fixed, this means that they are high relative to the amounts borrowed. This is why charges by commercial lenders serving the low-income market are high, mainstream lenders (banks and building societies) are reluctant to enter this market, and not-for-profit lenders with lower charges require subsidies. The key to lending to low-income borrowers is assessing and managing the risk of default. This means careful recruitment, collecting repayments in ways that minimise the risk of non-payment, and repeat loans to defray set-up costs.

Risk assessment

Lenders serving the low-income credit market have found that word-of-mouth recommendation brings the most reliable customers. And, unlike mainstream credit providers, they do not tend to rely on the use of automated techniques (notably credit scoring) to assess risk. Instead, they carry out face-to-face assessment of potential customers and small 'trial-run' loans of between £50 and £100. They also closely monitor new customers' ability to maintain payments, recording numbers of missed payments and how many times an agent had to call before successfully collecting the repayment. Although they have proved to be very effective ways of assessing risk in this market, face-to-face screening and monitoring of repayments add to lending costs.

Once a new customer has proved their ability to repay a loan, they can borrow increasing sums of money in subsequent 'step-up' loans. The application and monitoring procedures for repeat loans are generally less rigorous as well, because lenders have found that a borrower's past payment record is the best predictor of future default.

Some lenders in this market have been exploring the use of automated credit scoring systems. And, as the information that credit reference agencies hold on people on low incomes improves, it is likely to become more widely used to predict borrowers' behaviour. The danger is that increased use of credit scoring and credit reference agency data in this market will exacerbate credit exclusion among the poorest households. As companies become better able to ascertain relative customer profitability, they will increasingly move away from lending to less profitable customers, that is the poorest, highest risk and most vulnerable.

Risk management

Unlike mainstream lenders, credit providers specialising in loans to people on low incomes distinguish between those who are unlikely to repay in full and those who may, for genuine reasons, struggle sometimes to meet a repayment. The latter is a fact of life for people on low incomes, and these lenders have processes to accommodate it. Lenders aim to set repayments that their customers can afford. This amount is assessed at the same time as the decision about whether to lend. Most lenders would argue that this can only be done face to face.

As mentioned above, many lenders closely monitor new customers' repayments for the first 10-15 weeks. They also tend to offer very small loans initially, increasing the amount once customers have a track record of reliable repayment. Similarly, credit unions and savings and loans schemes require members to establish a regular pattern of saving before they can take out a loan.

Many lenders in this market 'manage' their customers' repayments, rather than relying on customers to pay on time. Traditionally, this means agents collecting the money from customers' homes. But home service is more than a means of payment collection. It is central to how these companies operate, as it provides a way to assess potential and repeat customers, sell products and chase arrears. Maintaining a network of agents is undoubtedly the largest single cost incurred by home credit companies. In contrast, the Social Fund is able to 'manage' payments by deducting them directly from people's benefit income, so that loan repayments are entirely outside the control of the borrower.

Many commercial lenders operating in this market are also prepared to reschedule loans for those facing genuine difficulties. Unlike mainstream lenders, they do not view this as default and do not usually levy additional charges for late payment. But the cost has to be covered, either as higher charges or, in the case of many low-cost, not-for-profit lenders, as subsidies.

Some lenders minimise the default risk by requiring collateral in the form of savings (credit unions and other savings and loans schemes) or valuables (pawnbrokers). This limits access to credit for many poor people, although it enables others to benefit from the somewhat lower charges usually associated with secured loans.

Extent of need for affordable credit

Data analysis by Policis (carried out for Collard and Kempson, 2005) indicates that up to 6.2 million low-income people aged 16-64 in the UK could not meet fairly modest expenditure without borrowing. In the course of a year, 1.8 million of them had borrowed money commercially. A million of these borrowers had very constrained access to credit, such that 750,000 had needed to use a high-cost lender.

These estimates are, however, likely to understate the potential demand for more affordable credit, as:

- they do not include people who need to borrow but who, because of changes in the market, find it increasingly difficult to access credit, even from high-cost lenders;
- more people may be attracted to use credit if it were more affordable, including people who currently only borrow from friends or family;
- they do not include pensioners, although levels of borrowing among older people tend to be much lower than among the working-age population.

The main credit need is for small, unsecured, fixed-term cash loans. People on low incomes want affordable weekly payments with no hidden or extra charges. They like automatic payments, but are wary of paying by direct debit as they risk high bank charges should the direct debit fail. The certainty of direct deduction from social security benefits is preferred. For the same reason, many users of home credit like collection of repayments from their home. They also welcome the facility to reschedule loans should they encounter temporary financial problems. In other words, potential borrowers want to reduce the likelihood of defaulting.

But their requirements inevitably add to the costs of borrowing, whether these are passed on to them or met by subsidies. No existing sources of credit fully meet these needs. Home credit comes close, but the charges are high and some people are deterred by home collection. The Social Fund meets many of the needs, but repayment levels tend to be high. The possibility of rescheduling Social Fund loans is not well known and is not straightforward. Community-based loan schemes could meet credit needs, but access is restricted and repayment methods do not always meet the desire for methods that reduce the likelihood of default.

Widening access to more affordable credit

There have been a number of attempts to develop low-cost credit products for people on low incomes in the UK, including credit unions; savings and loans schemes set up by housing associations; and community-based loan schemes. To date, take-up of these credit services has been relatively modest and none of them has made significant inroads into the customer base at the lower end of the sub-prime credit market.

Although the reasons for this are not well understood, it is clear that cost is not always the main consideration when people on low incomes decide where to borrow money from. The great majority of people who borrow from the home credit companies, pawnbrokers or rental purchase companies are aware of the price they have to pay (Rowlingson, 1994; Collard and Kempson, 2003). Even so, they often choose to use these lenders as they offer credit products that meet their particular needs.

Moreover, customer loyalty and resistance to switching among low-income borrowers make the development of a completely new credit product impractical. A more effective approach is to build on the providers that already exist: the home credit companies and other sub-prime lenders; credit unions and other not-for-profit loan schemes; and the Social Fund.

The final part of this chapter identifies the potential for widening access to more affordable credit in a viable way by a number of means: reducing the cost of commercial credit, increasing the availability and sustainability of not-for-profit lenders, and extending access to the Social Fund Budgeting Loan scheme.

Reducing the cost of commercial credit

A ceiling on interest rates has been heavily promoted in the UK as a means of reducing the cost of borrowing for people on low incomes who use high-cost lenders. On the surface, this is a simple and attractive idea that ought to benefit people on the lowest incomes. As we have seen, however, there are high costs associated with lending to people on low incomes who have a high risk of default. An interest rate ceiling could do little to reduce these costs. Instead, it is likely that the APR would be reduced by displacing these costs elsewhere, for example in the form of charges for default – the last thing that low-income borrowers would want.

It is also probable that more credit would become tied to the purchase of goods and consumers would be faced with high price mark-ups as retailers seek to recover the costs of supplying credit. Both of these would result in the total costs of borrowing being less transparent. Worst of all, there is a danger that lenders would move out of this market altogether, leaving more poor people prey to unlicensed lenders.

An alternative approach is to find a way of reducing the costs of lending in a high-risk market, which should then lead to lower charges for borrowers. It could also widen access by encouraging firms back into this market that have curtailed their lending to low-income borrowers. Of all the options this would, potentially, have the largest impact given the heavy reliance on high-cost commercial credit by people on low incomes.

The scope for reducing costs lies mainly in minimising the costs of managing risk, through the frequency and method of payment collection:

• moving to monthly rather than weekly repayments; and
• using automated payments rather than collecting the money in person.

The scope for moving to monthly payments, however, seems to be limited. People on benefits usually receive their income weekly or fortnightly; only a very small proportion of them are paid monthly. Consequently, most people on low incomes choose to budget by the week and, given the choice, they would repay their credit commitments the same way. Some lenders have found that monthly payments can greatly increase the risk of default among people on the very lowest incomes.

There is, however, some scope for moving to automated payments and two possible options are direct deduction of loan repayments from benefit income and direct debits.

Direct deduction of repayments from benefit is popular among people who borrow from the Social Fund. At the present time, in addition to Social Fund loans, payments can also be deducted at source for fines, rent arrears, current utility consumption and utility arrears. There is a limit on the total sum that can be deducted (25% of income) and an order of priority for creditors.

Adding other loan providers to the list of creditors able to access direct deductions seems an attractive proposition. Closer examination, however, highlights a number of potential problems. Substantial investment would be required to accommodate any significant increase in the use of direct deductions from benefits. Collecting payments when people move off benefit is also problematic. Finally, there may well be political opposition to a government agency collecting payments for commercial credit companies.

The other option is to collect loan repayments by *direct debit*. There are two potential difficulties with this. First, many people who pay the most for credit lack a bank account that has direct debit facilities. Without universal banking, therefore, widening access to cheaper credit in this way could deepen the effects of financial exclusion.

Second, experience shows that there is a much higher incidence of failed direct debits among people on low incomes. This could be addressed if the risk of default was removed at source. This would involve direct debit payments being triggered by the receipt of wages or benefits into a bank or building society account, so as to mimic the direct deduction of payments from income described above. At present, customers must nominate a day for payments to be debited and most people give themselves some leeway from the receipt of their income. The problem of failed direct debits therefore relates partly to the unreliability of direct credits to accounts and partly to people leaving insufficient income in their account to cover the direct debit. It is exacerbated by the time taken to clear payments into the account. Paying direct debits as soon as direct credits have cleared would help tackle these problems.

The ability to collect loan repayments either through direct deduction or a more certain method of direct debit would significantly reduce the costs of lending for commercial credit providers. Credit unions and other not-for-profit lenders would also benefit from these methods of collecting payments, as they would reduce their costs and make financial sustainability more attainable.

Widening access to not-for-profit lenders

Despite recent expansion of the not-for-profit sector, the UK is still a long way from having a national, coordinated and sustainable network of lenders that meets the needs of people on the lowest incomes. The main challenge for not-for-profit lenders is to reach a size where they can achieve economies of scale, including the provision of centralised administrative and accounting facilities. In recognition of this, in 2004 the government announced plans to establish a growth fund for not-for-profit lenders to increase the coverage, capacity and sustainability of the sector (HM Treasury, 2004a). The suggestions for reducing costs in the commercial sector, discussed above, could also minimise the level of subsidy required by not-for-profit lenders. This would both increase their likelihood of sustainability and ensure more rapid growth of this sector.

Within the credit union movement, there has been a move towards larger, more professionally run *credit unions* with prominent shopfront premises, which aim to benefit existing members but also attract new members. ABCUL, the main credit union trade association, has also encouraged the merger of employee-based and community credit unions in order to provide better access for people living or working within the common bond of the credit union, and to achieve economies of scale (Brown et al, 2003).

Despite these positive developments, credit unions will continue to have only limited appeal for people on very low incomes as long as savings remain the basis for securing a loan. An increasing number of credit unions are introducing 'instant access' loans, which require no pre-saving. Other credit unions have made changes to their lending policies to make it easier for members to access loans.

A further hurdle for credit unions is that there is a ceiling of 12.68% on the APR they can charge. Even given the fact that loans are generally underwritten by members' savings, credit unions that want to become more financially self-sufficient, and have paid staff, are unable to do so while charging this rate of interest. Understandably, the idea of credit unions charging a higher rate of interest is a contentious one, and any change would require secondary legislation. However, if credit unions (indeed community-based loan schemes generally) want to compete seriously with commercial lenders, they have to do so from a position of financial sustainability. In light of this, following a period of consultation the government announced in its 2005 Pre-Budget Report (HM Treasury, 2005a) that the maximum rate of interest that credit unions could charge on loans would be increased from 1% to 2% a month.

The newer *community-based loan schemes* that have been established in several areas of the country do not require borrowers to save before they take out a loan. Their loan capital is provided through partnerships with banks and they are free to set their own rates of interest, which generally range from 20% to 30% APR.

The challenge for these schemes is again one of scale. In order to be viable, it has been estimated (Collard and Kempson, 2005) that services have to be provided on a sub-regional basis at the very least. Alternatively, lenders could work in partnership with organisations such as housing associations, whose tenants are generally on low incomes. Some of the newer community-based loan schemes already have this type of arrangement with their local housing provider.

Extending access to the Social Fund

For those who are eligible, the Social Fund Budgeting Loan scheme is an important source of borrowing. But the scheme has long been criticised for its inadequacy in meeting the needs of people on low incomes. In particular, the rate of refusal for Budgeting Loans is high, and successful applicants often receive only a partial award.

One way of assessing the extent of unmet need for Budgeting Loans is to estimate the total level of borrowing from all commercial sources by people on low incomes. Analysis of survey data collected from people in the lowest household income quintile, who had no full-time earnings coming into their home, indicates that around 440,000 people had borrowed around £210 million in the previous year for reasons other than discretionary spending. The majority of these people had used high-cost credit sources (Collard and Kempson, 2005).

Arguably, most of this borrowing should have been met from the discretionary Social Fund. In 2004, the Secretary of State for Work and Pensions announced a £90 million increase in the discretionary Social Fund budget over a three-year period to 2005/06 (DWP, 2004). The estimates provided above suggest that this amount would have to be more than doubled if needs were to be met in full.

One way of widening access to the Social Fund is to raise further capital either from general taxation or through a partnership with banks or building societies, in much the same way as they currently provide loan capital for some of the community-based loan schemes. This additional capital in the Fund could be lent interest free as at present. Alternatively, the Social Fund Budgeting Loan scheme could be developed so that applicants have an initial credit limit that is interest free, after which they could borrow at affordable interest rates.

Conclusion

Whatever shape it takes, some intervention is required to ensure that poor people have access to affordable credit. Left to its own devices, the commercial market will continue to move towards more profitable customers and away from lending to the poorest people.

The biggest, most immediate impact would come from a system of guaranteed automated payments and further expansion of the discretionary Social Fund. This would require substantial investment, which could be met through public–private partnership.

A system of automated loan repayments would reduce the costs of both commercial lenders and not-for-profit credit providers. Safeguards would be needed, however, to minimise the risk of default.

Not-for-profit lenders also have real potential to deliver affordable credit. They need to reach a size where they can achieve economies of scale, including a centralised back office and accounting facilities. Moves towards larger, more professionally run credit unions and regional community-based loan schemes run in partnership with banks are particularly promising.

For the poorest people, however, the most appropriate solution lies in further increases to the discretionary Social Fund budget, either from taxation or using capital provided by banks. If the Budgeting Loan scheme is to meet fully the non-discretionary borrowing needs of people in the poorest households, its budget will have to be substantially increased over and above any additional funding that has been pledged by government so far.

Notes

[1] There are two groups of lenders in the sub-prime commercial credit market. The first tends to offer credit products that cater specifically for the needs of low-income borrowers. It includes some longstanding credit providers, such as home credit companies and pawnbrokers, and some newer entrants such as sale and buy-back outlets and rental purchase shops. This chapter focuses predominantly on these types of lenders. The second group comprises companies that offer similar credit products to mainstream (or prime) lenders such as banks. The difference is that they are targeted at people who have difficulty gaining access to the mainstream credit market because they have a poor credit record or history of bad debt.

[2] The APR is a measure of the cost of each credit agreement, taking into account all the charges made under the agreement, and expressed in the form of a yearly measure.

[3] This chapter is based on a study funded by the Joseph Rowntree Foundation (see Collard and Kempson, 2005).

[4] Until recently, credit union interest rates were fixed by law at 1% a month on a reducing balance, equivalent to 12.68% APR. Following a period of consulation, it was announced in the 2005 Pre-Budget Report that credit unions could charge up to 2% a month. Traditionally, the amount members can borrow has been determined by the amount they have in savings. Typically, this will be in the region of two or three times the amount saved.

[5] Mirroring developments in the US, there has been an expansion in the UK of the availability of sub-prime credit cards, targeted at people with impaired credit histories. To date, they do not seem to have been widely marketed to people on very low incomes. Sub-prime credit cards have APRs much higher than the mainstream, typically ranging from 20% to 60% APR, as well as lower credit limits. The APR may come down and the credit limit be increased once a customer has established a history of satisfactory repayment (Datamonitor, 2004).

NINE

Carers and employment in a work-focused welfare state

Hilary Arksey and Peter A. Kemp

This chapter explores the interaction between paid employment and informal caregiving in Britain.[1] The work–life balance, or how to reconcile caring responsibilities with paid work, has become an urgent one for policy makers concerned to maximise employment rates in order to maintain economic competitiveness. Moreover, as Jane Lewis points out in Chapter Two, along with childcare, the question of who will provide informal care has become increasingly important with the decline of the married male breadwinner family model and the increasing policy emphasis on paid employment as a route out of poverty and social exclusion. With a rising proportion of women participating in the labour market and an ageing population, there is also concern, as Glendinning points out in Chapter Ten, about who will provide the care that many chronically sick or disabled people need in order to live in their own homes. Thus, helping informal carers to participate in the labour market is an increasingly important issue for social policy and practice.

The structure of this chapter is as follows. The first section explores the risk of informal caring in Britain today, its implications for participation in paid employment, and its consequences for earnings and incomes more generally. The second section looks at what help is potentially available to carers, both in terms of cash and practical support. The third section draws on an empirical study of carers' aspirations and decisions about work, in order to compare policy with practice. The final section presents conclusions about carers and employment within the welfare state in Britain today.

The risk of informal caring

It is important to note that informal care is not just about 'elder care', that is, looking after frail or disabled older relatives. It also encompasses care provided to chronically sick and disabled children, spouses and other adults of working age. Indeed, the General Household Survey (GHS) conducted in 2000 found that, among people providing 20 or more hours of care per week in Britain, 18% of care recipients were children of the carer and 45% were their spouses (Maher and Green, 2002).[2] Thus although many carers are looking after older relatives, friends and neighbours, many are caring for chronically sick or disabled children and partners.

In Britain, the risk of becoming an informal carer is substantial. According to the 2000 GHS, 16% of adults (people aged over 16) in Britain were caring for a sick, disabled or older person. Altogether, 21% of households contained at least one person providing unpaid care (Maher and Green, 2002). Meanwhile, the 2001 Census found that there were 5.6 million carers in Britain.[3] However, there is considerable turnover among the carer population and, consequently, the number of people who experience caregiving during their lifetime is much larger than the number caring at any point in time. Indeed, using the British Household Panel Survey, Hirst (2002) estimated that over half the adult population is likely to be heavily involved in providing informal care at some stage in their lives.

Although 'care work' is often assumed to be a predominantly female activity, both men and women face a relatively high risk of becoming a carer (albeit one that is higher for women than for men). The GHS conducted in 2000, for instance, found that women accounted for 58% and men for 42% of informal carers. Men were as likely as women to be co-resident carers, but women were more likely than men to be extra-resident carers[4] (Maher and Green, 2002). This is in contrast to childcare, which is overwhelmingly provided by women. An analysis of gender and informal care using data from the GHS by Arber and Gilbert (1989), entitled 'Men: the forgotten carers', has itself been largely overlooked.

The amount of time that people devote to caring varies considerably between carers but in some cases is very substantial. According to the 2000 GHS, one in 20 adults in Britain was spending more than 20 hours per week caring for a sick, disabled or frail older person. Co-resident carers were very much more likely than extra-resident carers to be devoting a substantial amount of time to caregiving. In 2000, for instance, 62% of co-resident carers were providing at least 20 hours of care each week compared with only 10% of extra-resident carers (Maher and Green, 2002).

The evidence suggests that caring affects participation in the labour market among those whose caregiving extends beyond 20 hours per week (McLaughlin, 1991). For example, the Census of England and

Wales shows that 62% of people who did not provide care were in employment or self-employment in 2001. This employment rate compares with 65% among those who were providing between one and 19 hours of care per week, 48% among those who were providing between 20 and 49 hours, and only 29% among those who were providing 50 or more hours (cited in Arksey et al, 2005).

There are important gender differences in the extent to which working carers are in full- or part-time employment (Parker, 1990, 1993; Parker and Lawton, 1994; Arber and Ginn, 1995). Table 9.1 shows that a higher proportion of men than women with 'substantial' caring responsibilities (defined here as 20 or more hours per week) were in paid employment in Britain in 2000. Male carers were much more likely than women to be working full time and less likely to be working part time. It has been argued that the higher level of part-time working among female carers reflects both the selection of women into caring roles and the adverse effects of caring on their ability to participate in full-time employment (Arber and Ginn, 1995).

Switching from full-time to part-time work, or giving up work entirely in response to the demands of providing informal care, can have negative financial consequences for carers. A number of studies have indicated that there is a 'wage penalty' to caregiving, at least for co-resident carers, and particularly for men (Evandrou and Winter, 1993; Evandrou, 1995; Carmichael and Charles, 2003; Heitmueller and Inglis, 2004; cf Madden and Walker, 1999).

It is not just earnings that may be lower as a result of becoming a substantial carer; it is also incomes in general (Baldwin, 1995). This is because social security benefits do not sufficiently compensate for carers' lower earnings (McLaughlin, 1991; Shearn and Todd, 2000). Evandrou and Winter (1993), for example, found that the average net personal income of carers was lower than that of non-carers and this was especially true for men. There is also some evidence that the length of time spent caring can affect income levels. Thus, analysis of the 1988 Retirement Survey of people aged between 55 and 69 in

Table 9.1: Percentage of adults spending at least 20 hours per week caring who were working full or part time, by gender[a]

	Men	Women	All
Working full time	47	16	26
Working part time	7	26	19
All working	54	42	46

Note: [a] Adults aged 16 to 64 living in private households in Britain.
Source: Maher and Green (2002), table 4.7.

Britain found that the family incomes of people who had cared for 10 or more years were considerably lower than those who had cared for less than that time or not at all (Hancock and Jarvis, 1994).

Moreover, people who give up work to care and have no earnings of their own can find themselves financially dependent on the care recipient. The fact that entitlement to Carer's Allowance is based on the latter's benefit status can reinforce any feelings of financial dependency of the carer on the care recipient. This dependency can be a source of anxiety for many carers and generates particular concern about how they will get by if the care recipient moves into a residential or nursing home or dies (Glendinning, 1990). Such anxiety appears to have some foundation in reality, for caring episodes are shown to affect future as well as present incomes. For instance, a survey of Invalid Care Allowance[5] recipients and unsuccessful applicants found that, not only did carers have lower incomes than the general population, but former carers had substantially lower incomes than non-carers (McLaughlin, 1991). Thus, there can be a negative 'financial legacy' for former carers (McLaughlin, 1993).

The financial legacy of caring may also include adverse effects on pensions, especially for women. This can occur because of an interrupted or shortened working career or because of working part time instead of full time. The risk of this 'pension penalty' of caring (Evandrou and Glaser, 2003) is greater in relation to occupational and personal private pensions than to state pensions. This is because the social security system does provide, in certain circumstances, some protection to the state pension entitlements of carers, through Home Responsibilities Protection under the Basic State Pension and Contribution Credits under the State Second Pension (Ginn, 2003).

Not only is there a pension penalty to caring, but pension entitlements can influence decisions by carers about whether to give up paid work. Thus, a qualitative study of carers aged over 50 found that being able to retire early with a full occupational pension or favourable early retirement deal was a significant incentive to leave work in order to accommodate caring duties. This applied especially to men, as they were more likely than women to have a continuous employment career and hence to have built up sufficient pension entitlements to retire early. In contrast, having an inadequate pension entitlement was an incentive for female carers aged over 50 to stay on in work (Mooney et al, 2002). This is consistent with analysis of the 1988 Retirement Survey of people in Britain aged between 55 and 69, which found that female former carers who were over state retirement age were more likely to be in paid work than non-carers.

By contrast, male former carers were less likely to be in paid employment than non-carers (Hancock and Jarvis, 1994). This suggests that some female former carers may be working beyond state retirement age in order to make good the gaps in their pension contributions resulting from previous caring duties.

In summary, the risk of becoming an informal carer is relatively high, not only for women but also, to a lesser extent, for men. People whose caring responsibilities take up a substantial amount of time are less likely to be in paid work, and less likely to work full time, than those whose caring responsibilities are non-substantial or negligible. Meanwhile, many carers face both wage and pension penalties as a result of their caring responsibilities. This raises the question of how far the welfare state provides carers with income protection ('cash') or practical support ('care') to enable them to work while carrying out their caregiving duties.

Carers and the welfare state

The Beveridge plan for social security, and the post-war social security system on which it was largely based, made no explicit provision for people providing unpaid care for sick, disabled or frail older people. Indeed, the care of people living in the community was a major gap in the Beveridge report of 1942 (Baldwin, 1994). Such caring duties were implicitly a private responsibility and assumed to be the duty of women, whether married or single. In other words, informal caring was seen as a 'private risk' rather than a 'social risk' that should be addressed through the social security system. If caregiving was required, the implicit if not explicit assumption was that it would be undertaken by single women or would fall within the 'other duties' expected of married women within the male breadwinner family (Lister, 1994a).[6]

The introduction of Invalid Care Allowance (ICA) by the Labour government in 1976 was a major turning point in the recognition of unpaid care within the social security system. It was the first explicit recognition that informal caring was a social risk for which the welfare state should make some provision. Nevertheless this new, non-contributory social security benefit for people who were not in 'gainful employment' (defined as below a rather low earnings limit) incorporated assumptions consistent with the married male breadwinner model. Married women were explicitly excluded from eligibility for ICA on the grounds that they 'would be at home in any case' (DHSS, 1974, quoted in Baldwin, 1994, p 187). Carers over the state pension age were excluded too, presumably because they also would be at home and therefore available to care. Instead, ICA was for people 'of working age who would be breadwinners but for the need to stay at home and act as unpaid attendants to people who are severely disabled and need care' (DHSS, 1974, quoted in Baldwin, 1994, p 187).

Married women did not become eligible for ICA until 1986 and people over state pension age until 2002, by which time the benefit had been relabelled Carer's Allowance (CA). However, the fact that the gendered assumptions bound up in CA have been eroded does not mean the financial risks of informal caring have been adequately addressed. In the first place, the value of CA is well below that of minimum, means-tested social assistance benefits. Second, only a minority of people undertaking substantial caring responsibilities actually receive the allowance (McLaughlin, 1991). This is partly due to the fact that eligibility for CA is dependent on the cared-for person being in receipt of certain other qualifying benefits. It is also because of non-take-up among those who are entitled to CA and among those entitled to the qualifying benefits.[7] This limited social protection is carried over into means-tested in-work benefits such as Housing Benefit, which provides extra financial help for carers (via the 'carer's premium') but only if they are in receipt of CA.

People with substantial caring responsibilities who are in 'gainful employment' receive no financial help from the welfare state in recognition of their caring responsibilities. Meanwhile, apart from CA and the carer's premium, people who are full-time carers and not in gainful employment are largely invisible within the social security system. They may be claiming a range of benefits, including Income Support, Jobseeker's Allowance and Incapacity Benefit or living with a partner claiming them, but the Department for Work and Pensions does not publish statistics that enable them to be separately identified from other client groups. This invisibility has been largely replicated in many social surveys, in which economically inactive people who are caring are usually included in the category 'looking after the home'.

Until recently carers, like many social security benefit recipients, were also largely passive recipients of benefits. This meant that they could devote their time to caring while receiving a modest income from the state (in some cases via their claimant partner). However, since 1997, the social security system has moved towards a more active approach to welfare, with an explicit focus on helping to move people into work or closer to employability (Finn, 2003). The government's Welfare-to-Work Programme is a vehicle for achieving this, delivered through Jobcentre Plus offices, which provide an integrated service for jobs, benefits advice and support for people of working age.

Until November 2005 people who applied for CA were required to take part in a 'work-focused interview' as a condition of their claim, although this could be deferred to a later date or waived indefinitely in certain circumstances. Since then work-focused interviews for carers claiming CA have been voluntary rather than mandatory; however, people caring for a disabled partner in receipt of Incapacity Benefit or Income Support may still be subject to an interview in respect of their partner's claim.

Apart from the social security system, government policy aims to support carers in their caring role and enable them to continue caring, if that is their wish. Three Acts of Parliament focusing specifically on carers have been introduced since 1995, as well as a national strategy for carers (DH, 1999a). However, local authorities – the lead agency in supporting carers – have not been given any additional funding to help implement the legislation.

The 1995 Carers (Recognition and Services) Act gave carers who provided a 'substantial' amount of care on a 'regular' basis the right to request an assessment of their ability to care when the person receiving care was assessed for community care services. An assessment is an opportunity for a carer to discuss their situation with a social services practitioner, with a view to determining what can be done to make caring easier for them. However, there is no corresponding duty on local authorities to provide any services directly to carers, although additional services may be offered to care recipients, which could simultaneously help those caring for them. The overall emphasis of government guidance on the Act was on supporting carers to (continue to) care, rather than maintaining their attachment to the labour market (SSI, 1996).

The employment needs of carers were discussed in the national strategy for carers (DH, 1999a). The document emphasised the financial, social and psychological benefits to carers from participating in paid work. The government acknowledged the difficulties for carers in combining care and work and to that end emphasised the importance of developing flexible employment practices and leave arrangements, as well as support services to help carers remain in employment.

The 2000 Carers and Disabled Children Act strengthened carers' rights to an assessment of their needs and for the first time enabled local authorities to provide services directly to carers. The accompanying practitioner's guide highlighted the need for carers to be able to maintain employment, and emphasised that this issue should be a key concern in assessment (DH, 2001).

The 2000 Carers and Disabled Children Act also enabled eligible carers as well as disabled people to be offered 'direct payments', that is, cash payments instead of services in kind (see also Chapter Seventeen). The number of carers in receipt of direct payments themselves is low – just under 3,650 in March 2005 (CSCI, 2005b). However, there is limited evidence that direct payments (whether provided to the person receiving care or directly to the carer) have enabled carers to sustain paid employment when otherwise this might not have been possible (Stainton and Boyce, 2004; Arksey et al, 2005).

Most recently, the 2004 Carers (Equal Opportunities) Act aims to give carers the opportunity to enjoy the activities that many of us take for granted. In particular, the Act has helped raise the profile of the rights of carers to work, by making it a requirement that local authorities take account of carers' wishes in education, training, employment and leisure services.

The needs of carers who both work and care, or who might wish to return to work while still caring, have also been addressed in 'family-friendly' policy initiatives, which aim to help reconcile work and family responsibilities for all employees. First, time off for dependants, introduced under the 1999 Employment Relations Act, entitles staff to take a 'reasonable' amount of unpaid time off to deal with emergency or unexpected situations relating to those they look after. Second, the government's work–life balance campaign was designed to raise employers' awareness of the benefits to their organisations of policies and practices to help employees, including carers, obtain a better balance between work and their responsibilities outside of work (DfEE, 2000). Third, the Flexible Working Regulations, included in the 2002 Employment Act, gave parents of children under the age of six, or 18 if the child is disabled, the right to request flexible working, such as changing hours of work or working from home, after six months in service. The Work and Families Bill going through Parliament during 2006 proposes to extend this measure to carers of adults from April 2007.

In summary, there is increasing emphasis in government policy on supporting carers to work while caring. This seems to be largely motivated by the government's aspirations to reduce the number of people living on benefits and to raise the employment rate to 80% by 2010 (DWP, 2005b). However, given that at the same time a Green Paper on adult social care (DH, 2005) acknowledges that the formal care sector would be unable to cope without the caregiving activities of people looking after partners, relatives and friends, there is a clear tension between enabling carers to move into paid employment and ensuring that they provide essential, but largely unpaid, care in the community.

Helping carers to work

This part of the chapter draws on research evidence to illustrate how, in practice, the welfare state assists carers to remain in, or take up, paid employment. It is known that non-working carers lack confidence, have low levels of self-esteem and are therefore disadvantaged in taking up opportunities for training or employment (Arksey, 2003). As a result, many carers need encouragement and practical help to return to the labour market, whether during or after a period of caregiving. Furthermore, services such as day care or after-school clubs for disabled children can be crucial if carers are to both work and care (Kagan et al, 1998; Carers National Association, 1999; Seddon et al, 2004).

The evidence reported below comes from a study that explored carers' experiences of work and care (Arksey et al, 2005). The study included interviews with 80 carers of working age who were devoting at least 20 hours per week to caring, 43 of whom were also engaged in paid work of one form or another. In addition, 12 focus groups were conducted with frontline professionals (Jobcentre Plus personal advisors; social services practitioners; and people working in carers' centres and other voluntary organisations) who provided carers with advice and information.

Support from Jobcentre Plus

The services from Jobcentre Plus to which carers could gain access, either directly or indirectly, included help with obtaining a job and/ or improving their employment prospects; 'better-off' calculations to help establish whether or not paid work would make carers better or worse off financially, given the potential loss of means-tested benefits; benefit entitlement checks; and help to improve carers' confidence and skills to make them better able to compete for jobs.

Carers who had visited Jobcentre Plus offices held mixed views about their experiences.[8] For example, they praised the better-off calculations, but were critical of personal advisors who appeared to have limited knowledge of caregiving and did not understand the difficulties involved in combining paid work and caring. For their part, personal advisors took the view that the effectiveness of Jobcentre

Plus services for carers was limited because of organisational priorities that inhibited the support they could offer.

At the time of the study, work-focused interviews for carers making a claim for CA were still compulsory. Less than 15 carers reported attending a work-focused interview, which comprised a full benefits check with a financial assessor followed by a discussion with a personal advisor about returning to paid work. Carers who had experienced a work-focused interview did not understand why they were required to attend one to talk about their (future) work needs when they had substantial caring responsibilities (at least 35 hours per week in order to be eligible for CA). Moreover, like the carers interviewed by Davies et al (2004), they felt that the interviews were neither useful nor especially informative. None of the carers said they had undertaken training courses, employment or voluntary work as a result of attending a work-focused interview. The government's decision in November 2005 to make work-focused interviews voluntary rather than mandatory for carers could be seen as recognition that paid work is not a realistic option for some carers, given the other support that is available.

Support from social services departments

While some carers were full of praise for the support they received from social services, others were very critical. Some carers had chosen to manage without social services support. The reasons they gave for this decision were wide ranging, but common ones included feeling they would be letting their relative down by not undertaking the care work themselves; care recipients who were unwilling to accept help from paid carers, often because they did not want 'intruders' or 'strangers' in their home; services perceived as poor quality, inflexible and unreliable; and the cost of services that were seen as poor, expensive or for tasks carers could do themselves.

Not all of the 43 employed carers in the study were in receipt of support from social services, yet they were still able to combine work and care, in some cases holding down a full-time job. Other studies have also found that employed carers do not necessarily use services (Phillips et al, 2002). Our study found that services were provided in ways that did not meet the needs of all working carers. For instance, day care hours were too short to cover the full working day; brief home visits were available, but not longer substitute care services; services were provided but without any accompanying transport facilities.

Carers' assessments are intended to act as a gateway to social services. The importance of assessments in accessing services is intensified for carers who both work and care, or who want to start work. Despite guidelines (DH, 2001) accompanying the 2000 Carers and Disabled Children Act that stress the importance of addressing employment issues when conducting carers' assessments, there was evidence that social services practitioners were ambivalent about their role concerning carers and paid work. Social workers in two of the fieldwork areas stated that they did not routinely initiate discussions with carers about employment; one practitioner taking part in a focus group flagged up the dilemma they faced in that they needed carers to continue caring or otherwise (local) social care provision would break down. Some carers reported that their assessment had led to the provision of services intended to help them combine work and care, but one had been expressly told by her social worker that social services were not there to help her to work. Overall, the findings suggest that a change of mindset is needed on the part of some social services practitioners in the wake of the 2004 Carers (Equal Opportunities) Act, which aims to offer support to carers beyond their caring role, including employment.

Few of the carers or care recipients in the study received direct payments. Those who did were more likely to use the payments for befrienders or buddies to take the person receiving care out at weekends or evenings than for support services to make it easier for them to combine work and care. Social workers taking part in the focus groups believed that direct payments were a potential solution to help carers combine the two activities. However, because of the administrative and management demands of direct payments, practitioners did not consider them suitable for all carers.

Financial support

There was a consensus among carers taking part in the study that the monetary value of CA was much too low, especially if it was regarded as a 'wage' for caregiving.[9] Many of the carers who were working but not in receipt of CA were in professional jobs. For them, CA did not act as an incentive to provide (more) care. These carers commonly claimed that they could not afford to give up paid work to care because of their financial commitments.

A small number of carers in the study who were in paid work were also in receipt of CA. They were all women and generally had low-paid jobs (for example, residential care worker, school dinner lady, filing clerk) below their actual skill levels and experience. However, jobs with higher hourly rates did not fit easily with the earnings threshold for CA; consequently, they felt they had no alternative but to take low-level work, which many said did not give them a sense of self-esteem. The consensus among carers in this group was that the CA restriction on earnings was unfair and prevented them from working longer hours or getting better-paid jobs.[10]

About a quarter of carers who did not work were also in receipt of CA. Only in a handful of cases was this benefit an important factor in giving up work to care. In principle, the idea of resuming employment was attractive to some non-working carers. However, they were anxious about the impact of starting work, not only on CA but also on other means-tested benefits such as Income Support or Housing Benefit. Another concern was whether employment would reduce the number of hours spent caring to below the threshold of eligibility for CA.

There was a similar consensus among professionals taking part in the focus groups that CA was too low and that the benefit system in general acted as a barrier to paid work for carers. It could be hard for carers to make work pay, especially for those carers who stood to lose other means-tested benefits, such as Housing Benefit, once they started earning. CA also limited carers' access to full-time education to 21 hours per week of supervised study, which could serve as a barrier to carers wanting to improve their employability. This is a further example of tensions within government policy, given the aim to improve the competitiveness of business by encouraging a more skilled workforce.

Conclusions

The risk of becoming an informal carer is relatively high, with more than half of the population likely to be affected at some point in their lives. Many of the people devoting substantial amounts of time to caring find it difficult to combine this with holding down a full-time job. The net result is that some carers suffer a wage or pension penalty as a result of looking after a sick or disabled relative, friend or neighbour, especially those who are co-resident and/or providing substantial amounts of support. Nevertheless, in practice informal caring is still largely a private risk for individuals and their families, rather than a 'social risk' that is the responsibility of the welfare state to address.

The social security system does provide some help for carers who have little or no earnings or benefit income, but only a small minority of carers receive CA and the value of this benefit is in any case very low. The development of a more work-focused social security system and the aspiration to raise the employment rate have brought the issue of carers and employment to the fore. However, labour activation policies are not especially relevant to those with heavy caregiving responsibilities; they have already made the decision not to work while caring, often because it is just too hard or because of the restrictions governing receipt of CA. Moreover, personal advisors in Jobcentre Plus offices are generally not trained or knowledgeable about carers' issues and consequently often fail to understand the difficulties of combining work and care.

In principle, the social care system – in the form of social service provision, voluntary and carers' organisations – does assist carers. But, in practice, many carers do not receive such help. Even where they do receive an assessment of their needs, this often fails to address issues to do with paid work. Moreover, the evidence suggests that the state tends to see carers as a free resource (Twigg and Atkin, 1994) and is more concerned with sustaining their role as unpaid carers than with supporting carers to move into, or remain in, paid work.

Notes

[1] The term 'informal carers' is used in this chapter to refer to people who provide unpaid care for sick, disabled or frail older relatives, neighbours or friends. It is not confined to elder care and includes carers of chronically sick or disabled children, as well as people caring for spouses and other people of working age.

[2] The percentage for children includes children of any age; the term 'spouses' includes cohabiting as well as legally married partners; and of course some of these spouses – and their carers – will be older people.

[3] Estimates based on the 2000 GHS suggest that there are 6.8 million carers, which is much higher than the number found in the 2001 Census. The difference may be attributable to the fact that (a) the Census and the GHS questions about caring used different wording and (b) the GHS involved face-to-face interviews conducted by trained and experienced interviewers who were in a position to explain the meaning of questions, whereas the 2001 Census was, in effect, a self-completion questionnaire. On the one hand, it is possible therefore that the Census data under-represent the true extent of caring. On the other hand, whereas the Census is based on (almost) the entire population, the GHS is a sample survey that is subject to response bias.

[4] Co-resident carers are people providing care to a member of their household, while extra-resident carers are those providing care to someone in another household.

[5] Invalid Care Allowance is now called Carer's Allowance.

[6] It is important to recognise that assumptions did not necessarily match with reality; that some caring was probably undertaken by women in paid employment; and that some caring was almost certainly carried out by men, even if the vast majority of carers were women.

[7] To be eligible for CA, carers must be spending at least 35 hours per week looking after a severely disabled person who is receiving either Attendance Allowance or the highest or middle rate of the care component of Disability Living Allowance.

[8] Some of the carers' experiences may have pre-dated the roll-out of local Jobcentre Plus offices, so may not reflect current practice.

[9] In 2005, CA had a value of £44.35. The main rate of the national minimum wage for workers aged 22 and over was set at £5.05 an hour, which meant that the hourly value of CA was around one-quarter of the national minimum wage.

[10] In order to be eligible for CA, recipients must not be earning more than £79 (net of allowable expenses) per week from paid employment.

Part Four
Families, care work and the state

TEN

Paying family caregivers: evaluating different models

Caroline Glendinning

Introduction

This chapter provides an overview of different models of financial support for informal carers (that is, the kin and close friends) of older people. These models reflect the institutional and cultural traditions of the broader societies and welfare states of which they are a part. Thus, the underlying logic, rationale and form of different models of payment for informal care are shaped by wider welfare state institutional and cultural traditions, and by beliefs about the relationships between families (particularly the role of women within them) and formal, collectively funded state provision.

The chapter first argues that the issue of paying informal carers needs to be understood from several different policy perspectives. It then outlines four models of providing financial support for informal care, illustrated with examples from specific countries. However, as noted above, the rationales underpinning these contrasting models tend to reflect the dominant welfare arrangements in different countries (Lundsgaard, 2005). It is therefore difficult to engage in discussions of whether a particular model is 'better' or 'worse' than another, because of their embeddedness in specific policy logics and underlying assumptions. Instead, the chapter evaluates the different models against a series of questions relating to sustainability; the implications for economic well-being and concepts of citizenship that derive from labour market participation; the balance between individual, family and social rights and responsibilities; and the quality of care. Some of these issues, particularly those relating to gender and social rights, provide specific examples of the issues raised in Chapters Two and Three; the question of gender equity is also discussed in more detail in Chapter Eleven. Finally, the chapter argues that, in order to address these wider policy issues, a number of additional measures to paying informal carers of older people are required.

Payments for informal care – at the intersection of multiple policy domains

Payment for informal carers of older people is a complex issue because it is located within a number of different policy domains, each of which can be approached from different analytical and disciplinary perspectives.

First, payment for informal care is at the heart of debates about the sustainable provision of long-term care for older people; in almost all western societies the majority of primary caregivers of older people living in the community are close relatives. Population ageing is a key driver in debates about long-term care policy (CEC, 2005) and these pressures are expected to increase further as the post-war baby boom cohorts reach the oldest age groups over the next 30 years (Huber and Skidmore, 2003). Moreover, greater longevity means higher risks of serious disabling conditions and illnesses such as dementia. Consequently, the level of support needed by the oldest older people now (and in the future) is considerably more demanding than it has been in the past. An increasing proportion of informal carers are themselves older people, and possibly also frail. This is particularly true of older spouses, who constitute a growing proportion of informal carers (Hirst, 2001; Milne, 2001). Factors contributing to this trend include the increasing longevity of men and a decrease in multi-generational households in which older people have moved to live with their children.

In summary, both the volume and intensity of long-term care is increasing, as is the age of informal carers. Policy makers are therefore likely to avoid measures that might risk any diminution of informal care:

> Should the vast volume of informal care disappear and be
> substituted with paid care, the costs could be enormous.
> (Wiener, 2003, p 12)

Second, informal care is generally assumed to mean family care and is therefore embedded within wider cultural and political views on the respective responsibilities and rights of families and the state; these perspectives have strong gender dimensions (Lewis, 1992). At the core is the question of how far unpaid work – particularly that involved in caring for children and disabled and older people – is a private family responsibility, and what role the state should play in supporting and/ or compensating for this activity. This issue is at the heart of the 'ethics of care' outlined in Chapters Two and Three. However, there are substantial variations between countries in the extent to which they have explicitly attempted to strengthen the responsibilities of families or expanded public services to relieve families of some of their caregiving responsibilities (Leitner, 2003). Esping-Andersen (1999) refers to these variations as 'familialistic' and 'defamilialising' welfare regimes, distinguished by the extent to which public policy assumes that households or the state should and do carry principal responsibility for their members' welfare.

Third, payment for informal care intersects with labour market supply policies and, indirectly, with the social and citizenship rights derived from formal economic activity. These policies are partly shaped by wider forces, such as the demographic changes referred to earlier, and by pressures to sustain global market competitiveness. Associated with these pressures has been a recent dramatic increase in women's labour force participation in industrialised countries (see, for example, Jensen and Jacobzone, 2000). A growing challenge, therefore, is to reconcile the demands of the labour market with those for (increasingly intensive) informal care. Moreover, as societies have moved from 'one-earner' family policies to 'one-and-a-half-earner' – or even 'two-earner' – policies (see Chapter Two), there has been a tendency to equate concepts such as citizenship and social inclusion with active labour market participation (Lister, 2003). Models of payment for informal care that actively discourage simultaneous participation in formal paid work may therefore also affect carers' social inclusion and citizenship status through their impact on access to those rights and benefits that are secured via labour market participation.

Finally, payments for informal care intersect with widespread trends to promote choice and flexibility over care arrangements for both younger disabled and older people. As Chapters Sixteen and Seventeen show, disabled people have long argued for cash payments instead of directly provided services, with which they can employ their own helpers. In many countries, such arrangements are now being introduced or extended to older people as well (Lundsgaard, 2005). However, the conditions under which such payments are received and used and the role played by the state in regulating the relationship between users and informal carers are critically important for the rights, autonomy and social protection of both (Ungerson, 2003).

Different models and rationales

A number of writers have identified different types of payment for
informal care (Glendinning et al, 1997; Ungerson, 1997). Jensen and
Jacobzone (2000) differentiate between care allowances paid to an
older person and benefits paid directly to informal carers. Surveying
methods that offer older people increased choice, Lundsgaard (2005)
distinguishes between consumer-directed employment of care assistants,
care allowances that an older person can spend as they like, and Income
Support payments to informal carers.

These different analyses together allow us to identify four different
models of payment for informal care. It is the rationale or principle
underpinning each model that is important here, rather than the form
a payment takes or the conditions under which it is accessed (although
these will be closely linked). The four models will be briefly illustrated
with examples from different countries. Again, the aim is not to provide
accurate accounts of these examples as they operate in particular
countries, but to highlight the rationale underpinning each model
and the principles and assumptions that are embedded within them.

Personal budgets and consumer-directed employment of helpers

This 'routed wages' (Ungerson, 2003) model allocates the older person
cash instead of services in kind, with which they employ a personal
assistant or carer either directly or through a third party agency. As
Morris describes (Chapter Seventeen), this approach originated from
the demands of younger disabled people for choice and control over
their support through the employment of personal assistants. The
Netherlands, the UK and Flanders in Belgium (Chapter Twelve) have
payments of this type, although their take-up by older people in the
UK is low compared to younger disabled people (Glasby and Littlechild,
2002; Leece and Bornat, 2006) and the employment of co-resident
close relatives is prohibited; in Flanders, personal budgets are restricted
to people below the age of 65. However, in the Netherlands, instead
of receiving services in kind, older people can receive a cash 'personal
budget', which they can use to purchase services from formal public
or private agencies and/or to employ a close relative. The Dutch
personal budget scheme has proved very popular; by September 2002
about 10% of people eligible for home care services were personal
budget holders (Wiener et al, 2003). About half of personal budget
holders employ informal carers, and older people are more likely than

younger budget holders to employ close relatives (including spouses) as their service providers (Wiener et al, 2003).

Although the Dutch personal budget is calculated according to the level of home nursing and home help needed by the older person, a standard reduction of 25% is automatically applied on the grounds that informal arrangements do not incur the same overheads as traditional formal home care services; moreover, there is a ceiling on any personal budget equivalent to the costs of intensive nursing care. Consequently, the actual level of support provided by a close relative employed by a personal budget holder is likely to exceed what has been paid for by a considerable amount. This effect is graphically illustrated by Breda et al's comparison of co-resident informal carers and non-related personal assistants employed through the Flemish personal budget scheme in Chapter Twelve. In both countries, when personal budgets are used to pay close relatives, these tend to formalise and commodify care relationships that are already in existence (Ungerson, 2003).

Significantly, Dutch personal budget holders have to make formal contracts with their employees and adhere to normal labour market regulations concerning wage levels, taxation, social security contributions and liability insurance (Pijl, 2000). Ungerson (1997, p 370) describes these arrangements as the 'sharp end' of 'marketised intimacy' in which the state introduces an employer–employee relationship into an informal caregiving dyad.

Care allowances for older people

These are another form of 'routed wages' (Ungerson, 2003). Cash payments are made to the person needing care solely on the basis of their level of disability or the amount of help needed. However, there is no obligation to account for how the payment is used, only to secure adequate care. The state therefore assumes minimal responsibility either for ensuring that high-quality care is provided to older citizens or for safeguarding the citizenship and social rights of informal carers; rather, older people are trusted to use the allowance in whatever way best suits them.

This model is illustrated by the German long-term care insurance scheme (Glendinning and Igl, forthcoming). Once assessed as qualifying for long-term care insurance, an older person can choose between an entitlement to service 'assignments' up to a specified value, depending on the level of 'care dependency', or a lower value cash allowance, or a combination of the two. The Austrian care allowance is a similar unconditional benefit paid to the older person, whose only obligation is to secure an appropriate level of care (Chapter Eleven). In both countries, regulation of the amount or quality of care secured through these allowances is rudimentary.

In Germany, the cash allowance has remained the most popular option. The vast majority of older people choosing the cash allowance are believed to do so because they prefer to receive care from family and friends rather than strangers. One local survey found that half of all family carers received a regular payment from an older person in receipt of the long-term care insurance cash allowance, but in a third of these cases the payment to the family caregiver was less than the full amount of the benefit (Wiener et al, 2003).

This discrepancy indicates one of the major shortcomings of this approach, at least from the perspective of informal carers. All entitlements rest with the older insurance beneficiary and none with the carer, who is dependent on the discretion of the older person to pay as the latter considers appropriate. Moreover, the fact that any payment is derived indirectly via the entitlement of another person further undermines the status of informal carers, particularly in the German context where social insurance entitlements are important dimensions of citizenship (Glendinning and Igl, forthcoming). Finally, the cash allowance is considerably lower than the value of the 'in-kind' service benefit; similarly the Austrian care allowance falls short of the actual value of the care needed at all levels of disability. These arrangements reflect dominant beliefs and sustain traditional practice in both countries – that long-term care of older people is primarily a private, family responsibility preferred by both older and younger people alike, and depends heavily on the only partly remunerated work of women. In the case of Austria, this involves 'grey' immigrant labour as well (Chapter Eleven). Such labour is also unprotected by social and employment rights and risks the long-term poverty of carers.

Income maintenance approaches

Here, cash payments and other benefits are paid directly to informal carers to acknowledge, and compensate for, income from paid employment that is lost or foregone because of caregiving. The underlying rationale is to maintain a minimum level of income, despite being unable to have a (full-time) job because of providing care (and perhaps also despite being ineligible for other earnings replacement benefits). Some schemes, such as the Australian Carer Payment and the Irish Carer's Allowance, are only available for carers whose household income is low; the UK Carer's Allowance is payable to carers whose own personal income is low, regardless of the income or asset levels of a partner or spouse. Logically, earnings replacement benefits may be available only to working-age carers; however, the UK Carer's Allowance has been extended to maintain the incomes of older carers who have below minimum pension entitlements.

The most important feature of this model is that it explicitly acknowledges the rights of informal carers to an independent income, regardless of the circumstances of the older person. Such entitlements avoid the financial dependency of the carer on the receiver of care. In addition, if such payments are located within national social security systems, they are likely to be governed by universally applicable and largely categorical principles of rights and entitlements. Finally, because of their underlying rationale of income maintenance, they do not preclude either carers or older people from also receiving services (Glendinning et al, 1997).

Variations of this approach in Canada, Norway, Sweden and Ireland involve collectively funded income replacement benefits for employees who take temporary leave from work to care for a critically or terminally ill relative. Such schemes may be linked to statutory employment or sickness insurance schemes, and also usually safeguard carers' rights to return to work at the end of the leave period (Keefe et al, forthcoming).

Paying carers instead of formal social service provision

In countries such as Norway, Sweden and Finland that have high levels of both publicly funded formal social services and female employment, informal carers can be directly employed by the state on a similar basis to municipal home helps. In Finland, for example, the Informal Care Allowances have been introduced as a new social care service (Jensen and Jacobzone, 2000). The allowances are awarded on the basis of the older person's needs, but paid by the municipality directly to the carer. The carer enters into a contract with the municipality to provide care according to a jointly agreed service plan. These allowances have been effective in enabling older people, who would otherwise have entered institutional care, to receive intensive support at home. The vast majority of carers employed in this way are spouses or other close relatives and a third are aged 65 plus (Martimo, 1998). However, allowances are typically much lower than the costs of either institutional care or formal home care services. In practice they provide no incentives to begin caring; rather they are believed to encourage relatives to maintain existing caregiving responsibilities (Kröger et al, 2003).

These models of paying informal carers reflect different welfare state regimes and policy logics, particularly at the intersections between employment, care and family policies. The next section of this chapter discusses the implications of the different models. Moreover, the different payment models are generally accompanied by a range of other measures – social security, fiscal, service and employment related – that are targeted at or support informal caregiving. These additional measures are essential in addressing some of the wider policy issues outlined at the start of the chapter.

Evaluating different models of payment for informal carers

Because informal care constitutes such an important element of long-term care provision, a first consideration is the fiscal sustainability of different models within the context of demographic ageing. On the one hand, payments for informal care risk generating new demands for payments in respect of caregiving work that has previously been carried out wholly without remuneration (Askheim, 2005). Set against this is the fact that all the models outlined above involve far lower payments to informal carers than the actual value of the care provided:

> In many instances, the level of payment to informal caregivers is extremely low, or highly discounted against the cost of comparable formal services, and cannot be seen as real 'market compensation' for the amount of effort by the informal caregiver. (Wiener, 2003, p 14)

Thus, the lower value and greater popularity of the German long-term care insurance cash benefit option have been crucial to the overall financial sustainability of the scheme. Similarly, Kreimer (Chapter Eleven) and Breda et al (Chapter Twelve) show the discrepancy between the volume of work performed by informal carers and the levels of the care allowance in Austria and the personal budget in Flanders respectively. The UK's income replacement Carer's Allowance is paid at a rate so low that it falls below the minimum means-tested social assistance level.

Whatever the specific model, payments for informal care therefore constitute significant cost containment mechanisms within broader arrangements for long-term care funding. This also means that they do not – and cannot – provide incentives to start providing informal care. Instead, they offer symbolic recognition of the contribution of relatives and close friends to the provision of long-term care: as compensation for the opportunity costs of care (Jensen and Jacobzone, 2000); as (partial) compensation for the actual financial costs of family caregiving (Glendinning, 1992); and as an (again partial) attempt to maintain social equity so that those who provide family care are not substantially worse off than those who do not (Wiener, 2003).

A second issue is the intersection of payments for informal care with labour market policies. In the context of increased female labour market participation and anxieties about future dependency ratios, the key issue is not so much whether women's labour market participation threatens the supply of informal care, as whether there is adequate social and financial protection from the labour market-related consequences of providing substantial amounts of informal care. There is no evidence that the low levels of any of the models of payment for informal care constitute an incentive to give up paid employment in order to take up a care-related benefit (Jensen and Jacobzone, 2000) apart, perhaps, from the temporary income replacement models for short-term employment breaks.

There is, however, a substantial body of evidence on the difficulties experienced by carers in combining paid employment with extensive informal caregiving; some of this evidence is reviewed in Chapter Nine. Typically, carers have responded to these difficulties by giving up paid work, switching to part-time work, and making other adjustments to paid work in order to accommodate caregiving commitments. All of these responses can have long-term financial consequences for individual carers and their families and for the wider economy (Metlife Mature Market Institute, 1997; DH, 1999a). Thus, care allowances, as in Germany and Austria (Chapter Eleven), that assume the full-time availability of family carers may not be compatible with wider economic and workforce policies unless they are accompanied by other mechanisms for safeguarding the incomes of family caregivers in the shorter and longer terms. In this respect, the 'personal budget', 'income maintenance' and 'substitute social services' approaches all have the potential to safeguard the entitlements of carers to at least a minimum income and associated social protection rights. Nevertheless, as Breda et al (Chapter Twelve) point out, these rights may be minimal in the grey area between work and care.

Moreover, payment models that assume informal care to be largely incompatible with paid employment risk exposing carers to longer-term financial insecurity and social exclusion. Consequently, complementary social protection measures are important. Thus, Dutch personal budget holders must adhere to minimum labour market regulations in employing carers, whether close relatives or not. Carers of German long-term care insurance cash benefit recipients are entitled to relatively generous social protection in the form of accident and pension insurance contributions. In Finland, carers receiving Informal Care Allowance can join the municipal pension scheme. Nevertheless, informal carers who are formally employed under consumer-directed personal budgets (for example, the Netherlands) or by local municipalities (for example, Finland) still fare less well in terms of wage levels, working conditions and other benefits than formally employed carers working in conventional home help services (Wiener, 2003).

A third issue is the balance between the choices and rights of older people and informal carers. This is a difficult issue to resolve in policy terms. On the one hand, having choice and control over personal support is fundamental to human and citizenship rights, as Morris argues in Chapter Seventeen. On the other hand, as Land points out in Chapter Eighteen, recent research with older people highlights the importance of recognising and supporting interdependence and mutuality; this perspective may be particularly important as increasing numbers of older people themselves become informal carers for partners and siblings. As Parker and Clarke (2002) argue, some people will wish to have their personal support needs met through personal relationships and others will wish to provide such support. This involves a careful balancing of the choices, rights and autonomy of both older people and informal carers while simultaneously acknowledging and supporting those relationships in which family members wish to give and receive care from each other. Nevertheless, it is possible to identify some problems in some of the models described above.

For example, care allowances (as in Germany and Austria) that offer maximum direction and choice to an older person risk creating dependencies on the part of family caregivers, who are entirely dependent on the discretion of the older person for any income at all. To some extent, the same is true for informal carers employed under the consumer-directed personal budget model. As Breda et al point out (Chapter Twelve), even with the protection of a quasi-employment relationship it is difficult for informal carers to exit from an unsatisfactory employment situation.

Such situations may be acceptable for older partner carers in the context of marital relationships characterised by long-term, extensive and multiple exchanges of labour, resources and care (in the broadest sense). However, they are not compatible with the principle of defamilialisation, which has underpinned reforms in many European countries during the 1990s (Knijn, 2004). Defamilialisation aims to ensure that:

> ... individual adults can uphold a socially acceptable standard of living, independently of family relationships, either through paid work or through social security. (Lister, 1994b)

Thus, models that aim to compensate informal carers for loss of earnings from formal paid employment and/or for the additional costs of caregiving (as in the UK or Republic of Ireland), or that involve direct payments by the state to carers (as in Finland), do offer carers access to income sources that are independent of their family status.

A fourth issue is the relationship between payments for informal care and the range, availability and quality of formal services. Where payments for informal care are intended to constitute the main or the only form of support for older people, they risk effectively privatising care for older people within the family; this can have a number of direct and indirect consequences.

For example, models that aim to support informal care predominantly through care allowances (as in Austria – see Chapter Eleven) risk diverting attention and resources from formal services. Without such investment, services may not be available to support informal carers on a regular basis, or provide them with high-quality alternatives when they seek a break from caregiving. Formal services are a vital adjunct and complement to informal caregiving. A review of (mainly UK) literature on the effectiveness and cost-effectiveness of services for informal carers of older people examined the impact of services on carers' levels of psychological stress; the risk of the older person entering residential care; and the older person's views on the acceptability of services (Pickard, 2004). Pickard concluded that services aimed at the older person (such as traditional home help services) as well as services aimed primarily at carers (such as respite care) can be both effective and cost-effective in improving carers' well-being and delaying entry to institutional care. Providing services for older people is thus an important way of supporting carers and, because it helps reduce the most extreme risks of enforced and unsupported interdependency, is also consistent with both feminist and disability rights perspectives (Pickard, 2001).

There are other reasons for advocating a multifaceted approach that complements financial support with formal services. For older people without close relatives, or where relatives are no longer able to provide sufficient care, good-quality services are essential. However, an assumption that the majority of the long-term care that is required will be funded by payments to informal carers (whatever the model or rationale) risks relegating formal service provision to a residual status, as Kreimer shows in the case of Austria (Chapter Eleven). Similarly, in Germany, the popularity of the long-term insurance cash allowance has provided little incentive or leverage to improve the quality of either community or institutional services. How to fund and secure improvements in the quality of formal care services in Germany, particularly nursing homes, is now a major priority (Glendinning and Igl, forthcoming).

Safeguarding the quality of consumer-directed services purchased through care allowance models is another challenge. Conventional quality assurance mechanisms such as professional accreditation, agency regulation and inspection regimes are absent – and are arguably inappropriate in the context of care allowances intended to pay informal carers. Although both consumer-directed personal budgets and care allowances generally lead to high levels of user satisfaction, there is little robust evidence of their impact on quality indicators such as delays in functional decline or the avoidance of unnecessary hospitalisation. Moreover:

> … public agencies and disabled individuals have great
> difficulty disciplining poor performing relatives. It is difficult
> for government officials to insist that a daughter be fired.
> (Wiener, 2003, p 16)

Conclusions: payment for informal care is not enough

This chapter has outlined four different models for paying informal carers. Each reflects different configurations of relationships between the family (that is, women) and the state in the long-term care of older people. Whatever the model, the policy and practice of paying for informal care need to be evaluated in the context of wider policies: the development of sustainable approaches to the funding and provision of long-term care; labour market supply policies and related social and citizenship rights; and the balance between private, family-based care and formal service provision.

Drawing on these observations it can be argued that, on their own, payments for informal care are not enough. Additional policy measures are needed, to secure social justice and prevent social exclusion for both older people and family caregivers and to address these wider policy concerns. These additional measures include:

- A range of high-quality, publicly funded services for older people that are available whether or not an older person also receives extensive support from a (paid or unpaid) family caregiver (Pickard, 2001).
- An entitlement to breaks from family care, in the form of high-quality alternatives that are acceptable to the older person. Such entitlements are available to family carers of older people receiving long-term care insurance benefits in Germany, for example, and can involve paying a substitute informal carer rather than requiring temporary institutional admission.
- Payments to replace earnings from formal employment. In practice, these may take two forms: earnings replacement benefits because caregiving work is not regarded as employment or is incompatible with employment outside the home (as in the UK and in the temporary leave schemes of Canada, Sweden and Ireland); or payment of earnings for the work of caregiving (as in Finland). However, the principle underpinning both is the same. They provide family carers with an income which is paid by the (local or national) state and is independent of the person receiving care, and which therefore reduces the risks of financial dependence on a close family member.
- Payment of pension, accident and other social insurance contributions and other social rights normally attached to formal labour market participation. Some or all of these measures are available to family carers paid through consumer-directed care allowance arrangements such as the Dutch personal budget; to family carers in receipt of income replacement benefits such as in the UK; and to family carers employed instead of formal social service provision, as in Finland.
- Employment and workplace-based policies that facilitate a combination of paid work and family caregiving. Measures to support continuing labour market participation among parents of young children are unlikely to be wholly appropriate for family carers of older people (Anderson, 2004). The trajectory of caregiving is not predictable; institutional solutions such as nurseries are not appropriate; and there is a greater need for flexibility to meet fluctuating health problems and care needs. Instead, flexible working arrangements, including opportunities to start and finish work at different times, and entitlements to periods of leave without

jeopardising employment security are likely to be more appropriate (see Chapter Nine).

ELEVEN

Developments in Austrian care arrangements: women between free choice and informal care

Margareta Kreimer

Introduction

In comparative research, Austria has been classified as a strong breadwinner state (Lewis and Ostner, 1994; Duncan, 1995), among other reasons because of the low level of formal care services. Millar and Warman (1995) describe the Austrian care system as based on a nuclear family model. Bettio and Plantenga (2004) characterise Austria (and Germany) as a publicly facilitated private care system, with a large private informal care sector based on strong family obligations to provide care; within this the role of the state is to give financial support to the family. Thus, Austrian welfare policy is 'service lean' but very 'transfer heavy' (Esping-Andersen, 1996, p 67).

Consequently, informal care – mostly provided by women within the family – plays an important role. These informal caregivers have no or only limited access of their own to the social security system, and instead depend for the most part on a (male) breadwinner. However, there are increasing numbers of lone parents, and women living in poverty in Austria. These problems, together with debates about the crisis of the Austrian social security system, increasing demand for long-term care and the diminishing supply of informal family care, suggest that the breadwinner-oriented welfare state is no longer appropriate, particularly in the light of changing gender roles in the labour market and the family.

Since the early 1990s two important reforms have taken place: in 1993 the long-term care allowance was introduced and in 2002 a universal childcare allowance replaced the former parental leave benefit. Together with reforms in the social security system (such as the introduction in 1995 of pension credits for periods of childcare and leave entitlements to care for a terminally ill person introduced in 2002), it could be argued that the Austrian welfare state is beginning to assign a higher value to informal family care.

This chapter addresses two questions. First, the reforms described above are intended to improve the social security and income situations of informal family carers. Do they therefore represent a move towards 'caregiving parity' (Fraser, 1994) for informal carers? Second, the arguments in favour of these new payments for care have focused on their role in extending freedom of choice. Do informal carers and/or the people they care for actually experience greater freedom of choice now, compared to before the introduction of the cash benefits?

Apart from the fact that nearly all Austrian informal caregivers are female, they are otherwise highly heterogeneous. Unlike those countries which have introduced labour market and social security reforms of different kinds to facilitate a combination of paid work and providing care for older or disabled people (see, for example, Chapters Two and Ten), in Austria informal carers are defined as people who have left the labour market for longer than the maximum two years allowed for parental leave.[1] During the period of caregiving, informal carers have no independent status within the social security system, and are only entitled to benefits by virtue of their relationship to a breadwinner.[2] Full-time housewives and women with discontinuous labour market careers are the main groups of informal carers.

The chapter begins by discussing the concepts of 'caregiving parity' and 'freedom of choice'. It then examines the new childcare and long-term care allowances to see whether these reforms do indeed reflect a new approach to supporting care arrangements, based on these concepts. The chapter concludes that, although the Austrian care system does show some trends that challenge the male breadwinner model, it is still far from reflecting a new model of care.

Caregiving parity and freedom of choice

Fraser (1994) argues that the male breadwinner model is no longer appropriate and therefore contributes to the current crisis of the welfare state. She offers two alternative models for the post-industrial welfare state. The 'universal breadwinner' model aims to foster gender equality by promoting women's employment and depends on the widespread provision of day care and other services to enable women to become equal participants in the labour market with men. In contrast, the 'caregiving parity' welfare state model promotes equality between women and men by supporting women's informal care work. The centrepiece of this model is the state provision of caregiver allowances. Because of recent developments in Austrian care policy, the latter model seems particularly relevant.

The aim of the caregiving parity model is not to make women's lives the same as men's, but to make the differences between them cost-free (or at least significantly to reduce the costs otherwise borne disproportionately by women) (Fraser, 1994, p 606). Thus women doing informal care work should be able to be breadwinners by virtue of that care work, rather than being forced to adapt to a masculine model of work (see also Lewis, 2002). Measures to support caregiving parity could include: caregiver allowances; compulsory and subsidised social insurance for people working within the household; social rights derived from unpaid work; and an unconditional basic income. Continuity of access to all basic welfare and insurance benefits would need to be guaranteed. Furthermore, care-related benefits and allowances would need to be paid at a relatively high level in order to reduce by a significant amount the disparity between the rewards for market labour and care work.[3]

Although Fraser (1994) is mainly interested in the emancipatory potential of these models, it is nevertheless clear that the caregiving parity model could improve the status of informal care work and the social integration of informal carers considerably. As Lewis argues in Chapter Two, moves towards greater caregiving parity would help to establish a more care-centred system, with policies that value and redistribute care work (Lewis, 2002), and guarantee carers and care recipients new inclusive citizenship rights (Knijn and Kremer, 1997).

The other concept that is relevant for this examination of Austrian care arrangements is 'freedom of choice'. Freedom of choice is fundamental to (neoclassical) economic theory; individuals are assumed to choose the best alternative that maximises utility, within the constraints of their budget. Cash benefits are relevant to this concept because they increase the purchasing power of individuals who are able to participate in the market. In theory, the market will react to increasing demand for services by increasing supply. A perfect market will supply services in the amount and the quality required by demand.[4]

According to the principle of freedom of choice, carers and those receiving care should not be forced to use specific types of care services, but should be able to design the care arrangements of their choice. By paying care allowances, the welfare state delegates to the allowance recipient (part of) its responsibility for ensuring appropriate care arrangements (Daly, 1997). The result may be a tendency towards caregiving parity if recipients use the cash benefit to enable them to provide care themselves from informal sources; or towards the universal breadwinner model if the money is used primarily to buy formal care services (or a mixed arrangement of formal and informal services from different providers). The rationales that underpin different types of payments for care are discussed in more detail in Chapter Ten.

Austrian care arrangements are changing, but does this represent a shift from the male breadwinner to the caregiving parity model of informal care? Do informal carers or those who receive care experience greater freedom of choice? The following sections address these issues in the context of the new childcare and long-term care allowances.

Developments in childcare

Since 2002, all parents receive a childcare allowance of €436 per month until the child is three years old (if the parents share care, otherwise the allowance is payable for two-and-a-half years). Until 2002 only those parents who were entitled to parental leave from paid work were eligible for a flat-rate parental leave benefit of €407 per month, for a maximum of two years.[5] However, since 2002, the leave arrangements and childcare allowance have followed a different logic. Parental leave entitlement is still linked to previous labour market participation and provides protection against dismissal and a right to return to the job for a maximum period of two years. However, the childcare allowance is paid for a maximum of three years, regardless of labour market participation before birth. The earnings limit on the childcare allowance for parents who continue simultaneously to undertake paid employment (about €14,500 per year), and the complex interrelationship with the parental leave regulations, together restrict the universality of the benefit (Stelzer-Orthofer, 2001). Nevertheless, the childcare allowance is a relatively generous benefit, as can be seen from the fact that Austrian expenditure on family and child-related allowances are among the highest in Europe (Abramovici, 2003).

Two more reforms are relevant to this discussion. First, since 1995, carers can have their pensions contributions credited for four years for each child.[6] Second, in February 2004, a new right was introduced allowing parents to work part time. Employed parents with job tenures of at least three years, who work in firms with more than 20 employees, are now entitled to work part time and to have flexible working arrangements until their child reaches seven years of age or starts school, at which point they are entitled to return to their former working-time arrangements (Dörfler, 2004).

The childcare allowance is intended to strengthen family care for children below the age of three years – and it actually works. Studies (Lutz, 2003, 2004) show that the period of parental leave from work is gradually extending so as to become consistent with the maximum duration of the childcare allowance. But does this constitute caregiving parity, or a trend towards caregiving parity?

There are at least two arguments against this interpretation of the Austrian childcare reforms. First, the childcare allowance is far from high enough to reach parity with remuneration from paid employment. Childcare supported by the allowance does not guarantee economic independence; indeed, at €436 per month, the allowance is below the social assistance level. Consequently, poverty is a significant problem for women in Austria (Heitzmann and Schmidt, 2004). Moreover, the incentives to embark upon a career before starting a family and to re-enter the labour market after the period of leave are actually weaker than before the introduction of the childcare allowance. Instead, the incentives to stay at home beyond the period of two years' parental leave are relatively strong and this contributes to a growing female unemployment rate[7] and to the rise of so-called 'marginal' part-time work, where the earnings are too low to qualify for social security protection.[8] The ability to form a household and protection from poverty are only guaranteed as long as there is a breadwinner husband or partner.

Lone mothers who cannot rely on a breadwinner have high rates of labour force participation and very rarely withdraw from the labour force to become full-time carers (Kreimer and Schiffbänker, 2005). The employment situation of lone mothers reflects a parent/worker model (Lewis and Hobson, 1997); this model assumes that mothers are active members of the labour force and that care services and parental leave arrangements are available and affordable (Strell and Duncan, 2001). However, in Austria there are insufficient affordable childcare services and lone parents are disadvantaged in taking parental leave and care leave for sick children, in comparison to partnered mothers.[9]

The second argument against interpreting the childcare allowance as indicating a trend towards caregiving parity is that the incentive to take longer breaks from paid employment will increase the problems experienced by carers in the future, in relation to their social security entitlements and income status. Although there is some recognition of caring activities in the Austrian pension system,[10] carers' pensions will nevertheless be lower because of periods spent as informal carers, in part-time work and in jobs without social security protection. There are still about 400,000 women in Austria without pension rights of their own (BMFV, 1997; Mairhuber, 2000; Wörister, 2001). For women with low earning potential or discontinuous careers, the system only works well if there is a breadwinner. The Austrian care system is therefore suffering from a modernisation deficit, in assuming traditional patterns of breadwinner households while at the same time economic, social and cultural trends are weakening the male breadwinner model.

In examining whether these arrangements increase freedom of choice, it is necessary to look at the level of care services. In Austria, the supply of public childcare facilities is limited, especially for children under three years of age and for school-age children. Only about 9% of children under the age of three are in childcare institutions. Two-thirds of children aged three and four attend public childcare institutions, as do 94% of children aged five and six (school attendance begins at seven years). Full day care is limited for all age groups, although there are major differences between regions. Primary school ends at noon, without lunch. Only 8% of all school-age children attend after-school care (Statistik Austria, 2003a, 2003b).

In the second half of the 1990s, a special programme to increase the supply of childcare facilities was established with government subsidies. This helped to reduce the deficit of supply for children in the three- to six-year-old age group. The second stage of the programme – subsidies to increase the supply of care for children under the age of three and for those of school age – has not been implemented following a change of government in 2000. A 2002 survey showed a shortfall of 90,000 childcare places (BMSGK, 2003b).

The main shortage of formal childcare services is for children under the age of three – that is, the period when families receive the childcare allowance that is supposed to increase their freedom of choice. In fact very few families have the opportunity to choose, for example, between a day nursery, paid formal or informal childminders or family care. At the same time, the cash benefit makes it financially more attractive for second earners in couple families to choose to stay at home (OECD, 2003b) or to prolong their career break.

Carers who receive the childcare allowance can at the same time earn up to €14,500 a year. This relatively high earnings limit could allow mothers to combine part-time work with part-time care, and thus receive a more realistic level of reward for their care work. But this presupposes the availability of affordable childcare facilities while mothers work part time, particularly while their child is under the age of three. In addition, the earnings limit itself restricts freedom of choice, as well as the obligation to share the work of childcare with a partner in order to receive the allowance for the full three years.

In summary, the childcare allowance is not a measure that increases freedom of choice about how to provide care for children under the age of three (Kreimer, 2003). Genuine choice would require more than a relatively low cash benefit.

Developments in long-term care

Since 1993, a long-term care allowance has been paid to people who need at least 50 hours of care per month. The level of the allowance ranges from €148 to €1,562 per month, depending on the number of hours for which help is needed. The care allowance is payable irrespective of the cause of disability or infirmity, and is paid to the person in need of care. (See Chapter Ten for further discussion of the care allowance model.) The allowance is a tax-financed cash payment; it is not means-tested; and is not part of the insurance-based social security system. Four per cent of people receive the allowance, but only 12% of them receive one of the highest three (out of seven) levels. More than 55% receive the allowance at the lowest two levels – a maximum of €273 per month (Österle et al, 2001).

In 2002, an entitlement to care leave was introduced that allows part-time working or leave from work for up to six months to care for a terminally ill person (*Hospizkarenz*). This care leave is unpaid, but is credited for retirement pension purposes.

To what extent does the care allowance contribute to caregiving parity? In the area of long-term care it is much harder to argue that this policy contributes to caregiving parity, because providing long-term care on an informal basis does not guarantee access to social rights. No comprehensive rights to time off work exist that are similar to parental leave for childcare. Employees do have a right to one week's leave per year for care reasons (for relatives living in the same household). This is useful in cases of acute illness, but not long-term care. Consequently, many caregivers have to give up or to reduce their own paid employment in order to provide long-term informal care (Badelt et al, 1997). (Chapter Nine describes the similar pressures facing carers in Britain.) Furthermore, it is not surprising that the new unpaid leave scheme to provide terminal care has a very low take-up.

Only a small group of informal carers, namely those caring for someone receiving the care allowance at one of the higher levels (levels four to seven), receive any direct financial support, in the form of a subsidy for their pension insurance contributions. Even so, informal carers still have to pay their own part of the contribution, which means they must have access to some financial resources of their own. Alternatively, they must depend on receiving social security transfers (a pension or social assistance) or depend on a breadwinning partner.

As described in Chapter Ten, long-term care allowances have the potential to be converted into routed wages (Ungerson, 1997). This means that the payment can be routed, through the care recipient, to the informal carer because the care allowance provides the care recipient with the means to employ caregivers directly in an employer–employee relationship. In reality, however, only in a very limited number of cases are regular employment contracts established that would guarantee an adequate income (the direct payment or personal budget model described in Chapter Ten). Instead, most carers providing long-term care receive payment at a level that is merely symbolic (Österle et al, 2001). These payments increase inequalities more than they improve the situation of carers, because they tend to be used to fund cheap informal care or to purchase care services in the grey labour market, especially from migrants from neighbouring countries such as the Czech Republic, Slovakia and Hungary. These unofficial migrant workers can be paid at much lower levels and their availability currently maintains the supply of long-term care, particularly in Eastern Austria.[11] As far as the situation of informal carers is concerned, the long-term care allowance fits into the traditional breadwinner model; there is no trend towards a caregiving parity model.

However, the long-term care allowance is intended to contribute to developing the supply of care services, albeit in a flexible, unregulated way (Ungerson, 2003). In debates about the long-term care allowance, the idea that consumers – recipients of the allowance – would shape the market through their choices was always important, in contrast to the childcare allowance where no such expectations officially existed. How, therefore, did the market for care services respond to the introduction of the long-term care allowance? Before 1993, there was a relatively high level of some formal services such as home nursing in some provinces of Austria, but there was no general policy or strategy for developing a comprehensive system of social services. The result was a highly fragmented system with different providers, different types of provision, different regulations regarding access and finance and a substantial shortfall in social service provision. At the same time as the long-term care allowance was introduced, an agreement was reached between the central government and the provinces that gave the provinces responsibility for the development of domiciliary and residential care provision. However, the long-term care allowance has so far not fundamentally changed existing arrangements. The supply of institutional care in Austria remains low compared to other western European welfare states. In 1996/97, 3.8% of the population aged 60 and older (14% of long-term care allowance recipients) were in institutional care (BMAGS, 1998; BMUJF, 1999) and only 3% of older people receive home care services (Bettio and Prechal, 1998, p 35). In international comparisons of formal care services for older people, Austria ranks in the lower half (Bettio and Plantenga, 2004).

Half of all long-term care allowance recipients use formal social services (home help, home nursing, escorting services, meals-on-wheels) at least once a week (Riedel, 1999; Österle et al, 2001). However, these services only provide part of the full range of help that an older person needs, so additional help from a nearby informal carer is essential. Without such additional informal care, formal service provision would be inadequate to support a very frail older person to continue to live at home, and admission to institutional care would be the only option. The informal sector, therefore, still plays a key role in long-term care and the long-term care allowance has not stimulated the market supply of formal care services for older and disabled people.

One reason for this is the costs of formal care services (Hammer and Österle, 2001a). The introduction of the long-term care allowance led to an increase of more than 60% in total public expenditure on long-term care. This would seem to indicate a clear upgrading in the importance of care and an increased responsibility by the welfare state for long-term care. However, at the same time nearly all the formal services provided by welfare agencies or care providers and subsidised by the provinces increased in price. This means it is rational for older people to choose more rather than less informal family care and to use formal care services as additional supplements to, rather than substitutes for, informal care.

There are other ways in which costs affect choices. As a routed wage (Ungerson, 1997), the long-term care allowance is far too low. Only people needing care who have substantial financial resources can actually afford to choose between purchasing formal care or paying an informal carer a proper wage. However, most long-term care allowance recipients belong to the lower end of the income distribution, so their choices are particularly restricted (Hammer and Österle, 2001a). Moreover, many specialised formal care services, such as 24-hour and night-time care, do not exist and would in any case be very expensive to provide, given Austria's labour regulations. Instead, such provision is supplied informally by (mostly) foreign care workers.

As argued in Chapter Ten, long-term care allowances in principle maximise choice for care recipients. However, in Austria these choices are restricted in two ways: a wide range of affordable formal care services does not exist; and the incentives to use informal family care are greater than the incentives to purchase formal care services (or to articulate demand for them if the supply is too low).

There have been proposals to link part of the long-term care allowance to formal social services, for instance through making part of the allowance available in the form of vouchers. Such a link between cash benefits and the use of formal services could increase both the supply of care services and the opportunities for formal employment in caregiving jobs (Blumberger and Dornmayr, 1998; see OECD, 2003b, for similar arguments in the area of childcare). However, these proposals have not been implemented.

Hammer and Österle (2001b) use the concept of *defamilialisation* to analyse long-term care policies in Austria. This concept 'captures the potential of social policies to offer freedom of choice either to provide unpaid work within the family under conditions which secure an acceptable standard of living, or not to provide unpaid care work and to secure an acceptable standard of living via labour force participation' (Hammer and Österle, 2001b, p 3). The level of defamilialisation in Austria is very low because of the limited access to social rights and the income situation of those who provide long-term care. From a gender perspective, inequalities and the traditional division of labour are perpetuated. 'As social service provision is not adequate and female access to paid work often hindered, freedom of choice not to provide informal care still has a long way to go' (Hammer and Österle, 2001b, p 12). Again, a cash benefit alone does not guarantee freedom of choice.

Conclusions

Austrian social policy still supports the male breadwinner welfare state in many respects. One consequence of this is that a large proportion of care in Austria is provided on an informal basis. Since the early 1990s two important reforms have taken place; both have introduced new cash benefits for care. Although the long-term care allowance and the childcare allowance differ in many respects, these reforms may be interpreted as an attempt to change the Austrian care system from the male breadwinner model towards a new care model that values and rewards care much more explicitly.

However, this chapter has argued that these developments do not reflect a move towards caregiving parity; nor do either the providers or the receivers of care experience greater freedom of choice as a result. Although the two cash benefits and the related reforms may have improved the income position and social security of some groups of informal carers, there is no general trend towards caregiving parity. In the area of childcare, this conclusion has to be viewed in combination with the issue of freedom of choice. If there are virtually no alternatives to family care in the form of formal childcare services, then parents have no choice but to 'choose' to stay at home for three years, or to make complex arrangements involving 'marginal' part-time work, childminders and help from neighbours or grandparents. In the area of long-term care, the care allowance does not improve the situation of informal carers. Because of the rising costs of formal social care services and the low level of the long-term care allowance paid to the majority of its recipients, it is 'rational' for the latter to seek informal care arrangements that involve, at the most symbolic level, payments. Because of the decreasing provision of informal care by family members and the increasing demand for care by older people, the grey labour market is expanding, with a growing supply of care services by foreign workers from neighbouring countries. These informal carers have absolutely no social security protection in Austria.

What are the implications for further welfare reforms in the area of care? Should the cash benefits be abolished? Arguably, the problem is not the cash benefits themselves, but their role within the respective overall care systems. Although there are some proposals to improve the impact of the care allowances, much more work is needed to reshape the overall arrangements for care; as Chapter Ten argues, payments for care should not be considered in isolation from other policy measures.

From a feminist perspective, the issue of gender equality is of special interest. Caregiving parity is a welfare state model centred on informal care that aims, at best, to give care work the same value as paid employment. The potential disadvantage of such a model is not only the development of a marginalised labour market of carers, but also increasing gender segregation in the labour market and in society. Fraser (1994) argues for an alternative model that avoids these disadvantages – the universal caregiver model. Further research is needed to identify how to achieve such a model that guarantees a high level of gender equality – that is, that integrates care work into the lifecourses of women *and* men without discriminatory effects.

Notes

[1] Employees become informal carers if they quit their job to take on long-term care responsibilities, or interrupt their career for more than the maximum period allowed for parental leave (two years). If they return to paid work within this period, they remain protected by the social security system and have social rights of their own.

[2] If carers are related to a breadwinner, they have access to healthcare insurance and pensions insurance (including widow's pension) but, because they are considered to be dependants rather than workers, they cannot claim unemployment or industrial injuries insurance.

[3] Since care work rarely occupies the entire working life, continuing access to the labour market, particularly for part-time work, is also required. Flexible careers, like alternating periods of full-time employment, spells of full-time care work and periods that combine part-time employment with part-time care, should have equal outcomes to regular labour market careers in terms of income and social security entitlements. The consequences for carers, in the absence of such arrangements, are described in Chapter Nine.

[4] However, the market for care services is not a perfect market (Folbre, 1995; Folbre and Nelson, 2000; Jochimsen, 2003). For instance, the concept of children as public goods is analysed by Folbre (2004a). Moreover, the market does not act neutrally in respect of class and gender relations related to care (Folbre, 1994). The analysis of care work and care relations is an increasing focus of feminist economics (see also Chapter Three).

[5] Fathers can take parental leave as well as mothers (the latter in addition to maternity leave). Since 1996, six months of the leave is paid only if fathers take them; if parents do not share the leave, the remaining six months is unpaid (Städtner, 2002).

[6] To receive a pension, 15 insured years within the 30 years immediately before the desired age of retirement are required (the retirement age is currently 60 for women and 65 for men). Periods of childcare count towards these 15 years (BMSGK, 2003a).

[7] Based on the experience of the extension of the leave period from one to two years in 1990, increasing difficulties in returning to a full-time job or

long-term employment could be expected. Only one woman out of three returns to work immediately after parental leave; of these women, one in four loses her job within a year of returning (Neyer et al, 1999).

[8] Marginal part-time work is work that is not covered by social security legislation because of the low level of earnings (under €323 per month in 2005). Marginal part-time workers are covered by accident insurance, but not unemployment, healthcare or pension insurance. This form of non-standard work is increasing steadily and about three-quarters of marginal employees are women (Tálos, 1999; Mühlberger, 2000).

[9] Lone mothers have no partner with whom to share care work, so they can only receive the childcare allowance for a maximum of two-and-a-half years; they also have no partner who can take leave to care for sick children (one to two weeks per year).

[10] Non-employed parents can receive up to four years of pension credits per child (see note 6 above). From 2005, reforms to the Austrian pension scheme will give these years of childcare a higher value, making it easier for mothers to qualify for a pension in their own right, despite their discontinuous employment.

[11] This practice contravenes both the Austrian social security system and Austria's restrictive immigration policy (Österle et al, 2001).

TWELVE

When informal care becomes a paid job: the case of Personal Assistance Budgets in Flanders

Jef Breda, David Schoenmaekers, Caroline Van Landeghem, Dries Claessens and Joanna Geerts

Introduction

In Flanders (the northern region of Belgium), Personal Assistance Budgets (PABs) have been introduced for disabled people. PABs are cash payments that allow the recipients to employ their own personal assistants. Interestingly, no distinction is made between informal carers and other (unrelated) personal assistants. Under the scheme, relatives have no independent entitlement to financial compensation in respect of the care they provide, but must enter into a legal labour relationship with the budget holder. The PAB scheme is very similar to the Dutch personal budgets described in Chapter Ten.

This chapter examines how the PAB arrangement works in practice and the consequences for paid informal carers; where possible comparisons are made with the non-relative personal assistants who are also employed by budget holders. It begins by outlining a typology of arrangements for long-term care that sets PABs within a wider context. After brief descriptions of the PAB regulations and the design of a recent study into the operation of PABs, the chapter describes the profiles of budget holders and the people they employ. It then considers the principal reasons and motives for both parties to enter this paid caregiving arrangement. The chapter then describes the overall patterns of care received by the budget holders and the role of their paid caregivers within these wider patterns of support. Finally, the chapter discusses the outcomes of the PAB from the perspectives of budget holders and their paid carers respectively.

The Personal Assistance Budget: a hybrid scheme

According to the Independent Living Movement, systems of support for disabled people have traditionally been too driven by providers' perspectives. In the 1960s, groups of disabled students in the US began to organise themselves and arrange their own support services. Centres for Independent Living soon developed and spread the idea that support arrangements should start from the aspirations and preferences of the disabled person, rather than from the often patronising and disempowering assumptions of care providers and professionals (Waterplas and Samoy, 2001). (The social model of disability and its success in challenging traditional professional practice is described in more detail in Chapters Sixteen and Seventeen.) The independent living perspective argues that disabled people themselves should be able to recruit, select and supervise those who provide their support. As well as the independent living model, two other models of long-term care for disabled people can be delineated: the informal care model and the provider model.[1] The latter can be considered the opposite of the independent living model (Dejong et al, 1992) (Table 12.1).

Table 12.1: Models of long-term care for disabled people

Independent living model	Informal support model	Provider model
Consumer-directed	Family-directed	Provider-directed
Consumer role	Dependant role	Patient role
Accountability of consumer	Little accountability	Accountability of provider
No physician plan of treatment	No physician plan of treatment	Physician plan of treatment
No nurse supervision	No nurse supervision	Nurse supervision
Assistant recruited by consumer	Family/friends provide care	Professional aide provides care
Assistant trained by consumer	No formal training	Aide trained by provider
Social service benefit	No benefit	Healthcare benefit
Payment to consumer to assistant	No payment	Payment to provider

Source: Based on Dejong et al (1992)

Following a number of experiments, the PAB system of cash payments to adults with additional support needs was introduced in Flanders in 2001. The PAB is awarded to disabled people who are able to live at home with a reasonable amount of assistance. Anyone under the age of 65 can apply, irrespective of the nature of their disability. The size of a PAB ranges from €7,436.81 to €34,705.09 a year. The level of the annual PAB is mainly based on the level of support needed by the disabled person with activities of daily living; additional factors such as the family situation are also taken into account by the independent committee that decides the level of the budget. There is a ceiling on the level of a PAB equivalent to the costs of institutional care. The PAB can be used for just about any care activity as long as this does not give rise to double financing by the authorities. Thus, medical assistance is excluded from the scope of the PAB, and the use of the PAB to provide support in education or employment settings is also restricted.

With the PAB, the budget holder must organise and pay for their own assistance. As with the Dutch personal budget scheme (see Chapter Ten), the budget holder is required to enter into a contract with their personal assistant(s), thus becoming their employer. The budget holder can specify the detailed requirements of the job according to their own needs and preferences, as long as these requirements are compatible with labour law. The personal assistants, for their part, can offer their services under a range of different conditions – as self-employed people, temporary workers or agency workers. Thus, budget holders can avoid some of the administrative tasks associated with being an employer, but this means they also lose their role as legal employer; the formal relationship with a personal assistant becomes more like a service contract.

Since 2001, relatives have also been able to fulfil the role of a personal assistant under the same conditions as apply to unrelated assistants; in other words, a labour contract has to be drawn up between the disabled employer and the relative employee. Almost half (48%) of budget holders use at least part of their PAB to pay informal carers. As a result of this employee status, a considerable part of the PAB flows back to the government in the form of taxes and social security contributions. In households where the applicant for a PAB is a disabled child or young person, one parent is usually appointed as the budget holder while the other becomes the personal assistant, although such arrangements are not possible in lone-parent households.

As informal carers can be remunerated through a PAB, this approach appears to be not entirely compatible with the independent living model in its purest form. It is rather a hybrid model, containing elements of both the independent living model and the informal care model (Table 12.1). On the one hand, it includes features of the independent living model (a cash payment instead of direct social care services, which the 'consumer' uses to pay an assistant); on the other hand, it includes characteristics of the informal care paradigm, where care is provided by relatives and friends without formal training. Moreover, PAB recipients can also receive formal services at home as well and thus derive their care from each of the three models. However, PAB users appear to want to use their PAB to buy these services, thus extending the principles of independent living to the provider model.

Where the PAB is used to pay family carers, existing non-paid care is transformed into paid labour; this therefore represents a form of commodified care. Caregiving labour is commissioned indirectly through a payment that is made to the person needing support, who can then decide independently how that support should be organised (Daly, 2002, p 255). Ungerson (1999, pp 583-5) uses the terms 'routed wages' and 'paid volunteering' to describe new hybrid forms of relationship between 'work' and 'care'. Commodification, the process whereby private human relationships acquire an exchange value in the marketplace, usually implies that a product or service is withdrawn from the familial sphere and enters the public domain. However, in the case of paid informal carers there is a simultaneous process of familialisation, as particular familial relationships are given financial support by the government. Care thus becomes work, but only to a certain extent; the allowance is rarely high enough to provide a proper remuneration for every hour of work performed. The traditional dichotomy between paid and unpaid labour thus becomes less clear; previously unpaid care is now partly remunerated and sometimes acquires other characteristics of a paid job, but the carer is not paid in full for the work they actually perform.

The research reported in this chapter aimed to explore the relationship of the PAB to the independent living model and the informal support model of long-term care respectively. Does the PAB primarily benefit the budget holder or the paid relatives of the recipient? Does the budget holder acquire the role and the associated responsibilities of a consumer? To what extent does a PAB contract give rise to a relationship of authority, as between employer and employee, between the budget holder and a family member?

These questions were examined in a multi-method study. The study involved a large-scale survey of 229 budget holders and, for each, one of their personal assistants (PAB Survey). The sample was representative of the 431 people who had been working with a PAB for at least three months. In addition, a qualitative study was carried out consisting of in-depth interviews with 15 budget holders and, for each of them, three people in their immediate environment – the latter included close relatives and friends, professionals such as care managers and employed personal assistants.

In analysing the data from this study, first the personal characteristics of the budget holders and personal assistants are described. The analysis then examines the motives of both budget holders and personal assistants for acquiring and providing paid informal care respectively; and discusses the PAB within the wider context of the full range of the support received by the budget holders.

Profiles of the budget holders and their personal assistants

In the quantitative study, 48% of the budget holders ($n=229$) paid informal carers and 52% relied exclusively on unrelated personal assistants. A quarter of the budget holders in the study were children or young people, but there was no significant difference between these minors and the adults in their preferences for paid informal carers or unrelated assistants.

A third (36%) of the adults employing unrelated personal assistants lived alone, compared to just 14% of those using paid informal care ($X^2=16.693$; df=5; $p<.05$). A small majority of PAB users who relied on paid informal care (58%) lived with their parents. Most of the budget holders in the sample who were children and young people attended school, but only half of the adults in the sample had a regular activity outside the home.

Paid informal carers were usually relatives of the PAB user; in almost half of the cases with paid informal carers, the carer was a parent (see Table 12.2). Two out of three paid informal carers (68%) shared a household with the PAB user. In these cases, the paid informal carer was usually the mother, father or partner of the disabled person.

The majority of personal assistants were women. However, among the paid informal carers the proportion of men was slightly higher; 15% of unrelated personal assistants were men, compared to 24% of paid informal carers. The paid informal carers were also slightly more likely to be older; 15% were aged 60 or over ($X^2=38.077$, df=4, $p<.05$). Most of the co-resident paid informal carers were aged 40 to 49. In contrast, the majority of unrelated personal assistants were under 40

Table 12.2: Relationship between paid informal carer and disabled person (perspective of the personal assistant) (%)

Relationship to disabled person	Co-resident informal carer[a]		Age of disabled person[b]		
	Yes	No	Minor	Adult	Total
Partner	29	3	0	26	21
Child	2	14	0	7	5
Father/mother	59	24	50	47	48
Brother/sister	6	24	6	13	12
Grandparent	1	17	33	0	7
Other	3	18	11	7	7
Total	100(n=63)	100(n=29)	100(n=18)	100(n=74)	100(n=92)

Notes:
[a] X^2=34.364; df=5; p<.001
[b] X^2=31.654; df=5; p<.001
Source: PAB Survey

years old; the high proportion of parents working as paid informal carers explains this difference.

Only 4% of paid informal carers had never worked before becoming a paid carer; the rest had, on average, 20 years' experience of paid employment. Almost half had a degree from higher education. Paid informal carers were by no means less well qualified than unrelated personal assistants. Many of the paid informal carers had had a stable job prior to their appointment as a personal assistant; indeed, 71% had been working under an open-ended labour contract. Approximately two-thirds of all the personal assistants continued in their previous employment after beginning to provide paid personal assistance. However, an important difference was that the paid informal carers were more likely to have reduced their hours in their regular job (21%) while the unrelated personal assistants were more likely to have quit their previous job altogether (25%). Thus, there was no evidence of paid informal caregivers being individuals with poor employment opportunities who had been forced into taking quasi-domestic employment. Indeed, this probably explains why many had chosen to retain their previous jobs after becoming a paid informal carer, as there is inevitably a degree of uncertainty about whether they would be able to find similar employment after the period as a paid carer has ended.

Why do people opt for paid informal care?

The perspectives of the budget holders

Half of all budget holders cited the ability to remunerate informal caregivers as a reason for claiming a PAB, which they typically explained as follows:

> 'Does it provide a kind of recognition? Yes! People with a seriously disabled child ... are always hampered in their careers. They can't pursue them. Most are hampered by their situation.... Generally speaking, compensation for such people is in place.' (Peter, budget holder and husband of Mary, who was the paid informal carer for their disabled child – all names have been changed for confidentiality)

Only 6% of respondents who had indicated on their application for a PAB that they intended to appoint an informal carer in the end employed only unrelated personal assistants. However, the opposite was more common; a fifth (19%) of all PAB users in the sample said at the time of their application that they did not intend to appoint a paid informal carer, but eventually did so. A possible explanation for this is that paid informal care may have been a temporary solution while the budget holder was finding a suitable unrelated personal assistant, as the budget holder must hire a personal assistant within three months of being approved for the PAB. However, recruiting unrelated personal assistants is often difficult, not least because providing personal care is not a nine-to-five job. Other respondents asserted that their original intentions to recruit an unrelated personal assistant were (for the time being) unattainable, so they opted instead to keep their PAB and use it to pay an informal carer.

However, there were also intrinsic motives for choosing paid informal care, such as personal familiarity with the care provider. Given the nature of the relationship between a budget holder and a personal assistant, it is easy to see why the issue of familiarity is so important. Disabled employers are vulnerable to physical abuse and theft. In this kind of intense and intimate relationship, within the invisibility of the private domain, trust is absolutely essential (Ungerson, 1999). The importance of familiarity becomes very clear in relation to people with mental impairments, particularly those with autism or similar conditions, many of whom would find it difficult or even impossible to adapt to a different person or situation:

'With a stranger, it would take years.... And we also had to take immediate action when mum was admitted to hospital. John didn't have time to adapt to a stranger. It was already a difficult and emotional time for him.... We could have said: "Let's take him to the institution", because the staff were more familiar to him than a complete stranger.' (Ann, sister and John's paid informal carer)

'With his condition, continuity is very important ... and structure. In fact, it was always going to be Ann who would provide the care.... Considering who John is as a person, his total inability to adapt to strangers or a new environment, this is the best thing that could have happened to him.' (Liz, John's sister)

The perspectives of the personal assistants

The personal assistants were asked to name the two most important reasons for accepting the job (Table 12.3). Job-related motivations regarding the practical and content-related aspects of the job (items 1–6) as well as more personal and emotive-affective reasons (items 7–9) come to the fore.

However, there appeared to be a significant difference between the motives cited by paid informal carers and those named by unrelated personal assistants. Unrelated personal assistants tended to cite job-related reasons, whereas emotional and affective reasons were more common among informal carers. Differences between co-resident and non-resident paid informal carers were less marked; the non-resident informal carers tended to adopt a position in between co-resident informal carers and non-resident unrelated personal assistants.

The distinction between more job-related motives on the one hand and personal and affective motives (feelings, 'care as a duty' and so on) on the other reflects a fundamentally different perception of the job of a paid carer. It appeared that co-resident paid informal carers in particular did not consider their work to be a 'job' in the formal or businesslike sense of the word. Their high levels of emotional motivation made paid informal carers very dependent upon the care recipient, particularly as far as the duration and termination of the work was concerned, as this basically depended on the long-term prognosis of the PAB holder.

Table 12.3: Principal reasons cited by personal assistants for accepting the job, by use and type of paid informal care (%)

| Motivation for job as a personal assistant | Nature of the assistance[a] | | | | |
| | Paid informal care[b] | | | External | |
	Co-resident	Non-resident	Total	Personal assistant	Total
(1) Paid job	0	2	1	16	10
(2) Part-time paid job	1	8	3	7	6
(3) Sideline	3	2	2	3	2
(4) Wanted to change jobs	1	2	1	10	6
(5) Wanted an exciting job	1	2	1	13	8
(6) Preference for one-on-one relationship[c]				14	8
(7) To continue care	23	11	19	8	12
(8) Care for disabled person is duty	9	13	11	1	5
(9) Most appropriate for this disabled person	24	31	26	6	14
(10) Lack of personal assistants[d]	7	6	7		3
(11) Improvement of own financial situation	16	8	14	9	11
(12) Other	15	15	15	13	14
Total	100(n=63)	100(n=29)	100(n=92)	100(n=130)	100(n=222)

Notes:

[a] df=1 (in any case). The significance tests are significant for the following motives: (1) X^2=27.703, $p<.001$; (4) X^2=13.822, $p<.001$; (5) X^2=19.081, $p<.001$; (7) X^2=13.533, $p<.001$; (8) X^2=18.734, $p<.001$; (9) X^2=36.526, $p<.001$; (11) X^2=5.940, $p<.05$.
[b] df=1 (in any case). The significance tests are significant for the following motives: (1) X^2=4.441, $p<.05$; (2) X^2=7.982, $p<.01$; (7) X^2=5.744, $p<.05$; (11) X^2=4.285, $p<.05$.
[c] Item 6 was not included as a possible answer for the paid informal caregivers.
[d] Item 10 was not presented to the external personal assistants.

Source: PAB Survey

The overall support arrangements of the budget holders

The average PAB amounts to about €25,000 a year and almost 60% of PAB holders received at least this amount. How exactly was the budget spent?

Most budget holders who used the PAB to pay for informal care relied on only one relative, although some relied on two; and they usually also employed one or two unrelated personal assistants. Only a third of budget holders spent their entire PAB on paid informal care. While, on average, budget holders with a paid informal carer were able to call on 43 hours of paid support, those who used only unrelated personal assistants purchased an average of 30 hours of care per week ($t=-3.963$, df=217, $p<.05$). As previously mentioned, paid informal carers generally did not perceive their care work as a job and this was reflected in their working hours – they tended to carry out many more hours of work than they were actually paid for. Not surprisingly this was particularly the case for co-resident paid informal carers. The support they gave did not end with their contractual obligations; nine out of 10 co-resident paid informal carers claimed to provide more hours of support than were required under the terms of their contract, compared to only half (48%) of non-resident informal carers ($X^2=18.003$, df=1, $p<.05$). Co-resident informal carers continued to provide the same level of care as previously, while the PAB encouraged or enabled non-resident informal carers to increase the amount of care they provided.

Because they worked more hours (and more hours than they were paid for), the average paid informal care worker also performed a wider range of tasks than the average unrelated personal assistant. Paid informal carers were more likely than unrelated personal assistants to help with intimate tasks such as personal hygiene and nursing. Paid informal caregivers were also likely to carry out more domestic chores and meet the immediate needs of the PAB holder (for example with movement around the house). Unrelated personal assistants tended to do more extensive domestic chores, gardening or odd jobs.

Each budget holder employed on average two personal assistants and also received help from a number of other formal and informal sources. Seven out of 10 received additional (unpaid) informal assistance and eight out of 10 received further formal services. The overall pattern of support received by budget holders could be described as a 'mosaic of care'. Those who relied primarily on paid informal care were more likely also to receive other informal assistance; conversely those employing unrelated personal assistants were more likely to receive additional formal services. Budget holders who received no paid informal care, especially single people, were more likely to use formal domiciliary services and to rely more on personal alarm systems.

The outcomes of the PAB

The perspectives of the budget holders

On the whole, budget holders were positive about the PAB scheme. They were satisfied with the support they received and acknowledged that they now had more choice than they used to. The only difference between those relying on paid informal carers and other PAB holders was that the former were more likely to report a positive impact on their financial situation, since the wage being paid to a co-resident informal carer was making a contribution to the overall household budget. The most important problem was the administrative burden that the scheme presented to all budget holders.

A common desire among budget holders was to be able to combine the PAB with receipt of other support services; currently there are many restrictions in this respect. Almost half of the respondents felt that combining the PAB with other support services would be desirable; particularly those support services that offer greater autonomy and independence than traditional residential care. In effect, budget holders wanted to combine some elements of the provider model with the PAB. Combining the PAB with short-term residential care, whether in specialised respite care institutions or not, would also be of benefit to some carers. The wish to combine the PAB with some formal services was the same among PAB users who relied on paid informal care as among those who employed unrelated personal assistants. However, further analyses revealed that among those using paid informal carers, the desire to combine the PAB with other formal services was greater if the level of the PAB was considered inadequate; if the budget holder belonged to the same household as the paid informal carer; and if the relationship between the two was intergenerational. (The latter two variables were independent of each other.) On the other hand, factors relating to the level of burden experienced by the carer – both the objective amount of work and the subjective feelings about this situation whether perceived from the budget holder's perspective or from that of the care provider – did not appear to affect levels of demand for additional formal services.

The perspectives of the paid informal carers

Three-quarters of the relatives providing paid care did so under an open-ended labour contract. For paid informal carers, the PAB can have positive financial benefits as it provides an (additional) income and enables carers to accumulate social security rights.

Paid informal carers could be called upon more easily than unrelated personal assistants to provide support at unsocial hours (during weekends or at night). This is a reflection of the flexible and continuous care they provided – an important reason for making use of paid informal care. However, they were also less often remunerated for this unsocial work; they had no training opportunities; no holiday entitlement; and often no possibility of replacement in case of illness. Their labour conditions were therefore not consistent with the requirements of formal employment and the labour contract would appear to be merely for form's sake. On average, an unrelated personal assistant earned €10.79 an hour; if the actual hours worked are taken into account, a paid informal caregiver received an average of €7.59 an hour.

Paid informal carers were less likely than unrelated personal assistants to view their current employment as a career-related opportunity ($X^2=21.261$, df=3, $p<.05$). They also felt they had less freedom to quit the job should they become dissatisfied with it ($X^2=41.693$, df=3, $p<.05$). Moreover, this feeling was even more common among co-resident informal carers than non-resident carers ($X^2=12.496$, df=3, $p<.05$). It was also apparent that where informal caregivers had become personal assistants, role tensions could arise. What, for example, should the attitude of a mother/personal assistant be towards her daughter/employer? Such conflicts could be avoided if there were clear agreements about the respective roles and responsibilities of both employer and employee:

> 'I made it clear from the beginning that I would not be ordered about and that I was not going to play the role of an "assistant". She also has to adapt to our [domestic] situation.' (Mark, father and personal assistant of Eve)

Figure 12.1 shows that the 'burden'[2] on co-resident paid informal carers was clearly greater than that on non-resident carers ($t=3.780$, df=90, $p<.05$). This burden on paid informal carers was both psychological and physical in nature. Moreover, many also felt under pressure of time, so their social lives were affected.

Figure 12.1: Burden of care for paid informal carers (%)

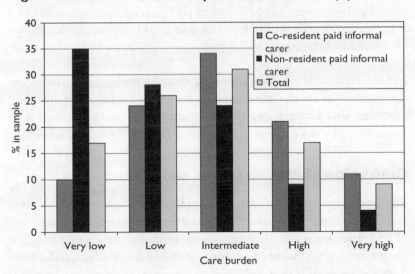

If the total hours of care work plus the hours spent working in a standard job are taken into account, it was clear that paid informal carers were under a greater 'burden' as the total number of 'active hours' increased (Pearson's r=.227, p<.05). However, the correlation was even greater when the number of hours that the informal carer spent in the company of the disabled person was included (Pearson's r=.440; p<.001). This suggests that it is important for informal carers to have a regular break from the work of caregiving, even if this involves a second paid job. This other work should ideally be easily compatible with their care responsibilities; those who found it easy to combine care work and another paid job showed a strikingly lower burden than those who found the combination problematic (Pearson's r=.373, p<.05). The problems of combining paid employment with informal caregiving are also described in Chapter Nine.

The qualitative interviews suggested a contrast between those paid informal carers who were the disabled person's only assistant, were frequently under pressure and who had often become a paid personal assistant for financial reasons; and part-time paid informal carers for whom paid care work was a sideline. A good example was Patrick, who transferred the money he received for his care work into his children's savings account:

'My job isn't really a job. Charles and Jenny aren't colleagues. I'm here in part to help and in part to relax, in my leisure time.' (Patrick, brother-in-law and paid informal carer of Charles)

Indeed, other authors have observed that the pressures of caregiving are greater – as are the consequences for carers' health and well-being – among sole or principal informal carers, than among those who belong to a broader caregiving network (Lloyd, 2000, pp 147-8).

Conclusions: between labour and care

For different reasons, half of the budget holders relied on paid informal carers, who usually constituted one of their two paid carers. Ungerson (1999) raises some important questions about this aspect of paying for care: what is the quality of labour performed by relatives; and where does the locus of power lie?

First, there is the issue of remuneration for care work. Under the PAB, previously unpaid work is now paid for, but only to a partial extent. The actual hours of work contributed by informal caregivers are so extensive that it would not be financially feasible to pay properly for them all. Moreover, the other conditions of labour for paid informal carers (lack of training opportunities, holiday entitlements or formal work job description) suggest that they are located on a continuum between 'work' and 'care'.

Second, and in contrast to the original intention under the independent living model of empowering the service user, it is debatable whether power and control over the care process has shifted towards the budget holder when the PAB is used to employ an informal carer. Certainly the study reported here found that few changes were apparent, compared to the situation prior to receiving the PAB. The relationship between the paid informal caregiver and the budget holder is, first and foremost, a familial one. Moreover, within the context of such relationships it appears that problems relating to the extent of the informal carer's commitment are common. Thus it is not clear how much the budget holder can demand or what the paid informal caregiver can refuse.

Given the level of personal involvement, it is hard to terminate a commodified care relationship; as Ungerson (1999) puts it, paid informal caregivers lack the power to exit. She considers this to be the main drawback of a care budget system. In addition, there is an inherent risk of undermining the caregiver's future employment prospects because paid care work within the family is unlikely to be given equal recognition and value alongside fully-fledged commodified labour in the conventional labour market (Ungerson, 2004). Feminist researchers have argued that policies based on an 'ethics of care' approach would help to end this unequal value attached to caregiving, as Wærness argues in Chapter Three.

Although paid informal caregivers in theory become formal employees, in practice familial relationships continue to dominate in accordance with the logic of care needs. It is true that a distant relative who becomes a paid assistant may show greater commitment to the budget holder because they now have a number of hours' paid work to perform. However, a household member who becomes a paid informal carer through the personal budget scheme is likely to be motivated to provide care at any cost, including that of their own social life or health:

> In those schemes which allow relatives to be paid, the
> relationship, and the work of care, may most resemble that
> of informal care – a relationship based on kinship and affect
> rather than contract, and one that provides holistic care.
> (Ungerson, 2004, p 192)

Returning to the model developed by Dejong et al (1992) (Table 12.1), we would argue that the market terminology of the independent living model, in which the disabled person is characterised as a 'consumer', is not applicable to the budget holder who employs informal caregivers. Rather, the PAB seems to have the effect of increasing the level of family assistance characterised by the informal support model. The PAB is thus often used as a means of obtaining additional assistance; but this rarely replaces the work of relatives. While the income from the PAB that is received by a co-resident informal caregiver can boost the overall household income, the budget is rarely used to mobilise additional formal support services that might reduce the subjective burdens experienced by family caregivers.

In practice, since the introduction of the PAB, budget holders draw on all three models represented in Table 12.1 in organising their support needs. They are enthusiastic about the demand-based independent living model; at the same time they appreciate the continuity provided by the informal support model; and they also continue to make use of formal care services that reflect the provider model. In the provider model, the relative security of care for clients is combined with good working conditions for frontline care workers. Paid informal caregivers, for their part, lack any such protection. Crucial elements, such as rights to regular breaks from caregiving work, need to be introduced for this group of carers. A similar view is expressed by Lloyd (2000), who argues that the term 'respite' should be replaced by the term 'break' to indicate the need for frequent, short interruptions in caregiving responsibilities as part of the normal work experience of the caregiver (see also Chapter Ten, where the potential lack of access to services is highlighted as a particular drawback of the care allowance approach). If such entitlements were introduced, they could enable paid informal caregiving to be empowering for both the disabled person and the informal carer.

Notes

[1] Dejong et al (1992) call this the 'medical model'. However, as they themselves point out, its characteristic feature is not so much the dominance of the healthcare sector, but of professionals in general. In the context of this chapter, the term 'provider model' is more appropriate.

[2] The 'burden' on informal carers was measured by means of a scale that is also used by the Dutch Social and Cultural Planning Bureau (Timmermans, 2003). The scale contains 11 items and has a high internal consistency (maximum score = 44 and $\alpha=0.89$).

THIRTEEN

Better off in work? Work, security and welfare for lone mothers

Jane Millar

Introduction

Increasing employment and reducing child poverty are two central goals of current government policy in the UK, and lone mothers – with their relatively low employment rates and relatively high poverty rates – are one of the key target groups for both. Since 1997 there has been a substantial investment in government support for lone parents in work, including a dedicated labour market programme (the New Deal for Lone Parents), increased financial support for those in work (the Child and Working Tax Credits), and an expansion of childcare services (the National Childcare Strategy).

These policies have had some success in the context of a favourable economic and social context. The employment rates of lone mothers, although still below those of partnered mothers, have risen quite rapidly, from about 44% in 1997 to about 54% in 2004. Their poverty rates – defined as net incomes after housing costs of less than 60% of the median – although still higher than those of couples, have fallen from about 57% in 1997/98 to about 46% in 2003/04 (DWP, 2005a). Material deprivation and reported hardship have also fallen (Vegeris and Perry, 2001; Barnes et al, 2005).

Thus, the context in which lone mothers make their decisions about employment – about when and how much to work – has changed quite rapidly in recent years. There is much more support for employment, but there is also much more pressure to work. The Labour government has repeatedly stressed the value and importance of employment – 'work is the best form of welfare' (Blair, 1997) – and has set a target that 70% of lone parents should be employed by 2010. Work-focused interviews, in which lone mothers discuss employment options and agree an 'action plan', are compulsory for all lone mothers receiving social assistance benefits. There are various further measures being piloted, including additional financial incentives for job search and for taking up employment. The Department for Work and Pensions' Five Year Plan (DWP, 2005c) signals the intention to require some work-related activities for lone mothers with children of secondary school age, with the introduction of an 'automatic payment of a £20 activity premium ... conditional on undertaking the agreed activity' (DWP, 2005c, para 70). Work requirements for lone mothers in the UK are still much less than in many other countries (Millar and Ridge, 2001; Millar, 2005), but there has been a distinct shift towards an employment-based model in both policy and rhetoric.

However, promoting an employment-based model for lone parents is not uncontroversial. On the one hand, there is good research evidence to support this approach. The government, for example, points to research that shows the benefits of participation in paid work for lone parents, especially the financial gains, the promotion of social inclusion and the creation of a positive role model for children (DSS, 1999). Lone parents themselves identify similar reasons for wanting to be in paid work – the financial benefits, hopes for improved self-esteem and independence, and the chance to give their children a better future (Finch et al, 1999; Dawson et al, 2000; Lewis et al, 2000). Those in work are less likely to be poor than those not in work and the gains from working compared with living on Income Support have increased since 1997, even with the increases in the allowances for children in non-working families (Brewer and Shephard, 2004).

On the other hand, however, the actual financial situation of each family depends on a number of individual factors, including their wages, childcare costs, transport costs, other work-related expenses, housing costs and child support payments (Harries and Woodfield, 2002; Farrell and O'Connor, 2003; Woodland et al, 2003; Graham et al, 2005). Some families are not receiving the Tax Credits to which they are entitled and the Childcare Tax Credit pays only a portion of the costs of registered care. Being in work may also place other pressures on lone parents, including lack of time and difficulties in managing childcare (Skinner, 2003; Bell et al, 2005). Many lone mothers who do work are in service sector jobs, often quite low paid, and so work itself may be stressful and/or boring and repetitive. Evans et al (2004) show that lone parents tend to have higher job exit rates than average and the risk of job exit is particularly high in the first 12 months after entering employment. Children with parents who move in and out of employment may experience more poverty than those in more stable situations (Adelman et al, 2003).

Current policy is based on the premise, or promise, that paid work will not only reduce income poverty but also improve well-being and quality of life. This chapter draws on in-depth interviews with 50 lone mothers who had recently started work,[1] in order to explore whether or not they felt themselves to be better off in work, and what they meant by this. These mothers clearly felt a strong push away from Income Support, with employment seen as a route to independence, which living on benefits did not provide. The women wanted to work for more money but also for social contacts, for self-esteem and autonomy, and to feel that they have a purpose in life. Some were also looking to the future, hoping to buy their own home, planning for their pensions, thinking about the time when their children would grow up and leave home. But on the other hand, many of the women were also anxious about leaving the relative security of Income Support for what were often potentially insecure, sometimes temporary jobs, about managing financially while waiting for wages and Tax Credits to stabilise into regular payments, and about coping with the demands of work. Here we start by placing the move into jobs of 16 or more hours per week in the context of the mothers' employment and family histories more generally, and then go on to look at issues of income security and welfare in work.

The sample consists of 50 lone mothers in receipt of Tax Credits, all of whom had left Income Support or Jobseeker's Allowance between October 2002 and October 2003, and taken a job (or jobs) of 16 or more hours per week. Most had school-age children only, as the sample was selected to include families with at least one child aged between eight and 14.[2] About half had been lone parents for five years or more. Two women were bereaved, nine were single mothers and 39 were divorced or separated. Five of the women came from minority ethnic backgrounds and a further three had mixed-heritage children. Interviews were carried out in various areas of England, both rural and urban.

Paid work: family and employment histories

The women were included in our study because they had recently entered work. However, this one event – leaving Income Support for jobs of 16 or more hours per week – was just one part of each individual employment history. For example, the sample included women who had always worked regularly and who had been unemployed for just a few months, women who had not worked for some years while bringing up children and women who had gone back to higher education as mature students and were now re-entering employment.

Despite this diversity, however, there were a number of common themes in the employment experiences of these lone mothers.

First, almost all the women had previous experience of employment but, like most women with children, their paid work had been fitted in around their children. Most had therefore either had breaks in employment before they became lone mothers and/or had mainly worked part time while they were with husbands and partners. Almost half – 21 women – had families of three or more children (although not all were living at home at the time of the interview). Women with large families are more likely to have periods out of paid employment, even if they are living with partners.

Second, becoming a lone mother often had a direct impact on employment. Some had started working during the period they were separating from their partners, as one woman said 'to get me out of a bad situation'. But becoming a lone mother was more likely to mean leaving work, sometimes only for a few months but more often for a year or more, in part depending on the ages and number of children and the circumstances of the separation. Half of the women had left work around about the time that they separated from their partners. Employment histories were thus closely bound up with family histories, with responsibility for children and with lone parenthood.

Third, although 35 of the women had been on Income Support for a year or more (the longest period was 14 years), this did not mean they had no engagement with the labour market during that time. Just over half of the women had experience of working part time, doing voluntary work or studying while they were receiving Income Support. The Income Support rules allow work of up to 16 hours per week for lone parents, and they can earn up to £20 per week without any impact on the level of benefit they receive. Thirteen of the 50 women had worked part time, 15 had done some training and eight had done some voluntary work (seven women had done more than one of these three activities). For some, this provided a direct route into work – they worked as volunteers or did training placements and were then offered paid jobs – and was part of a longer-term strategy to get better jobs. For others, the goal was more immediate; to boost their income a little and get a break from housework and childcare, but the part-time hours could sometimes be increased to cross the 16-hour threshold, which took them off Income Support and onto Tax Credits. Thus, for many of the women the move off Income Support and into jobs of 16 or more hours was part of a gradual process of re-entering employment, rather than an abrupt shift from no paid work to full-time jobs.

This is also illustrated by their experiences in their most recent jobs. By the time we interviewed them (about 10-12 months after they had left Income Support for work), seven of the women were out of work again, six had changed jobs, two had had substantial time off (one for sickness, the other for maternity leave) and three had changed their hours of work. In total, therefore, there were 18 women whose jobs had changed in some way since they left Income Support, and to these can be added another five women who were expecting their jobs to end soon, either because they were due to be made redundant or because they had temporary contracts. This is almost half of all the women, suggesting that finding security in employment is not an easy or quick process, even for those who have recent training and qualifications.

Being better off in work?

Like many other employed mothers, these women were mainly working in just a few occupations and industries. Most – 36 women – worked in care homes, offices, shops, catering or cleaning. One woman was self-employed, one worked from home selling by telephone and one was driving a school bus. However, there were 11 women in professional or semi-professional jobs, all in care or education, most of whom had completed some further education or training. Most of the women worked part time, with just 13 in jobs of over 30 hours per week. Six women had more than one job, usually because this was the only way in which they could get above the required 16 hours for Tax Credits. Four women were working nights (all of them in care homes) and five were working weekends (some on rotas rather than every weekend). The highest-paid women earned about £11 to £12 per hour, the lowest were paid at national minimum wage levels (£4.40 per hour). But pay was typically about £5 to £6 per hour, which is about average for women in part-time work, but which is close to the commonly used low pay threshold of the two-thirds of the hourly median for all workers.[3]

We asked the women whether they were better off financially in work, and what this means to them. Being better off was generally defined in quite minimal terms. It meant being able to pay bills, not having to worry so much about money, being able to redecorate their homes, having a bit more money for treats, especially for the children but also for themselves, and being able to afford holidays, Christmas and other religious festivals. Being better off was also set in the context of their previous circumstances, and in particular the usually very difficult experience of trying to make ends meet while living on Income Support. For example, Ruth had been on Income Support for nine years, and was now working as a care assistant. She talked a lot about how she could now afford 'the little things':

> 'A lot better off than I was. I'm not rich but I can do little things like a takeaway or take the kids to pictures and things like that.... We've had the best Christmas ... bought them a PC and just bought myself a microwave, it's just little things that a lot of people take for granted ... I can have a night out myself maybe ... I can let [my son] go to snooker, whereas before ... all his friends would go off to snooker and he couldn't go. Things like that. Just little things that you take for granted. Now I can just do it.'

Wendy had had two spells on Income Support as a lone mother – the first for about three years and the second for about a year – and was now working as a medical secretary:

> 'I just feel like I am better off. I don't write everything down but, compared to when I was on Income Support, I couldn't do anything, really, I didn't go out, I didn't have a bottle of wine, or take the kids out, or give the kids pocket money, um, stuff like that, or buy the latest DVD that's come out, couldn't do anything like that. Whereas now, I can do things like that, so you know, and I am not in any great debt through doing it either, so, I think I'm definitely better off....'

The women were about equally divided between those who said that they were financially better off in work and those who said they were not, or that there was very little difference. However, the way the women talked about whether they were better off or not was often quite complex and ambivalent:

> 'I don't actually feel better off but I am.'

> 'I am better off but the money does not always make up for the amount of pressure and the lack of time.'

> 'I would say it's about the same. But, as I say, the benefits were what it [going to work] did for me mentally.'

'It is swings and roundabouts really. I am better off because obviously I'm at work but I'm not as better off as I thought I was going to be.... But I am better off, I mean I feel better for working.'

Thus, in thinking about whether they were better off or not, the women were not just making a simple financial calculation between income levels at different points in time, they were also taking into account other aspects of their situations, both financial and non-financial. Looking first at the financial side, there were three key factors that affected how the women felt about their circumstances: income security, debts and budgeting especially for additional costs in work.

Income security

Income packages in work were often quite complex, with money coming in from different sources at different times of the week or month. All the women were receiving Child Benefit and all were receiving Tax Credits, although they were not always sure whether this was Working Tax Credit or Child Tax Credit or both. Nine were receiving Childcare Tax Credit. Nineteen were receiving child support (that is, maintenance from non-resident parents), although not always regularly. Nine were receiving Housing Benefit. Wages and tax deductions were often unknown or unstable at first. For example, Hayley pointed out that:

'You are a month without money, you don't get paid for a month and you're not sure how much you're going to get ... the way they calculate the wages ... it's quite complicated and you don't actually get what they say you're going to get, you actually get quite a bit less.'

As they moved into work, most (32 women) received some financial help – one or more of Income Support run-on, Housing Benefit run-on, back-to-work bonus or child maintenance bonus. For about half of the women, accessing this financial help went quite smoothly, although it usually took some time, and Jobcentre Plus personal advisors were very important in providing information and practical help at this point. Most of the women (32) saw a personal advisor and about half got some help with their Tax Credit, or other in-work benefit, claims. But delays and wrong payments were also common, both for Housing Benefit and Tax Credit claims, and when this happened the women often had to try and borrow money to keep going.[4] The lack of information about Tax Credits added to the insecurity:

> 'There is no breakdown so you don't know what you should be getting or why.'

As did receiving letters that gave different information and, in particular, the sudden receipt of large amounts of money that the women were unsure whether or not they were really entitled to have. Hayley had received a payment of £1,300 and said that:

> '... the Job Centre have said to me, don't spend it. The Lone Parent Advisor said when you start getting your Tax Credit payments, there will be an overpayment of around £1,000, whatever you do don't spend it, because come April the Inland Revenue will want it back.'

This had happened to Joanne:

> 'I qualified for Child Tax Credits last April, which was tremendous, I mean the amount I received really surprised me it was that much. It was like another wage.... But then unfortunately because my wage had gone up [and] ... I found out they'd overpaid me. So they stopped at Christmas, I've not got anything since then, which is awful, because I got £800 odd from them and now I don't get anything and I don't understand.... My wage went up but the actual difference in my net amount I receive is ... about £100 ... and also my childcare went up because my dad stopped helping out.... As I say they've overpaid me so I've not got anything ... which I don't understand myself and it certainly made me think because well I don't know what I'm going to do, because I can't pay the bills now, I can't pay them all. Let's see what happens.'

Child support payments were another potential source of insecurity. As with Tax Credits, the income received via child support was generally very important to those women who were getting payments. But there were often difficulties in establishing regular payments, and there was very little help available from the Child Support Agency. Irregular child support was therefore a problem for some, especially if this had been part of the theoretical 'better-off calculation' but was not actually being received.

Overall, it took some time to sort out incomes in work:

> '… it's slowly settling down, you need to be aware there is a running in period when you start work.'

One woman said that it took at least six months before she knew how her income would work out; another said it was more like 18 months.

Debts: paying the past

Few of the women had been able to avoid at least some debt when they were living on Income Support, and at least two of the women had been declared bankrupt. Some also had debts from when they were living with their former partners, or had gone into debt when they separated, trying to keep their housing for example. These debts did not go away in work, as Jean, working in two jobs and relatively well paid, put it:

> 'You see I imagine that the perception is that once you start work everything suddenly changes, and they haven't thought, well no why would it, because all the things you've not done and not paid for are all there with you still. And this extra money, albeit it's there, is still in the past, to pay the past.'

Indeed, debts sometimes became more pressing when the women started work. Beverley, for example, was being asked to repay a Social Fund loan that dated back several years, and this was an unexpected – and unwelcome – expense as she was struggling to make ends meet anyway and felt she was no better off in work. Debts were not always entered into the 'better-off calculations' that the women had from their personal advisors, sometimes out of embarrassment, so the impact of paying back debts may not have been foreseen.

Budgeting: new or extra costs

As discussed above, the move from the relative simplicity and regularity of Income Support to the more complex working incomes was something that often took time and some energy to sort out. Coping financially was also made more difficult because being in work generated some new, and sometimes unexpected, costs. Paying off debts was part of this, as noted above. Some women started running a car. Mortgage payments went up for some women. Council Tax was often more than expected. Few of the women qualified for Council Tax Benefit (apart from the single person rebate) and paying Council Tax was seen as particularly difficult:

> '... the only thing that was letting me down was my Council Tax.... If you didn't have this high Council Tax to pay you would be so much better off. The real problem is the Council Tax.... It's going to be more than my mortgage.'

In various ways, the costs of children rose. Some women were paying for formal childcare and the full costs were not met by the Childcare Tax Credit. Others were paying for informal childcare, and consequently were not eligible for the credit. School meals were a significant cost, especially for the large families, and child transport costs – the bus or train to school – could also be substantial.

Worries about money were still common. For example, Angela felt she was better off on the whole but:

> 'Being in work is a challenge I would enjoy ordinarily but I haven't got the luxury, money is at the forefront of your mind when you're on your own, because you need to make enough money to live.... It's a double-edged sword really, I enjoy working and it's a challenge and it's quite nice to prove myself, but it's also quite stressful.'

Some of the women were really struggling to meet all their costs. Rose was thinking of giving up work:

> 'The money's no better, no better at all.... I went to the government and asked them if it would be worth my while to go to work, and they said, "yes, it would".... And for three months it was. And then one day I just got a letter saying, no more benefits. Live on what you've got. Full rent, full Council Tax. I pay the same amount of Council Tax a couple does, I mean, it's only £100 less. I'm paying £50 out for my two children to go to high school, £50 out for my child to go to childcare, £50 on rent.... I'm not earning enough money to survive.... So I'm thinking

of just packing my job in so that I don't have to pay anything out.'

However, most of the women were coping financially and, once past the initial in-work period, were finding that they could manage better. One of the most positive aspects of being in work was that they felt that they could spend a bit more freely, and also that they were entitled to do so. In this way, changing expectations played a part in changing spending patterns. Treats for children – computers, toys, clothes, holidays, days out, school trips – were very common and spending on children was a clear priority in the first few months in work. There was a feeling of liberation for some of the women, an opportunity to spend:

> 'I think I've just relished in the chance of having big wads of money.'

And especially to spend on larger items such as going on holiday, house improvements and cars. For some women, being in work made it possible to obtain credit and hence access to items they would not otherwise have been able to buy. More generally, some of the mothers just relaxed a little:

> 'I could not afford to be in debt on Income Support.'

They also felt that they should be able to afford more if they were working. As Tracey put it:

> 'If we're talking purely financially, I'm probably worse off in some ways, but I think the trouble is my expectations of what I want to do have risen. When I was on Income Support ... I think I restricted my spending a lot more because I was so worried about how am I going to bring up these three children.... So I've changed, and I suppose I am less disciplined about money now than I was, simply because you can't be so stringent for, you know, so many years.'

Security and stability

For most of the women, the fact that they were not better off or only marginally better off was compensated by other aspects of being in work – the feeling that it was better for their children for them to be working, their interest in their jobs, their pleasure at not being on Income Support, and their hopes for the future. Thus, for example, Amy had recently returned to work after higher education:

> 'I wasn't going to be much better off. I knew that.… I was looking at the big picture and not at what I'm going to earn this year, I'm looking at when I've moved up that ladder a stage, I will be getting less benefits for the children because the children will, may not be school age by then. So I was really looking at getting my foot in the door and using my time constructively.'

Jean was in similar circumstances and was also looking ahead to when she would be better off:

> 'If I'm honest, if I thought I was going to stay in this position then it would be very, very tempting to think well, you know, sod it. I'm knocking myself out here and I'm not really that much better off.… I could just go back to being on the social for two or three years and then do this again.'

These women were looking ahead to a time when they could feel better off and a key aspect of that was their future security. Seeking security was an important issue for the women in general, both now and in the future. All of the women had experienced major family change in becoming lone mothers, and for some this was still fairly recent. Some were still involved in sorting out financial and other issues with ex-partners, sometimes in very difficult and stressful circumstances including violence and threats of violence. Whereas almost all the women looked back on their time on Income Support as difficult financially, there was more ambivalence in respect of leaving the security that it offered. Faith had been on Income Support for about seven years:

> 'And though it was never enough, I would not have, certainly not have survived on Income Support without the back-up from my family.… But the good thing about it, and I've learnt since I've gone out to work, is mentally you've got that support and it took an awful lot of sleepless nights to make the decision to come off Income Support.… While you're on Income Support as a single parent you

get so much.... If something happens to me, at least the roof is over the children's head. But now it's not. And that's what makes it even worse and more of a mental strain.... Saying from experience now, having gone back to work, there's no describing the mental support you get knowing that somebody is actually paying to have the roof over your head.'

A number of the women had taken temporary jobs and so were unsure about their future employment:

'The fear of just ending back up on Income Support makes me feel very depressed ... I need a permanent, full-time job.'

Some were struggling to find work that matched their qualifications, although others were settling for jobs below their qualifications in order to be able to work nearby or suitable hours. Work was often seen as insecure and this was not unrealistic since, as noted above, many of the women did experience job loss or change and they often worked in sectors of employment with high labour turnover.

Conclusion

The expectation that lone mothers, especially those with school-age children, will engage in at least part-time employment is being increasingly accepted and public opinion is broadly supportive of current policies to encourage lone-parent employment (Taylor-Gooby, 2004). The women becoming lone mothers are themselves very likely to have been in employment while with their partners and, although the actual transition to lone parenthood can disrupt employment, many do expect to work once they are more settled.

The policy environment now provides much more support for employment, with higher levels of financial support in work, better access to childcare services, and more practical and personal help with the transition to work. This has clearly made an important difference to many lone mothers and has made employment, especially part-time jobs, much more possible. Ongoing wage top-ups are particularly important for these often low-paid workers. Several of the women we interviewed said that they could not have worked without the additional income from Tax Credits. Some said that they had tried before but found it impossible financially, others that they would have returned to work much sooner if the current levels of support had been available then.

But being in work, even with Tax Credits, does not always mean being – or feeling – better off financially. Compared with Income Support, most of the women felt that they could afford a better standard of living for themselves and their children. But only about half said that they thought they were clearly better off in work. In making this judgement, the women were not only thinking about the level of their current income. They were also thinking about income security, which was particularly important during the initial transition to work. They were often paying off past debts, and sometimes incurring new debts. They had new costs to meet in work, especially for housing, for travel, for school meals and school travel for children, and, for some, childcare costs. Achieving security – in the family, in the labour market and in their incomes – was an important aspiration to the women but also often a major challenge, which took time and persistence and sometimes a willingness to put up with difficulties now in the hope of better things in the future. Helping to create the conditions for security in work is an important policy challenge and one which should be at the centre of policies to support incomes in work, including the three key areas of childcare and housing subsidies, child support and the effective delivery of Tax Credits. More fundamentally, higher wages – a higher minimum wage, access to better-paid jobs – would reduce the reliance on these other sources of in-work income and provide much greater security for these low-income families.

Notes

[1] The research is funded by the Economic and Social Research Council (Reference RES-000-23-1079).

[2] This age range was chosen to facilitate the interviews with children, since one-to-one interviews are not very suitable for younger children, and older children may be facing their own transitions out of school and into the labour market. See Chapter Fifteen by Tess Ridge. The sample was drawn from official records of Tax Credit recipients and we are grateful to HM Revenue & Customs for their help in this.

[3] Median gross earnings in April 2004 for women were £7.95 per hour, £9.46 per hour for those working full time (30 hours plus) and £6.27 per hour for those working part time. For all workers median gross earnings were £9.21 per hour (ONS, 2004a).

[4] These women were entering work just as the new Tax Credits were being introduced. There is mounting evidence of substantial problems in delivering Tax Credits (CAB, 2005; National Audit Office, 2005; Parliamentary and Health Service Ombudsman, 2005).

FOURTEEN

Reciprocity, lone parents and state subsidy for informal childcare

Christine Skinner and Naomi Finch

Introduction

The Labour government in the UK aims to increase the lone parent employment rate to 70% by 2010. To help achieve this aim, a state subsidy for childcare through Tax Credits has been introduced. However, the subsidy has been restricted to formal childcare, despite evidence that the majority of lone parents use informal care, are more likely to rely solely on this form of care than couple families, and that deficiencies in formal childcare provision in relation to quality, suitability and affordability still act as a significant barrier to lone parents' employment.

This chapter investigates the potential of a state subsidy for informal childcare. Utilising evidence from a study of 78 qualitative in-depth interviews and eight focus groups with lone parents, it explores preferences for informal care and how such care is negotiated in families. The study found that lone parents held deeply embedded preferences for informal childcare based on trust, commitment, shared understandings and children's happiness. It is important, therefore, for government to support informal as well as formal care. However, the evidence also shows that the way informal childcare was negotiated involved complex notions of obligation, duty and reciprocity, suggesting that a subsidy could potentially intrude upon private family relationships. Yet, on closer examination, we found that care was negotiated differently depending on who was providing it, with lone parents tending to favour paying for childcare provided by other family members and friends than by grandparents. This has implications for the state childcare subsidy, and this chapter seeks to cast light on the potential complexities by relating the findings to theoretical explanations on how negotiations between kin work.

Background

A variety of labour market policies have been introduced by the Labour government that focus on increasing lone parents' employment rates. These include financial incentives via Working Tax Credits, practical help via the New Deal for Lone Parents and a National Childcare Strategy that aims to expand formal childcare provision and improve quality, suitability and affordability. These measures have been introduced with the understanding that structural factors are the main inhibitors of lone parents' employment. Significant progress has been made, with 55% of lone parents in employment in 2005, an increase of nine percentage points since 1997 (HM Treasury, 2005b).

This improvement has been achieved despite policy limitations. In particular, the National Childcare Strategy remains inadequate. There are wide regional variations in childcare places for pre-school children, ranging from 11 to 58 places per 100 children across local authorities. There is also insufficient flexible provision to cover evenings and weekends, for disabled children and for children living in disadvantaged areas (National Audit Office, 2004, p 6). In relation to costs, the childcare subsidy has been partially successful, but problems remain. Increasing numbers have claimed childcare expenses through the Tax Credit system;[1] however, only 70% of the costs are covered up to maximum limits[2] (rising to 80% in 2006). The Daycare Trust argues that families in the UK still pay proportionally more for their childcare; 75% of the costs compared to an average of 25%–30% in many of the Organisation for Economic Co-operation and Development (OECD) countries (Daycare Trust, 2004). Also, of the 1.06 million lone parents receiving Working Tax Credit (WTC) only 223,800 were claiming the childcare element in April 2005 (HMRC, 2005, p 15). The outcome is that work may not pay and many lone parents could even be worse off after paying childcare costs (Work and Pensions Committee, 2003, p 24).

The childcare element of WTC is restricted to registered formal childcare such as playgroups, day nurseries, childminders, out-of-school clubs and childcare workers who are approved to provide care in parents' own homes under the Home Childcarers Scheme (introduced in April 2003). Childcare provided by family members (including grandparents, non-resident parents and other kin) and friends/ neighbours is not covered by the subsidy, even if care is provided on a full-time basis. Thus, it is not maximising its potential to make childcare more affordable or to increase employment participation rates in low-income families. While the government did seriously consider subsidising informal care as part of its concern to meet welfare-to-work and anti-child poverty strategies, the idea was rejected.

The House of Commons Work and Pensions Select Committee's inquiry into an informal childcare subsidy (Work and Pensions Committee, 2003) rejected the idea as a contentious option, believing that costs could spiral out of control,[3] that it would be too difficult to police administratively, that it would potentially undermine the drive for improved standards in formal childcare, and that it would not expand the number of childcare places because informal carers would 'simply provide the care they would have provided anyway' (Work and Pensions Committee, 2003, para 100). A possible solution was to extend the current Home Childcarers Scheme to 'non-registered childcarers' (potentially all informal carers and nannies), allowing them to become eligible for the childcare subsidy. This would also improve standards and expand formal provision, as these newly registered carers could take on more children (Work and Pensions Committee, 2003, para 103). In the end, a slightly adapted proposal was accepted and a new 'Childcare Approval Scheme' was implemented in April 2005. It is less rigorous than the Home Childcarers Scheme, and involves proving the pre-existence of a childcare qualification or undergoing an induction course, gaining a first aid certificate, being vetted by the Criminal Records Bureau and being re-approved on an annual basis (DfES, 2004a, p 9). The new approval scheme, however, is not open to all; it is aimed primarily at 'nannies' rather than family and friends (that is, the majority of informal carers) (DfES, 2004a, foreword). Its potential is limited and it does not figure greatly in the new ten-year strategy for childcare, which concentrates on improving the quality of formal provision, regulation and inspection frameworks, availability, affordability and the integration of childcare with education (HM Treasury, 2004b). It falls short of demands made by the Daycare Trust for a state investment in informal childcare, and for family and friends to be encouraged 'into the fold' through the provision of a fast-track registration process (Daycare Trust, 2003). This is in line with making formal care more attractive to parents to meet new targets of 50% usage of formal care among low-income families by 2008 (HM Treasury, 2004c, p 6).

The plan, therefore, is not to bring informal childcare within the scope of the WTC because:

> The Government recognises the huge contribution that informal care makes to family life. However it is not the Government's role to offer financial support for care that

is freely given within families and it would also be extremely intrusive to make appropriate checks for payments between family members or friends. (HM Treasury, 2004b, p 37)

This argument is not in line with childcare usage; most parents rely on informal childcare and lone parents are more likely than couples to rely solely on informal care (see Figure 14.1). As Land (2002, p 19) argues, an expansion of formal care will not necessarily reduce the need or wish for informal care. This might especially be the case where informal care supports the coordination of formal services, for example where friends and family transport children across different formal childcare and educational settings (Skinner, 2003, 2005; Bell et al, 2005). The importance of this coordination role is acknowledged by the government as 'the glue' that holds complex childcare arrangements together (HM Treasury, 2004b, para 5.13), yet it has not endorsed informal care. The interesting question is whether an important opportunity to support diversity and choice in childcare, and thereby employment opportunities, has been missed. To answer that question, we need to understand more about parental preferences for informal childcare, how it is negotiated among lone-parent families and the potential of a state subsidy to support this provision. It is within the process of negotiation for informal childcare that the notion of payment might be discussed between the giver and receiver, and therefore this is an area that needs further exploration in order to understand how a subsidy might impact on childcare usage. Thus, the next section begins with a discussion of other theoretical work that has explored how negotiations for care operate in families.

Studies in negotiating care

Finch and Mason's (1993) seminal work on kin relationships explored the nature of family negotiations between adults, children and their older parents over informal care. They found that, in offering support, family members did not operate on a basis of fixed rules or norms, but rather entered into an implicit process of negotiation whereby they relied on certain criteria or guidelines to help them work out the 'right thing to do' under the circumstances. Their evidence demonstrated the centrality of principles of obligation and reciprocity in working out the 'right thing to do'. They also found that reciprocity operated differently depending on the nature of relationships in families, and identified two kinds: 'balanced reciprocity' whereby an immediate return is expected for services offered; and 'generalised reciprocity'

Figure 14.1: Source of childcare used by lone parents and couples (2001)

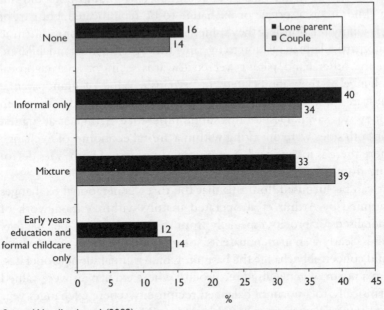

Source: Woodland et al (2002)

with no expectation of an immediate return. Close kin relationships, such as between a parent and child, tended to operate under the latter, as there is either a longer timescale in expectations of returns or no return is expected at all, so there is more tolerance of imbalances in exchanges. However, Finch and Mason focused on adult negotiations about the informal care needs of older parents, not the childcare needs of dependent children to enable their parents to undertake paid work. It may be that reciprocity within families operates differently in relation to childcare, especially as three generations are involved when childcare is provided by grandparents – the most common providers of informal care (Woodland et al, 2002). In-depth research on grandparents suggests this might be the case.

Arthur et al (2003) explored the nature of reciprocal relations across three generations for grandparental contact and childcare. They found that grandparents tended to strongly resist the idea of reciprocity in relation to any expectation of a return for childcare. Grandparents were keen to point out that they offered childcare for the love and enjoyment of their grandchildren, and to help their adult children take up paid work. They rejected any offer of payment (gifts or cash) and some felt cash payments would turn their caregiving into a 'job', which they did not want (Arthur et al, 2003, p 67).

From this evidence, Arthur et al argued that grandparents did not see childcare as a service or exchange to be reciprocated, but part of their family relationship; they valued it for its own sake, for its intrinsic value, particularly in relation to the time they spent with grandchildren. On the other hand, parents veered towards seeing it as a reciprocal exchange as they appreciated the extrinsic value of grandparental childcare; they knew the costs of private childcare and how much money was saved. Despite this subtle difference, Arthur et al suggest that both sides were operating within a 'moral economy' of exchange where there is intrinsic value in mutual support and both sides derive value from the exchange.

It can be surmised from this that the three generational exchanges examined by Arthur et al operated mainly within a framework of generalised reciprocity, especially from the grandparents' perspective. This is clearly seen in grandparents' strong resistance to payment, which could conceivably change the basis on which mutual support operates, from a norm of generalised reciprocity where exchanges were valued intrinsically, to a norm of balanced reciprocity where exchanges veer more towards extrinsic value judgements. Thus, balanced reciprocity was strongly regarded as inappropriate by grandparents – mainly grandmothers – in their role as givers, but not always by parents in their role as receivers, as some expressed a desire to pay for grandparental childcare. This set of exchanges is illustrated in Figure 14.2.

Figure 14.2: Nature of intergenerational relationships and exchanges

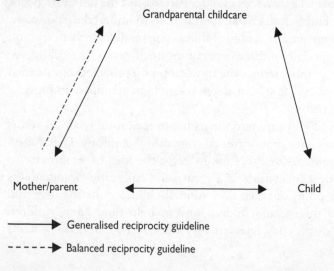

Grandparental childcare

Mother/parent   Child

——————▶ Generalised reciprocity guideline

- - - - - ▶ Balanced reciprocity guideline

It is not clear from these findings about reciprocity whether a lack of a state subsidy for informal childcare concurs with, or diverges from, attitudes and behaviour in families. The research reported in this chapter on lone parents attempts to understand more about parental preferences for informal childcare and how negotiations over it operated within family – mainly grandparents – and friends. The findings contribute to the debate about whether informal childcare should be subsidised.

Lone parents and informal childcare

The study involved 78 qualitative, in-depth interviews and eight focus groups (involving 69 respondents) with lone parents (mainly mothers) in urban, rural and inner city areas in England. The sample of lone parents was drawn from people who took part in the Family Resources Survey where they had agreed to participate in further research studies. To capture the saliency of childcare needs and preferences, only lone parents who had at least one child aged 10 years or less were included. The data were analysed using 'Framework', a grid method that uses a thematic approach to classify and interpret qualitative research. We start by presenting the findings on lone parents' preferences for informal care.

Preferences

Childcare preferences are shaped by a myriad of factors that include practical considerations such as availability and costs (Woodland et al, 2002; Kasparova et al, 2003) but also ideas about good mothering that are socially, geographically, morally and culturally embedded (Duncan and Edwards, 1999; Duncan, 2003). Our interviews with lone parents show that some of them held strong preferences for informal over formal childcare. Four broad reasons emerged as to why this was the case: trust, commitment, shared understandings and children's happiness.

Trust

Concerns about trust and safety were among the strongest determinants of some parents' preferences for informal over formal care. This is consistent with other evidence (Duncan and Edwards, 1999; Woodland et al, 2002). Our study shows that a distinction was made between childcare providers as people they knew versus 'strangers', mirroring a division between those they 'trusted' and those they did not. Thus, family and friends were often singled out as more trustworthy than formal childcare providers. In some cases, this was underpinned by a sense of fear about the potential maltreatment of children 'behind closed doors' in formal care settings such as nurseries or by childminders. This was fed by media scare stories highlighting the neglect and maltreatment of children in particular formal settings, but it could also arise as a result of previous experiences of poor care of their children or from negative memories about the poor care received by themselves as children in formal care. Negative experiences were very powerful, with some parents determined never to use the particular type of formal care. Yet, there were some positive attitudes too. Some lone parents' fears over formal childcare had changed after trying out a formal provider, and others felt more reassured about their child's safety when providers used web cameras or sent digital photographs via email.

Commitment

Views on the commitment of providers also appeared to influence informal care preferences. Family and friends were often seen as providing childcare 'out of the kindness of their hearts' or of being able to 'stick by you' or would 'rally round' when required. That these people might actively *want* to look after the children and could be relied upon, even at short notice, acted in favour of informal childcare to such an extent that in some cases formal care was never even considered. But contrary views were also apparent. Some lone parents expressed concerns about family/friends providing support out of a sense of reluctant duty/obligation rather than willingness, and they believed this might compromise the quality of care given. Others were worried about 'putting on' people to provide regular care or they felt 'guilty' about relying on them. For grandparental care in particular, there were some concerns expressed about it not being their role to provide childcare: 'they brought us up, why should they bring mine up?' All these beliefs could limit the use made of informal care.

Shared understandings

Having shared values over childrearing practices also influenced preferences for informal care. For example, it has been shown that grandparents are often seen as the 'next best thing' to the parent

(Woodland et al, 2002). Certainly, in our study lone parents were concerned about childrearing practices that carers might use, for example how they might discipline children and the values they might instil. They appreciated having a shared understanding on these issues with informal carers, especially grandmothers. As one respondent said of grandmother care:

> '... and [she] bring[s] them [the children] up the way I want her to and ... they get 80% or 90% of the same treatment as they would with me....' (Lone mother of twins aged nine, worker)

However, not all family and friends were considered to hold the same values and approaches to childrearing. Some negative views were expressed about family/friends having different parenting styles and about grandparents having not brought *them* up very well when they were children. Grandparents could also be seen as having a tendency to 'interfere' with the lone parents' childrearing practices. Yet, at the same time a further influencing factor for informal care was the belief that the carers should have experience of parenthood themselves in order to be capable providers of care.

Children's happiness

Children's happiness, as well as their safety, was also an important factor shaping informal care preferences. The lone parents frequently talked about their children's 'happiness' and about 'wanting them to be happy'; having children cared for in familiar surroundings was often seen as key to their happiness. This was viewed as being more easily achieved in informal care settings than in formal care. Also, that friends, family and especially ex-partners – mainly fathers – had affection for or 'loved' their children, and would thus give them special attention, was seen as an advantage of informal over formal provision. Some parents said that their children would be 'safe and cared for completely' with informal carers. For a few lone parents, a non-resident father's close relationship with their child before the breakdown of the parents' relationship meant that it was important for the child that the father continued to have an input into the child's upbringing and care.

However, there were other reasons why parents thought that family members in general – and grandparents in particular – might not easily facilitate a child's happiness. This was often related to perceived inabilities to provide desired activities or stimulation, leading to boredom and unhappiness in the child. A further disadvantage of some informal care was the lack of opportunity for social interaction with other children, which was considered to be a major benefit of group-based formal provision such as out-of-school clubs, nurseries, playgroups and crèches. Such opportunities for social interaction were considered especially important for an only child and for younger children whose older brothers and sisters had already started school. The socialising function of nurseries in particular was also considered important in order to prepare children for the 'shock' of starting school.

The evidence on childcare preferences demonstrates that there is no particular norm operating among lone parents that always favours informal over formal care. It does show that preferences for informal care were related to beliefs about what is best for children in relation to safety, commitment, shared understandings over childrearing practices and happiness. On these dimensions at least, formal childcare seemed to be more problematic in meeting lone parents' expectations of quality, with the possible exception of social interaction, which was seen as an advantage of formal group-based care. Preferences for informal care were also inhibited, however, by concerns about asking for too much support ('putting on' people) or of feeling guilty if it were provided. Such inhibitions suggest that negotiating arrangements was not straightforward. A greater understanding of these inhibitions might provide insights into whether an informal childcare subsidy would be useful in enabling lone parents' employment.

Negotiating childcare

Grandparents

Lone parents' negotiation over childcare with grandparents to cover employment needs tended to be a very implicit affair, and was therefore not easily explained. Many described how arrangements had 'just happened', that grandparents had 'just offered', or 'just rallied round' or gave support out of the 'kindness of their hearts'. Even so, it appeared that a number of subtly different expectations were operating where some lone parents thought that grandparental care *should* be offered – almost regardless of the grandparent's other commitments or ability to provide it – while others were merely hopeful that it *might* be offered and said they would 'not ask' for it.

Hoping that help *might* be offered was more common. Under these circumstances it seemed that grandparents were left to decide to offer childcare; and, when they did, lone parents typically accepted that they were willing and able to do so. Exceptions arose where grandparents were perceived to be incapable of providing care due to ill-health, or frailty (where looking after children was considered as being 'too hard') or had other commitments such as caring for another relative or being in employment. In some cases, grandparents themselves were said to place limits on the amount of childcare they were prepared to offer for the same kinds of reasons. More rarely, where lone parents believed that it *should* be given (even when grandparents were said to be no longer capable or willing to provide it), this tended to be related to perceptions that formal care was unaffordable and not a realistic option. Under such circumstances tensions could be created, leading to family rows.

In some cases, however, expectations were more explicitly balanced and reciprocal in nature. One lone parent said she expected no support from the grandmother but qualified this by saying that, if the grandmother were to offer to provide childcare, she would pay her to do so. In this more unusual case, the expectation of reciprocity appeared to be connected to the fact that the grandmother was relatively young and had a dependent child of her own, and she and her daughter cared for each other's children on an equally reciprocal basis for purposes other than paid work. This may explain why this lone parent wanted to pay for the care. Her lack of expectation of support may also have been related to a perception, echoed by some other lone parents, that grandparents should only provide childcare if and when they are genuinely willing to do so:

> 'I think sometimes they [grandparents] feel obligated as well and that puts a strain on the relationship, like if you're asking them to look after your child and then they don't really want to, there's somewhere else they really want to be but they don't really want to say no to you at the same time.' (Lone parent, worker)

Despite this, it was very uncommon for lone parents to pay grandparents for providing childcare (only one did so). Although some had offered money, it had been declined. Sometimes, efforts were made to pay grandparents back 'in kind' by taking them shopping or buying small gifts.

Overall, there appeared to be two strands to expectations regarding grandparental childcare – one where lone parents seemed to put the needs of the grandparent above the needs for childcare, and the other where the needs for grandparental childcare came first. It was not possible to tell from this data the full interplay of factors underpinning these differences, except that in some circumstances the grandparents' health and well-being were seen as prime concerns.

Other relatives and friends

Negotiations with friends or other relatives about childcare appeared to operate differently from those with grandparents, and seemed to be underpinned by a clearer expectation of reciprocity. When lone parents used other relatives or friends for regular rather than occasional childcare, they were more likely to have offered payment of some kind or expressed a wish to do so. Some said this was to make their arrangements more 'businesslike'. In general, lone parents offered gifts, childcare or other forms of support rather than money 'in return' to friends or extended family members. The phrase 'in return' suggested that support should be paid back, and that any exchanges should be kept in balance. As one parent described her relations with her sister-in-law:

> 'Yeah, and I felt like 'cos it was my sister-in-law doing it and my sister couldn't obviously she had like, she was doing a hairdressing course, I mean she was full time, she was busy, and so I felt, yeah, I did, I felt like, you know, in return I had to put a lot of effort in making sure that my brothers were OK, do you know what I mean, like keeping everybody happy.' (Lone parent, worker)

Thus, in negotiations with friends or extended family members, unlike those with grandparents, reciprocity was more explicitly expressed. Some lone parents even suggested that informal carers (other than grandparents) ought to be eligible for the childcare subsidy via the WTC, as this would make them feel more confident about asking for care from these sources and, hence, more likely to take up work or increase their working hours. Others expressed a sense of injustice or considered it illogical that the government was prepared to support parents financially to leave their child with a 'stranger', but were not prepared to do the same for family members.

Conclusions

Overall, the findings show that negotiating informal childcare was a complex process that varied depending on whether it was with a grandparent, other family member or friend. Applying the theoretical work of Finch and Mason (1993) to this evidence, it could be argued that the onus was more often upon grandparents as the potential givers of childcare, to negotiate and make the decision to provide care, rather than on the lone parent. This can be seen where most lone parents' expectations were founded on the idea that childcare *might* be offered, or where they would 'not ask for it'. The implicit nature of this negotiation process also shows why it was difficult for lone parents to explain how decisions for childcare with grandparents were made. Implicitness was also a feature of the reciprocity underpinning negotiations, although this varied depending upon the relationship. 'Generalised reciprocity' appeared to operate in negotiations with grandparents, and there was ambiguity about what, if anything, should be paid back. This could be because grandparents were reluctant to accept payment, as childcare was more about spending time with grandchildren and loving them; or because childcare was provided out of a sense of duty or obligation. However, it could also be that lone parents had limited financial capacity to pay.

'Balanced reciprocity' seemed to operate with other family members or friends; here it was clearer that something had to be paid back. However, here too affordability of cash payments could be a problem. Even if lone parents wanted to reciprocate 'in kind' – childcare in return for childcare – they were also likely to be short of time if in employment and unable to do so. This explains the hesitancy expressed by some lone parents regarding childcare preferences, where they were worried about 'putting on' people, or about feeling guilty if they received free informal childcare regularly. Indeed, survey evidence shows that friends and other family (not grandparents) are much more likely to receive cash payments; 11% of friends compared to 8% of other relatives and only 3% of grandparents do so (La Valle et al, 2000). This has implications for the idea that government should offer a childcare subsidy for informal care.

It seems that lone parents are inhibited from explicitly asking grandparents for childcare support, and that grandparents are unwilling to accept payment from their adult children. There appears to be less reluctance to ask for informal care from friends or other relatives, but it is more important to pay this back, thus raising difficulties regarding affordability in cash or payment in kind. In both circumstances, a childcare subsidy from the state given directly to the carer could ease negotiations and encourage greater use of informal childcare. The givers of informal care would therefore not actually be taking money from parents. Rather, a state subsidy would help to put informal care on a 'businesslike' basis, enabling more lone parents to use more of it and thereby expand this type of childcare provision. This conclusion is contrary to that of the Work and Pensions Select Committee (2003), which assumed that there was limited capacity to expand informal provision as the childcare would be given anyway, irrespective of a subsidy. Such an assumption is likely to be flawed if the attitudes and behaviour of the lone parents in this study are typical. It also shows that the Committee might have been mistaken in lumping together all types of informal childcare as if they are the same thing.

Even so, Land (2002, p 13) argues that 'Rewarding, regulating and sustaining providers of informal care raise complex and controversial issues'.

It is also possible that a state subsidy for grandparental childcare could create unease in relationships as it could create pressure on grandparents to provide care where they feel they have a duty but may not be especially willing to do so. Certainly, the evidence suggests that some grandparents felt obliged to provide more childcare than they wanted to in order to help their lone-parent daughters (Bell et al, 2005). The state therefore runs the risk of being an undesirable interloper in these private exchange relationships, particularly if it also has a role as a regulator or approver of such care provision. It would also be very difficult to police such a subsidy and the potential for fraud would be considerable; as such it would fly in the face of the government's principle of 'progressive universalism' where some support is offered for all 'and most support for those who need it most' (HM Treasury, 2004b, p 4).

We know that informal childcare is the most common form of childcare used by lone parents and that they are more likely than couples to use informal care on its own rather than in combination with other formal care. For this reason, supporting informal care is important; not least because many lone parents genuinely prefer informal childcare to all forms of formal care, and that, in some cases, it may be the most appropriate and effective option for them (for example, in the evenings and at night).

Another argument in favour of an informal childcare subsidy is that it could help promote childcare and work choices, thereby extending the rewards of paid employment to more lone parents and helping to reduce child poverty. For example, payment for informal childcare could encourage some lone mothers into employment instead of being constrained by a lack of trusted formal care. More pragmatically, such a subsidy could be used to tackle the problems experienced by parents in coordinating working hours and travel arrangements with available childcare. Paid, informal provision could provide wrap-around childcare and help with transporting children between formal childcare/ education services and the home (see Skinner, 2003, 2005; Himmelweit and Sigala, 2004; Bell et al, 2005). It therefore has the potential to help informal childcarers to tie together disparate formal childcare/ education provision and to fill gaps in out-of-normal childcare hours. This kind of coordination support is still likely to be needed, even if universal state-funded childcare were provided. The government may therefore be too dismissive of the importance of the 'glue' of informal care that binds formal arrangements together and aids employment. The debate, however, has been prematurely cut short by the government's decision against subsidising informal care. As the Equal Opportunities Commission (2003, para 63) previously argued:

> Before conclusions are drawn either way on the role of informal care, further work is needed to investigate what is meant by quality childcare, and to understand more fully parental expectations and preferences.

We would add that, in the light of the evidence presented here, the ways in which an informal childcare subsidy might work in practice merit further investigation by the government.

Notes

[1] The subsidy was originally called the Childcare Tax Credit but was renamed the 'childcare element' of Working Tax Credit in changes made to Tax Credits in April 2003.

[2] In April 2005 the maximum childcare costs covered increased from £135 to £175 a week for one child and from £200 to £300 for two or more children. Consideration is also being given to extending entitlement to parents who work less than 16 hours (HM Treasury, 2004b).

[3] Costs were estimated to rise from existing expenditure of £195 million to between £263 million and £8.2 billion under different scenarios (Work and Pensions Committee, 2003, para 82).

FIFTEEN

Helping out at home: children's contributions to sustaining work and care in lone-mother families

Tess Ridge

Introduction

This chapter presents an important dimension to our understanding of unpaid care, by focusing on the role of children as active caring agents within their families. In general, children's active agency within households and the contributions they make to family life have tended to be neglected or ignored. Policy discourses have tended to constitute children as passive, dependent family members in need of appropriate adult care and control. Where children have gained recognition as caring family members, it has been as 'young carers' caring for sick or disabled parents (Becker et al, 1998). In particular, children living in working families have been treated as problematic and as burdensome responsibilities, and in workless families as potential obstacles to employment. Parents, especially mothers, are seen as struggling to manage a satisfactory work and family life balance, and this struggle is often characterised as a double shift or a double burden. In these discourses children appear mainly as problems to be resolved, part of the burden, as needy, largely passive individuals who are the main family members in need of care and attention. As a result, the issue of children and parental employment has been mainly confined to a policy agenda focused on adult employment. While acknowledging the challenges that working and caring presents for working parents, especially women, this dominant perception of children as passive and needy within families presents a very one-dimensional view of the complex social and relational dynamics that exist within households, between parents, children and siblings.

This chapter is based on children's accounts of their contributions to family life and reveals their involvement in a complex range of care and support within their families; including childcare, domestic labour, financial assistance and emotional sustenance. As such, it provides us with an opportunity to explore a very particular set of social and familial relationships, and gain some insight into the roles children can play in sustaining family cohesion around issues of work and care. The issue of children's perceptions and experiences of maternal employment is an important one, especially for children in lone-mother households.

As discussed in Chapter Thirteen by Jane Millar, the UK government has set two key policy goals directly affecting the lives of many women and children: to increase lone-parent employment to 70% by 2010, and to eliminate child poverty by 2020. The two are closely related, with the government espousing paid employment as the best route out of poverty (DSS, 1999). However, although there has been much research on the barriers to employment for lone mothers, we still know little about the impact of paid work on the lives of their children or about the factors that help or hinder lone-parent families to stay in paid work. We know still less about the role of the family unit in sustaining employment or the impact of employment on children and mothers who are trying to balance the ongoing and sometimes conflicting demands of work and family life.

Furthermore, while there has been much research into work–life balance from a parental perspective, there is little that looks at parental employment from a child's perspective (see Galinsky, 1999; V. Lewis, 2001, for some exceptions). Various studies have sought to identify the impact of mothers' employment on educational, employment and demographic outcomes for children (for example Joshi and Verropoulou, 2000; Ermisch and Francesconi, 2001; Marsh and Vegeris, 2004). However, none of these studies has examined how children themselves experience their mothers' employment and the impact it has upon their everyday lives as children and as active family members.

The family is a group enterprise, and within each family individual members will have key roles to play in managing and sustaining collective endeavours. As Brannen et al (2000) have shown, within families children are often engaged in a complexity of interactions and negotiations with their mothers and their siblings. Furthermore, the children in this research study are from lone-parent families and all of them have experienced a period of time on social assistance (Income Support or Jobseeker's Allowance). Both of these characteristics – their lone-parenthood family status and (given the low level of social assistance benefits) their poverty – may have an impact on these negotiations and on how they construct their identity as a family. Children in lone-mother households may develop very particular relationships with their mothers (Brannen et al, 2000; Smart et al, 2001). Poverty can restrict children's social environments and limit their access to economic and material resources (Middleton et al, 1994; Davis and Ridge, 1997; Roker, 1998; Ridge, 2002). Low income can also have implications for the relationship between children and their parents (Ridge, 2002).

The research

The research reported here comes from the first stage, begun in 2004, of a new qualitative longitudinal study of working family life involving interviews with 50 lone mothers and their 61 children. It explores their expectations and experiences of paid work over a period of several years.[1] The main aims of the project are to examine the impact of paid work – and, for some, job loss – on family life and living standards over time; and to explore whether and how these families negotiate the everyday challenges of sustaining low-income employment over time.

To gain an insight into working family life that was grounded in children's lives and experiences, the study employed a distinctive child-centred approach, which treated children as informed social actors in the context of their own lives and within their families (James and Prout, 1997; Christensen and James, 2000). This chapter focuses on the first round of interview data from the 61 children in the study. The children were aged between eight and 15 and their mothers had all left Income Support (or Jobseeker's Allowance) within the previous 12 months and were receiving Tax Credits.[2] There were 31 girls and 30 boys; six children came from minority ethnic backgrounds and a further five had dual heritage. Interviews were carried out in various areas of England, both rural and urban (including Leeds, Halifax, Bradford, Hull, Sheffield, Birmingham, Bristol, Swindon, Cornwall and Plymouth).

Maternal employment and children: understanding the context

Overall findings from the interviews with children focusing on their perceptions of their mothers' move into employment, indicate that many of them are more buoyant and content with their lives in comparison with children living in families receiving Income Support interviewed in the late 1990s (Ridge, 2002). This was apparent in a number of areas including financial satisfaction, school engagement and overall perceptions of well-being. For those children whose mothers had moved into what seemed to be relatively secure employment, the increase in income was significant and appreciated. However, despite the initial increase in income (which our findings show often leads to extra spending and treats for children in the early stages), they are still living in families that are relatively poor. Children whose mothers had not secured stable employment, or who were unable to manage the transition satisfactorily, were not buoyant. They shared many of the characteristics of concern expressed in Ridge's previous study, including uncertainty, insecurity and fears about social exclusion and difference. Research by Adelman et al (2003) shows that some of the very poorest children live not in families on long-term Income Support, but in families where there is frequent movement into and out of low-paid work.

Although children given the choice indicated that they would change aspects of their mothers' working, especially in relation to having more money and having more time together, overall they felt it was important that their mothers continued in work. This finding needs to be understood in the context of children's experiences prior to their mothers' recent employment. Many of the children were able to recall with great clarity the fears and concerns they had had about being poor and being identified as poor. Their accounts showed clearly the impact of economic and material deprivation on their lives, including their feelings of social and economic vulnerability, their fears of being left out and unable to join in with their peers, and the challenge of having no money, and for some being in debt. For these children the prospect of a return to such a financial situation seemed daunting. These concerns can be seen particularly in children's heightened fears about what would happen if their mothers stopped working. Hussain's experiences illustrate this well (names have been changed to protect anonymity). He is eight years old, and here he is talking about why he thinks it is important for his mum to keep working:

> 'Because then we'll have enough money and we'll have enough food. Because sometimes we run out of food and then we don't have enough money to get some and so like if the power went out and we had no money we wouldn't be able to get another ticket for it.'

It may well be that children who have had very little in the past, and are now experiencing a time of increased financial well-being, greater social engagement and treats, have a strong incentive to ensure that their mothers' employment is sustainable. It is in the light of these past (and for some children still very present) experiences of poverty, coupled with their experiences as children in lone-mother households, that we should try to understand their roles as active caring agents within their families.

What roles do children play in low-income lone-mother households?

When children talked about their family lives and the roles they played in working lone-mother households, their accounts revealed a complex range of caring and supporting activities. These contributions to family life tended to fall into four key categories:

(1) Helping around the house – this included domestic chores, cleaning, washing and cooking.
(2) Financial support – through the moderation of needs to reduce financial pressures, children's own work contributions and money sharing.
(3) Childcare – part of children's responsibilities within families was to care for themselves, some of the children were also engaged in sibling care, and others were involved in a diverse range of formal and informal types of care.
(4) Emotional support – for parents and other siblings.

Looking at each one of these areas of care and support, it is possible to see that children can play a very active role in their families.

Helping around the house

One of the issues confronting working mothers, especially lone mothers, is the double burden of work and care that they are shouldering. A key component of this is the everyday practice of household tasks, the maintenance of the family home and the undertaking of the domestic chores that keep homes running smoothly; cleaning, washing and cooking are central activities in the practice of doing housework. But when we look at children's accounts of their activities at home, almost all of the children in the sample are engaged in some form of housework to sustain their family well-being.

This was not gendered; boys as well as girls were performing housework practices; cleaning, tidying up, vacuuming, dusting, polishing and washing the car. This increase in responsibilities was identified as an outcome of their mothers' employment; they were not doing as many household chores before their mothers were working. But in order for families to sustain work and maintain family life, the responsibility for keeping the house tidy and clean has to be shared between children and mothers. Children like Lucas (eight years old) are well aware that their mothers' efforts at work need to be supported by increased efforts at home:

> 'Like we have to pick up all our stuff now because Mum's been at work and she wants a rest, so we pick up all our stuff and take it all upstairs, then do the dishes and all that.'

Some children are helping on a regular basis, often working to a rota of chores. This is Lauren, who is 14 years old, talking about her chores and her responsibilities when her mother is working in the holidays:

> 'Tidying up my bedroom more and like washing up dishes when she's not here and vacuuming ... if she leaves in the morning and like she leaves about half seven, she leaves us a note on the side telling us what to do before we can go down [to where her mother is working].'

As well as cleaning, some children are also doing the washing and laundry; in some cases washing their own school uniform.

Some children were also doing the cooking on a regular basis, producing food for themselves or for their families. For example, Ella is 12 years old; she has a baby sister who she helps to care for. As well as cleaning, she cooks the tea for her family every other evening. Many children were making their own food, especially their own sandwiches for school or making themselves tea when they came home before their mothers got home from work. For some children, like Roshan (12 years old), this has meant learning new skills and taking on new responsibilities:

> 'Coming home, using the key, locking up, um drying up the dishes and all that, making my own food using the grill and the oven and what do you call it, the cooker thing. Yeah, using the matches to do that, I learnt those ages ago.'

Shannon, who is 15 years old, had taken on responsibility for looking after exchange students who were lodging in her house to help increase their family income. This meant carrying out a range of general chores as well as cooking the lodgers' food in the evenings when her mother was still at work.

Responsibilities within the home are constantly negotiated between children and their parents (Such and Walker, 2004). In general, children's chores appeared to be undertaken freely, but there are pressures within families and mothers who are working are often stressed and under strain at work and at home. Without another adult to share the tasks, ensuring that children take on more responsibilities can be essential. However, while some children indicated that they felt under pressure to do domestic chores, in general children just identified them as extra responsibilities taken on since their mothers were working.

Financial support

Children were also engaged in trying to alleviate financial pressures where and when they could. This was particularly the case for children whose mothers were no longer working, and for those who were in particularly low-paid employment. The issue of children's roles and engagement in financial support in the family is a complex one, and can take several forms.

One of the key ways in which poor children can act to alleviate financial pressures within their families is by moderating their wants and needs to diffuse tensions and ease the strain on already overburdened family finances (Ridge, 2002). This strategy also shields them from disappointment, and protects their mothers from worry. Previous research shows that parents try to protect their children from the experience of poverty in childhood (Kempson et al, 1994; Middleton et al, 1997; Goode et al, 1998), but research shows this act of care is also reciprocal (Ridge, 2002). For many of the children in this study, life before their mothers' recent employment was characterised by poverty and exclusion, and although children in general felt better off financially since their mothers were working, some of them did not. Several of them were still clearly managing and restricting their needs and expectations, some overtly, but others more covertly. This is Courtney (15 years old) explaining how she tries to manage her needs without asking her mother for extra:

> 'Well, I don't like asking Mum for money that much so I try not to. Just don't really ask about it…. It's not that I'm

scared; it's just that I feel bad for wanting it. I don't know, sounds stupid, but, like, sometimes I save up my school dinner money and I don't eat at school and then I can save it up and have more money. Don't tell her that!'

Moderating behaviour can manifest itself in unusual ways. Some children in the study were clearly making careful judgements about their health. If they felt ill, they were trying to make decisions about whether or not to tell their mothers and have time away from school. Although we might think children love nothing better than time off school with a minor sickness, some of the children in the study, like Lewis (12 years old), were clearly weighing up the economic consequences for their families of their mothers losing a day's pay to look after them. Lewis worries that if he is away ill his mother might not get paid:

'Once I had really bad tonsillitis and I just went to school because my Mum, like, was getting paid that day and she had to work.'

Another way in which children in low-income families sought to contribute financially to the household was through their own employment. How to gain access to their own autonomously controlled money is a key issue for poor children whose lives have been characterised by constraint and financial restriction. Previous research has shown that children who are on a restricted income at home use their own employment to increase their social and economic well-being (Middleton et al, 1994; Mizen et al, 2001; Ridge, 2002).

In general, children in the study showed a keen understanding of the financial situation in their families, revealing their acute awareness of the costs of everyday essentials like food, petrol, electricity and gas. This everyday knowledge, ordinarily the preserve of adults, can have a profound impact on their perceptions of financial well-being. Many were living in households that had cut down in the past on food, clothes and other social activities; for some, bills remained ever present and pressing. So even with an increased income from their mothers' employment, some children in the study were still trying to mitigate the worst effects of being poor. Taking on employment enabled them to buy clothes, pay for their own transport and leisure activities, use their money to go out with friends, go to the shops, go to the cinema and sometimes to pay for school trips and school items. For children like TK (12 years old), who was working on the market every Sunday picking up litter, the money he earned was used to buy his weekly magazine, and some clothes. Therefore children who were working were playing a significant role in easing some of the financial strain in their families.

Sometimes children were receiving their own incomes from other sources such as non-resident fathers or grandparents. This gave them access to more money than they would normally receive from their mothers' income, and this could at times be used to help their mothers financially. These are significant contributions from children who do not have easy or regular access to money. Some children are helping overtly, like Abiola (11 years old) who used to split the money he got from his father half and half with his mother, and Jake (10 years old) who has lent his mother money but knows that she can't pay him back:

> 'I'm getting used to it though, not, like, paying back things, 'cos she ain't got enough money yet. She's got to work, work, go to Asda and everything, so she hasn't got time yet really to pay me back.'

Others are giving money more covertly, like Ella (12 years old) who helps her mother when she can. She gets pocket money from her grandmother and tries to pass some of it on to her mother – a gentle, caring and altruistic gesture:

> 'If she ever buys me things I always say I'll pay her and she won't let me pay so in the end I get the money out of my money box and put it in her purse, and then she takes it because she doesn't realise it's in there, and then she spends it.'

Childcare

How to balance work and care responsibilities is a traditional area of concern for mothers, and central to this is the issue of childcare. Employment presents considerable challenges for lone mothers, including time pressures and the challenge of finding and managing appropriate after-school care for their children (Skinner, 2003; Bell et al, 2005). Many mothers in the sample had arranged their work so that they were mainly employed during school hours, reducing the need to draw on childcare; however, for others, successful after-school arrangements were a vital component of sustaining work.

Because of the need for after-school care, children in the study had a wide range of caring experiences occurring in different spatial and temporal locations. Many, especially the older children, were caring for themselves, letting themselves in at night, or leaving last in the morning. They were taking responsibilities, as we have seen, for cooking and cleaning for themselves as well as their families. For some older children in particular, self-care and time alone (without adults) brought greater freedoms as well as responsibilities.

As well as undertaking self-care there were also children in the study who had the responsibility of caring for their siblings. Fourteen children identified that they were responsible for caring for their siblings while their mothers were working. For some of the families, brothers and sisters caring for younger siblings was an integral part of sustaining their mothers in work and provided a vital component in the family-work project. Other children were carers on a more irregular basis, making sure that their mothers had time off and a break from responsibilities and care of young children when they were not at work. Sibling care did not always mean younger siblings; and one girl of 15 whose mother worked nights was getting her older brother up in the mornings to make sure he went to college. Harry (12 years old) cares for his younger brother on Saturday and Sunday nights when their mother is working late in the pub. He likes the increase in responsibility, although he sometimes falls out with his siblings. Here he explains the rules he has established for Saturday nights:

'They can watch Casualty and then they have to go to their rooms, and then they can do what they want there.'

Other children in the study were experiencing a range of different caring situations, including care by older siblings, aunts, grandparents, family friends or their fathers. Younger children were often receiving formal childcare mainly from after-school clubs or childminders. Some children whose mothers were working late, or working nights, were staying overnight with close relatives (often a grandparent) on a regular basis. What is often overlooked in policy and research is the role played by children themselves in ensuring that care regimes work. While childcare can be a valuable and enriching experience for some children, for others it is not. Although many children in the study were too old for formal childcare and were involved in managing self-care, those who did require childcare were often enduring formal care that seemed to be unsuitable and inadequate for their needs. The issue of childcare and after-school clubs is important for children, and yet some of them viewed provision of care very disparagingly. Where after-school clubs worked well, they were a valuable opportunity for children to make and sustain new friendships outside of school. However, for those who did not like school, or who were being bullied at school, the prospect of staying on for after-school clubs was not welcomed. After-school clubs were often seen as boring and restrictive, and for older children the presence of younger children often meant poorly targeted play opportunities.

Emotional support

Employment, particularly low-income employment, presents real challenges to the well-being of families, especially when mothers are under pressure at work or are still struggling to manage their income or deal with debts. Under these circumstances, some children were clearly spending time nurturing and providing emotional support to their mothers. On one level we understand that lone mothers often come home to a household where there are no other adults to share the stresses and strains of the day, but what we sometimes forget is that there are children in the house, and these children often play a vital role easing and absorbing emotional pressures. The children provided emotional support in a myriad of ways; making sure that the house was tidy, that chores were done and siblings cared for. They provided simple acts of kindness – cups of tea, cooked food, quiet time without demands.

Tiredness and stress from work was one of the key concerns that children mentioned in relation to their mothers' working, and financial stress and debt was still a worry for many. Although the majority of the children felt financially better off since their mothers were working, their families were still on relatively low incomes and they still had concerns about having sufficient money, employment security and, in some cases, debt. This can mean that some children are sharing some of the heavier financial and emotional challenges that working lone mothers face. Here is Jake (aged 10 years), who is the oldest child in the family, talking about his mother sharing her worries with him:

'Sometimes when Mum's struggling and she needs to talk to us all, I help.... I like ... talk to her with my brother and sister in bed, and we have a really good chat about what's happening and everything.'

Several children in the study were concerned about their mothers' well-being at work, and had seen their mothers being depressed and stressed; others were unhappy that their mothers were being bullied or were unsafe at work. This can result in uncertainty and insecurity about work. (Eleven-year-old) Josie's mother has changed her employment because she found the work too demanding. For her daughter this was a period of concern about her mother's well-being:

> 'She was, like, really stressful when she came home, 'cos they pushed her too hard I think, 'cos she worked for a hotel and I think that they made her work too hard and she came home, like pretty stressed.'

In the absence of another adult partner, children sometimes appeared to be assuming the role of parent as well as confidant. The mother–daughter dyad was particularly strong in some cases, and girls' discourses on caring showed close similarities to discourses on mothering. Protection and 'mothering' sometimes extended to keeping tabs on their mothers, trying to ensure that they were content at work, happy at home and safe when they were out socially. Here is Merlene (14 years old) talking about how protective she feels about her mother:

> 'I'm very close to my Mum ... I get very worried when she goes out and stuff, and I can't wait to hear her key coming in or stuff like that or hear her coming in through the door. Like I'm always going to her bedroom as well, I sleep in her bed and make sure that I wait for her to come back. I'm really protective of my mum and she knows that as well.'

In general, children were both protective and supportive of their mothers and clearly understood some of the challenges they faced trying to manage work and home life.

Conclusions

By positioning children as active social agents within their families, we are able to have a more holistic understanding of family life; one that embraces children's agency and perspectives alongside those of their parents. It is evident from the accounts of children in this study that they have an active engagement with duties and responsibilities, and that their individual strategies of care and support all contribute towards sustaining working family life in lone-mother households. To understand children's contributions to sustaining family cohesion around issues of work and care, we need first to acknowledge their commitment to the family-work project and their understandings of their roles within it. If we look at the contributions of children across a range of areas – domestic chores, financial support, childcare and emotional care – it is apparent that these children are making considerable contributions to the well-being of their families. They are helping out in the home across a range of domestic practices, including cleaning, washing and cooking. They are also engaged in strategies of financial support; often moderating their own needs and desires to reduce pressure and to alleviate financial worries. They are competent self-carers and, in some cases, carers of their siblings. They also accept complex spatially and temporally challenging childcare arrangements, which may be unsuitable for their needs and impinge upon their time with their mothers and their friends. They are also competent and thoughtful emotional carers, sharing confidences and supporting and protecting their mothers where and when they can.

Far from being passive and needy family members, it is apparent that these children are actively participating in constructing and reconstructing family life under very particular social and financial circumstances. These are low-income children who have experienced periods of poverty and exclusion. The experience of poverty in childhood is a damaging one, and we still know very little about how children mediate the experience of poverty or the impact a spell of poverty can have on children's future perceptions of security and well-being. For these children there are clear incentives to try and sustain the family project of work, despite the hidden costs evident in increased practical, social and emotional responsibilities. These are also children living in lone-mother households who have in many cases experienced family upheaval and change. Children's concerns and strategies of support may well reflect in some ways the intensity of reciprocal caring relationships that can develop within lone-parent households. Finally, these findings also have implications for policy, not least in relation to the quality of social and economic support that lone mothers and their children are given, and the suitability of after-school childcare that is accessible for children.

Notes
[1] Funded by the Economic and Social Research Council (Reference RES-000-23-1079). Jane Millar's chapter (Chapter Thirteen) is based on data from the interviews with parents in the same study.

[2] The sample was drawn from official records of Tax Credit recipients and we are very grateful to HM Revenue & Customs for their help in this.

Part Five
From welfare subjects to active citizens

SIXTEEN

Making connections: supporting new forms of engagement by marginalised groups

Karen Postle and Peter Beresford

Introduction

This chapter explores the implications of two competing discourses on participation: the consumerist discourse and one concerned with empowerment, democratisation and liberation. These discourses are situated in the context of their relationship to welfare provision and changes therein since the 1980s. Drawing on recent research, the chapter connects participation in political activity with the development of movements of people using health and social care services.[1] It discusses the implications these may have for the nature of involvement and, indeed, of democracy. It therefore illustrates some of the more theoretical issues about the role of service users, and the knowledge they contribute to policy and practice processes that were raised in Chapter Four. This chapter also considers the changing role of care professionals in relation to forms of participation that can liberate and empower rather than construct people who use services or give care/support solely as consumers in a care market.

Context: the residualisation of state welfare provision in the UK

In 2005 a major new political discourse was initiated about welfare provision in the UK (see also Chapter Seventeen). Social care tends to be marginalised in political debates but this discussion emanated from the Prime Minister's Strategy Unit, bearing his formal imprint. Its initial focus was on disabled people but its influence is spreading across a range of service user groups (DH, 2005). This new discussion focuses on 'individual budgets', converting services to notional or actual entitlements that can be used flexibly to secure the range and types of support that an individual prefers. As the Prime Minister makes clear, the proposal to introduce individual budgets is at the heart of government thinking about 'improving the life chances of disabled people':

> I asked the Strategy Unit to look at what more we can do to improve disabled people's opportunities, to improve their quality of life and strengthen our society. Despite considerable progress, disabled people are still experiencing disadvantage and discrimination. Barriers ... still have to be overcome by disabled people, reducing their opportunities and preventing them fulfilling their potential. Too many services are organised to suit providers *rather than being personalised around the needs of disabled people.* (Prime Minister's Strategy Unit, 2005, p 3; emphasis added)

This is the latest in a series of developments going back 25 years in the UK. All reflect a shift away from the dominant view that the state should be the main organiser and provider of health and social care, to an emphasis on the private market as a key funder and provider of services. During this period two related, often overlapping, discourses of the market and of participatory approaches in health and social care have also emerged.

These debates raise some important issues for long-term users of health and social care services. This chapter examines these two discourses, and their relationship to each other, drawing on material from recent research. This research is described in detail elsewhere (Postle and Beresford, 2005; Postle et al, 2005). In summary, it ascertained the views and experiences of a range of people, including long-term users of health and social care services, about citizenship and political participation. The research took place in two phases. The first was conducted in 1998, one year after the election of a Labour government in the UK following 18 years of Conservative governments. The second phase was in 2001/02 and coincided with the General Election preceding Labour's second term in office. This enabled comparisons to be made over time and some account to be taken of the impact of New Labour policies. The research comprised discussion groups in England and Scotland.

Challenges to traditional public welfare provision

The shift to an emphasis on marketisation in welfare policy began with the election of a 'New Right' Conservative government in the UK in 1979. This has had an enduring effect on public policy. Three themes shaped government attitudes to welfare during the 1980s: concern about the costs of public services; distrust of a 'nanny' welfare state, which was thought to create and perpetuate 'dependence'; and 'dislike' of inefficient government intervention and a preference for a greater role for the private market in welfare (Means and Smith, 1998).

This led to the residualisation of social services provision (Walker, 1997). Social care, constructed as 'community care', became a vanguard policy for advancing the welfare ideology of the New Right. The funding of welfare services now became an explicitly ideological issue. Restricting public expenditure, charging people for services and fostering expectations that people should make their own provision for welfare were all presented as virtues (Means et al, 2002). The new role of the 'care manager', replacing that of social worker, was part of a rationing, rather than a facilitative, process (Gorman and Postle, 2003).

Disquiet and dissatisfaction with existing public provision came from several quarters and was not solely driven by the ethos of successive Conservative governments. While not necessarily sharing the same political agenda and desire to reduce public expenditure, their rhetoric chimed with many wider concerns. Thus, there was broader public concern about the cost, lack of responsiveness and poor quality of much public welfare provision. In the early 1980s, public services were criticised for being bureaucratic, over-centralised and dominated by professionals. This critique resonated with both the public in general and with progressive commentators (Hadley and Hatch, 1981).

Welfare professionals and other workers wanting to work in different, more egalitarian ways were unhappy about the inflexibility and lack of accountability that characterised the practices of their employing agencies and advocated anti-paternalistic ways of working (London Edinburgh Weekend Return Group, 1979). New kinds of support services demonstrated that different, more reciprocal arrangements were possible. The growth of self-directed and self-managed lesbian help/support lines, rape crisis centres, women's and black women's refuges, and advocacy and buddy schemes based on more equal relationships between service users and providers met needs that had previously not been addressed and were also often run in more collaborative ways.

New philosophies gave greater force to, and emphasis on, inclusion and participation. 'Normalisation' or 'social role valorisation', emphasising social integration and a valued life, offered a coherent value base for services (O'Brien and Tyne, 1981). Although criticised for its dependence on prevailing values, this approach was influential for people with learning difficulties and other groups of social care service users in challenging traditional segregating and paternalistic approaches to policy and services.

Service user movements: the growth of active citizens

A concurrent, significant development was the emergence of strong service user movements. People pressed for a greater say about their lives and the services they used. Movements included those of disabled people, people with learning difficulties, young people in state 'care', older people and mental health service users. They were frequently unhappy with services offered to them or which they were forced to use, and they wanted changes (Morris, 1991; Oliver, 1996; Shakespeare, 2000).

The growth of movements of people using social and health services at local, national and international levels was marked by a shift from self-help and mutual support activities to direct involvement in service provision and in campaigning and direct action for service improvement (Barnes, 1997; Carter and Beresford, 2000; Turner et al, 2003). This shift epitomised the change from people using welfare services being passive recipients to active citizens (Prior et al, 1995; Barnes, 1997).

Thus, two key discourses developed concurrently, both concerned with welfare provision. One, energised by the New Right, was concerned with the organisation and funding of services. The other, initiated by service user movements and their allies, focused primarily on service users' perspectives and concerns. While these two discourses and developments overlapped, their underpinning ideologies, aims and objectives differed. Only the latter explicitly constructed people as active citizens capable of shaping their own lives.

However, these two discourses had a meeting point; both advocated a shift from service-led provision to user-centred services. Both placed considerable emphasis on user involvement as a means to achieve this. As a result, user involvement has become a key concept in health and social care, with increasing requirements for it in legislation, policy, practice, professional education, research and service provision.

Competing concepts of involvement

'User involvement' does not have an agreed meaning within the different discourses of service users and the New Right. Rather, it represents an area of struggle where disagreements and tensions between the two ideologies are enacted. This section examines different approaches to user involvement, in order to understand its complex and contested meanings. Historically, typologies of participation have highlighted the extent of involvement (Arnstein, 1969). Here, the focus is on the ideological underpinnings of different approaches to participation.

Currently, the different approaches to participation are frequently confused and conflated. A predominantly managerialist and consumerist model has emanated from the New Right's ideological approach to public policy. It is exemplified in the Griffiths Report's recommendation that people receiving help should have a greater say in what is done to help them, and a wider choice (Griffiths, 1988). The report heavily influenced the Conservative government's approach to community care, which has continued, essentially unchanged, within current Labour social policy. Its focus is the service system and its concern is to ensure that service users inform the nature of services and provision. The approach is technicist in nature and presented as a neutral means of information gathering akin to market research, where the emphasis is on information gathering rather than action. There is no suggestion of a redistribution of power to service users in this approach.

In contrast, the democratic approach to user involvement originated in the disabled people's and service user movements' struggles for liberation and is consistent with active citizenship. It is much more concerned with improving people's lives. This approach highlights the need for people as actual and potential users of services to have more say over services and more control over their lives in general. This approach has been influential and contributed to change, but nonetheless represents a counter, rather than a dominant, discourse (Beresford and Croft, 1996). In sharp contrast to the managerialist and consumerist approach, the democratic approach addresses power imbalances.

The dominance of the managerialist and consumerist discourse has led some service users to become highly critical of initiatives for service user involvement, feeling over-consulted and reluctant to continue getting involved when frequently few significant changes and improvements in social care policy result (Bewley and Glendinning,

1994; Campbell, 1996; Carter and Beresford, 2000). Fundamental concerns have also been raised about the common failure to evaluate what, if any, difference such involvement makes in social care services (Carr, 2004).

Declining conventional political participation

The development of debates around user involvement in health and welfare policy and practice, and the increasing emphasis upon this, have coincided with growing concerns about people's reduced participation in conventional political processes like voting and membership of mainstream political parties. Few attempts seem to have been made to examine the relationship between these apparently contradictory discourses and developments. However, both have significant implications for service users' participation in the design and delivery of services.

The rise of new social movements, such as movements of service users, has taken place at the same time as a decline in participation in traditional forms of political activity (Todd and Taylor, 2004). This decline is exemplified by voter turnout in UK General Elections. Turnout peaked at 84% in 1950, but declined to 77.7% in 1992 and 71.6% in 1997 (Russell et al, 2002), leading the government to establish the Electoral Commission and investigate strategies for increasing voter turnout. A further drop to 59.4% in the 2001 General Election exacerbated concerns and intensified efforts to increase voter turnout. Considerable effort has focused on increasing voter turnout through techniques such as electronic, Internet and postal voting (Wintour, 2001; Hetherington, 2002; Ward, 2002). Another indicator of declining interest and involvement in traditional political activity is the reduced number of people joining mainstream political parties, which now compares unfavourably with membership of organisations such as The National Trust or the Royal Society for the Protection of Birds (Walker, 2001).

This disenchantment with traditional politics mirrors similar disaffection in the US (Herz, 2001). Herz notes that poorer people and sections of communities that are particularly marginalised are least likely to vote – despite the fact that these same people will have benefited least from government policies and most need to see changes in service provision.

The research summarised earlier in this chapter (Postle and Beresford, 2005; Postle et al, 2005) indicated two broad factors contributing to the lack of involvement in conventional political activity: immediate obstacles and a sense of disenchantment. Examples of immediate obstacles included the use of unfamiliar language and/or jargon; the lack of time required to attend or get involved; the timing of meetings; the stamina required to participate; and cost. Often, the things people described as preventing them from participating in political activity mirrored the physical and attitudinal obstacles which people in marginalised groups experience as contributing to their exclusion. To take the example of language and jargon:

'I know that some deaf people go to political meetings, but they always say ... "If you find an interpreter I will attend that meeting" ... sometimes it's hard for them to actually find an interpreter.... When they have, like, the annual conferences for Labour or Tories, yes, they provide an interpreter at those large gatherings, but at a local level I don't think they provide interpreters.' (Man, disabled people's group)

'The problem is that to get more people involved you need first of all people who are articulate in English, OK, because that is the nature of the meetings. There might be a person who is quite capable of attending the meeting but they don't have the English ... there is no one to support them, to translate for them.' (Man, minority ethnic forum)

'Half the words they say you can't understand what the hell they mean.' (Man, young people's group)

'They've got to stop using some jargon ... not treating as if the general public are stupid but saying it, perhaps, in terms that we can understand ... perhaps explaining things a bit better.' (Woman, disabled people's group)

Both time and costs also proved obstacles to participation:

'[Support/caring responsibilities are] 24 hours a day, 365 days a year.' (Woman, adult mental health carers' group)

'[Taking part in political activity is] a heavy burden on you, the time, the cost.' (Man, minority ethnic forum)

'You find there are an awful lot of people out there and they are not allowed to participate because they get their benefits cut because they are taking too much time; they're not classified as available for work, people who can't take expenses because they're taking too much money in a week ... it's ridiculous.' (Woman in group involved in activities associated with Single Regeneration Budget funding)

'For me to attend all these meetings, I have to pay my own money to travel to get there and back whatever ... not many people could be able to afford to do that ... how can you tell people you have got to take part but you have also got to be out of pocket?' (Man, minority ethnic forum)

These obstacles may appear obvious but what causes concern, however, is their persistent nature. This is particularly worrying because the very people whose lives are likely to be affected by the outcome of political debates find themselves excluded from them (Lister, 2000).

The other major obstacle to participation in political activity cited by most people was disenchantment. This was expressed as ineffectiveness or powerlessness, mistrust of politicians and political systems and politicians' lack of interest. It compounded the immediate obstacles outlined above, leaving people feeling excluded from political processes:

'I voted when I was 18. It's a waste of time. They're professional liars.' (Man, young people's group)

'The party I joined, they've got less and less democratic. They don't want to listen to the ordinary members and, when they complain about the lack of people going out to vote, I think they should just look at themselves.' (Man, pensioners' forum)

'They [politicians] don't take that much interest in people with disabilities.' (Man, disabled people's organisation)

Young people's disaffection, as exemplified by the young man quoted above, is particularly interesting because it has often been labelled as 'apathy'. This issue is complex because there is evidence that young people are certainly engaging in forms of activity that they consider political, such as signing petitions, going on demonstrations or taking part in protest actions within schools (National Centre for Social Research, 2000; CYPU, 2002; Park et al, 2004).

Despite the initiatives noted above, voter turnout continues to cause concern. The root of the problem seems to be that key issues of disenchantment and disaffection are not being addressed. As one research participant summarised it:

> 'It's not because it's not easy for people to vote. They don't vote because they can't be bothered. Not because it's difficult. It's because they're disillusioned. It's because they don't feel they can change anything – will my vote make any difference?' (Man, 'Area Parliament' initiative)

People acknowledged that there had been some improvements, such as new ways of voting. However, they felt that, overall, improvements were not significant or had only come about as a result of their own campaigning activities. For example:

> 'I belong to a group [of activists] and some people went to the polling stations to make sure they're accessible.... We had to fight for it.' (Man, disabled people's group)

These examples reflect the reasons given for not participating in conventional political activity. People interviewed were, however, often taking part in activities that some people described as 'political, with a small p'. These are now described.

Successful involvement in political activities

While some service users reported negative experiences of 'getting involved', the picture emerging from this research was more complex. Although many expressed negative views about conventional political participation, they also felt that they had achieved real gains from engaging politically in different ways, some of which equate to forms of user involvement. People talked of gaining strength and encouragement from successes achieved through campaigning and direct action and reported a number of examples.

For example, an adult mental health carers' group, whose original aims were self-help and mutual support, had lobbied Parliament and made their views heard about changes in mental health legislation:

'The most important change, and it actually did come initially from our carers' group, is that with the new Mental Health Act, they're actually pushing through that people will be accountable and have to give reasons. For example, if you ask "can my relative be on this particular medication?" and it is expensive and you are refused the medication, they will have to put in writing the reasons why you were refused the medication ... and that did actually come from this carers' group, and it has fed up to government....'
(Woman, adult mental health carers' group)

The young people's group had achieved a local community centre:

'We got a petition together, and what have you, and got everyone's points that wanted a community centre. After a long period of time we got it built ... there was a load of us that did it and we all stuck together.' (Man, young people's group)

Disabled people had secured accessible polling stations; had successfully campaigned for accessible council meetings and a road crossing; and had gained the involvement of some politicians. For example:

'The group has done very good things for access problems in this part and they've achieved paving up the parking [to level the area and improve access] on the high street. It took them two years to do it but they did it.' (Man, disabled people's group)

People in a minority ethnic community forum had achieved provision for cultural and religious needs within local hospitals and, through this, become involved in improving provision nationally:

'[We are now] having Halal food and a place for prayers, and all those have come about because we have participated in their consultation and working together.... I have been invited onto the national body to represent the housekeeping and the good food in the hospital project.' (Man, minority ethnic forum)

The older people's forum was campaigning on a number of issues:

'We've had tremendous campaigns on the pensions. I can't tell you how many thousands of signatures we've got over the years on the question of TV licences, heating allowances, health and community care. We organised two very well-attended conferences prior to the 1993 Act coming in on health and community care. We've transport, we've campaigned on transport....' (Woman, pensioners' forum)

These examples all illustrate increasing use of forms of direct or participatory democracy, in contrast to traditional, representative democracy with which there was widespread disenchantment.

Managerialist/consumerist approaches to participation: outcomes and impact

Significantly, the kinds of successful political participation reported above tended to be based on a democratic model of involvement rather than a managerialist/consumerist one. They were examples of people taking control about issues concerning them, rather than relying on conventional political processes from which they often felt alienated. This should raise a note of caution, considering that most user involvement initiatives take a managerialist/consumerist approach. Other research raises further concerns about the degree to which opportunities for involvement in policy and provision have actually led to improvements in the quality of social care and broader social conditions facing service users. Two studies are briefly mentioned here.

In research commissioned by the Department of Health to ascertain people's views of, and proposals for, social care (Beresford et al, 2005), service users described the current social care system as grossly underfunded. They reported poor-quality provision and charges that prevented people from obtaining the support they needed. Service users talked of struggling to get help, patchy provision, inflexibility, excessive red tape and staff who were frequently unreliable and of poor quality, with private agencies a particular cause for concern. People with learning difficulties described fears of being bullied in the services they used. Many service users said they received personal care that only met their bodily needs, rather than social care that enabled them to go out and participate in their community.

Second, the Disability Rights Commission commissioned research into the barriers facing disabled people (Sutherland et al, 2005). 'Disabled people' included people with learning difficulties, mental health service users, people with physical and sensory impairments, older people with impairments, young disabled people and palliative care service users. All participants reported facing barriers of different kinds. These included attitudinal barriers created by non-disabled people and barriers relating to the built environment, transport, access to goods and services, education and training, employment and in health, social care and welfare. Care, support and welfare services, including the benefits system, presented huge barriers. Problems of inadequate social care services, poor-quality services, cuts in services and lack of interpreters were all reported.

On the basis of what service users reported in these two studies, it is difficult to conclude that arrangements for user involvement have led to significant improvements in social care and related services. However, a further issue relates to the conceptualisation, construction and terminology of social care. Social care is still essentially framed in the same traditional terms as when it was primarily a free public service, rather than a largely market-driven service for which users are expected to pay means-tested charges. Where this conceptualisation has changed, it has been the consumerist approach that has predominated, rather than the democratic and liberatory approaches advanced by service users. The development of direct payments exemplifies this.

Direct payments, instigated by disabled people themselves, represent a major innovation resulting in a radically different approach to social support and service provision. Based on a social model of disability, the idea is that disabled people control their own package of support, enabling them to live as independently as and on as equal terms as possible to non-disabled people. Direct payments were seen as part of a broader strategy to secure the rights of disabled people, which would also include resourcing local centres for independent living controlled by disabled people, one of whose roles would be supporting people to access direct payments (Hasler et al, 1999; Hasler, 2004). Despite the origins of direct payments in a human rights-based philosophy, this is not how they appear to have been understood or implemented. Instead, a mixture of professional and consumerist models have been applied. Increasingly direct payments have been treated as though they are an individualised process for the purchase of care akin to the care management model. The process of assessment has continued to be professionally dominated; arbitrary and inequitable cash ceilings linked to the cost of institutional care are widely imposed; and private agencies have increasingly been brought in to manage direct payments schemes.

Democratic approaches to participation: seeds of optimism

Direct payments exemplify continuing tensions between managerialist/consumerist and democratic approaches to service provision and user involvement. The example also raises concerns about how much is being achieved to improve social care support in response to service user organisations' proposals and preferences. The prevailing managerialist/consumerist model of user involvement does not seem to be working to achieve this. The people interviewed in the study reported above who felt that they had made progress tended to have done so through methods more often associated with democratic approaches to participation. This suggests that a more helpful route for developing social care services in line with what service users want is a more participative politics, which includes, and is related to, a democratic model of user involvement.

There is little evidence to indicate that UK governments are taking steps to support the kind of critical democracy which 'is characterised by increased participation and empowerment, often on the part of people normally excluded from political activity' (Blaug, 2002, p 106). Participatory democracy offers opportunities for people, as active citizens, to make a real impact on policy decisions affecting their lives. It enables them to move beyond endless ineffective consultation processes (Carter and Beresford, 2000). As one man said:

> 'Our main concern is, is it consultation or is it just verification of what is going on? ... Positive action, if it is there, will encourage people to say, "Ah we can see the results, we are not here only as a talking shop".' (Man, minority ethnic forum)

There are some notable exceptions such as Better Government for Older People (2003), but overall little has been done to address the difficulties, such as lack of confidence and time constraints, which people experience when they want to become involved in campaigning activity (Birchall and Simmons, 2004). This will need to change if social care policy initiatives like direct payments and individual budgets are to take progressive rather than regressive forms and service users are to exert effective influence alongside other stakeholders. Participation that is not integrated into the reform of broader political processes is ultimately unlikely to be effective.

UK governments appear to have recognised the importance of

service user involvement in the design and delivery of social care services and responded by establishing various initiatives to ensure that people's voices will be heard in social care provision. This is exemplified by including people using social care services as key stakeholders in the design and delivery of the new social work degree programme introduced in the UK in 2003 (DH, 2002). The danger here is that such involvement can be reduced to a managerialist/ consumerist model of 'ticking the box' when people who use services have been consulted about their views.

As this chapter has argued, for participation to be meaningful and empowering and to have the potential to liberate, this cannot be an appropriate model. Rather, social care professionals and their managers need to challenge dominant market/consumerist ideology and explore ways of working with people that build their capacity for strength and growth. This can include, as the participants in our study told us, supporting them in their campaigning activity. There are seeds of optimism in such ways of working but they require a shift away from predominantly individualistic approaches, towards approaches that work much more closely with and within communities.

This chapter began by citing the Prime Minister's Foreword to *Improving the life chances of disabled people* (Prime Minister's Strategy Unit, 2005). In the 2005 Green Paper on adult social care services, the government set out plans for extending cash payments or their equivalent entitlement to support up to a specified value, with which individuals can secure the services of their choice (Department of Health, 2005). This suggests a brokerage model of social work/care management for those people needing advice and/or support in choosing and managing their support arrangements. Such a model may superficially appear potentially empowering; it gives service users power and control over their support, in forms of their choice. In reality, as with direct payments, resource constraints and lack of real choices mean that individual needs may remain unmet and a passive relationship between service user and provider is perpetuated (Huxley, 1993). Furthermore, a brokerage model overlooks the skill and complexity of the social work task and its potential to work in ways that can challenge users' disempowerment (Braye and Preston-Shoot, 1995; Smale et al, 2000). These developments risk perpetuating the consumerist model, which has done few favours to people using services or those giving care/support. The model minimises the social work role and ignores the full scope of its potential for emancipatory and liberatory work consistent with models of participation encompassing direct democracy.

Note

[1] This chapter uses the term 'service user'; however, we recognise that, for some people who use services, this is not their preferred term (see Beresford, 2005).

SEVENTEEN

Independent living: the role of the disability movement in the development of government policy

Jenny Morris

Introduction

During 2005, the British government committed itself to achieving independent living for disabled people and set out proposals for delivering this aim. This chapter[1] examines the role of research evidence and the disability movement in influencing government policy, situating the discussion in the context of wider debates on citizenship, human rights and the role of the state. It also asks whether these new proposals further an individualist and consumerist approach to meeting needs, thus undermining the collectivism and public service ethos that have been such an important part of the welfare state; or whether they will help disabled people to achieve the active citizenship that previous social policies have failed to deliver. It therefore illustrates the changing role and nature of 'evidence' in the policy process described in Chapter Four; and extends some of the arguments on choice, consumerism and citizenship set out in Chapters Sixteen and Eighteen.

The government's proposals

In January 2005, the Strategy Unit in the Cabinet Office of the British government published a detailed report and proposals for a 20-year programme of change entitled *Improving the life chances of disabled people* (Prime Minister's Strategy Unit, 2005). At the heart of these proposals was a commitment to promote independent living for disabled people and introduce 'a new approach' which:

- addresses all aspects of needs for support and/or equipment or adaptations;
- is personalised according to individual need and circumstances;
- is underpinned by the principle of listening to disabled people and acknowledging their expertise in how to meet their needs;
- maximises the choice and control that people have over how their additional requirements are met;
- provides people with security and certainty about what level of support is available;
- wherever possible, minimises disincentives to seek paid employment or to move from one locality to another;
- uses existing resources to maximise social inclusion (Prime Minister's Strategy Unit, 2005).

This 'new approach' aims to give individuals choice and control over how their support needs are met, replacing the existing fragmentation of needs across different central and local government agencies and departments by introducing individual budgets. Individuals would be allocated a budget, based on eligible assessed need, and they would choose how to use this budget, with advocacy support where needed. The budget could be taken as a cash payment or in the form of services, or a combination of the two.

Individual budgets would enable a range of support needs to be met: personal care; family roles and responsibilities; and access to community, employment, voluntary work, training and education and leisure activities. The budgets could be used to purchase equipment, personal assistance, transport, adaptations and/or advocacy. The report also called for a cultural shift on the part of social care professionals, to promote self-directed support; and for each locality to have a user-controlled organisation, modelled on the existing Centres for Independent Living.

What are the factors that have brought these policy changes about?

The analytical and final reports (Prime Minister's Strategy Unit, 2004, 2005) on which these proposals are based reflect fundamental changes in attitudes towards disabled people. Up until the early 1990s, it was not commonly accepted that people with physical and/or sensory impairments, learning disabilities and/or mental health problems were unfairly discriminated against; now a legal framework (the 1995 Disability Discrimination Act) exists that recognises such discrimination and declares it to be unlawful. Until that time it was generally assumed that poor life chances were an inevitable consequence of impairment or illness; now the policy framework recognises that people are disabled by negative attitudes and unequal access to resources, rather than by impairment or illness in itself. This acceptance of the social model of disability (albeit often accompanied by an incomplete understanding of the approach) has long been campaigned for by the disability movement.

This is not to deny the limitations of the Disability Discrimination Act (DDA). The DDA does not deliver full civil rights and uses a medical model to define who is covered by the legislation. However, by including within the legal definition of discrimination failures to address barriers that exclude disabled people, the DDA requires positive action to be taken to enable disabled people to have equal access to opportunities. Anti-discrimination measures for disabled people are not about being treated the same as non-disabled people but about the additional action required to address disabling social, environmental and attitudinal barriers.

The adoption of the goal of independent living by the *Improving the life chances of disabled people* report is also a reflection of the success of the disability movement in challenging the notion that the need for assistance in daily life renders a disabled person 'dependent'. Instead, disabled people have argued that independence is achieved by having choice and control over the assistance they require; and that this choice and control is essential to enabling people who need support to access their human and civil rights.

The influence of the disability movement in bringing about a fundamental shift in policy has been threefold: a change in attitudes towards disabled people; practical demonstrations that giving people choice and control works; and research evidence that this is an efficient use of public resources. The history of independent living is therefore the history of a grassroots movement struggling against political and professional institutions and winning over those institutions to its perspective and aims. As McLaughlin argues in Chapter Four, the reshaping of the welfare agenda since the early 1990s has not just been played out within the politics of Old Labour, New Labour and the New Right, but has also been profoundly influenced by grassroots movements among those groups who are particularly reliant on the welfare state for their life chances (Williams, 1999, p 668).

The role of research evidence in influencing government policy

While the disability movement has had some major successes in influencing the development of policy, developments in the funding and conduct of research have also played key roles.

In the late 1980s and 1990s there were important changes in the relationship between research subjects and those commissioning and conducting research – changes that had a profound effect on research in the field of community care. The main arena in which this happened was the research-funding activities of the Joseph Rowntree Foundation (JRF); but changes in the way the Foundation funded community care research were also adopted, to a greater or lesser extent, by some other funding bodies. The limitations of both JRF's approach and that of other funding bodies have been criticised (Oliver, 1997). Nevertheless, it was research primarily funded by JRF and based on the social model of disability that influenced the Strategy Unit's report – rather than research that had remained uninfluenced by the politics of the disability movement.

The relationship between the disability movement and JRF was a natural one, in the sense that the Foundation's funding activities have always been determined by the principle that research should 'provide the tools and the impetus for change towards a more just society' (Ward, 1997, p 32). In 1988, the Foundation set up a Disability Committee (later called the Community Care and Disability Committee), which adopted some important principles:

- including disabled people with relevant expertise in the membership of the Committee;
- consulting with disabled people and their organisations;
- funding applications to take a social model approach to disability and demonstrate the involvement of disabled people in both setting the research agenda and influencing the conduct of research;
- 'staying with' research issues, so that programmes of research were developed with a view to influencing policy and practice.

JRF funded the influential work by the British Council of Organisations of Disabled People, which made the case for anti-discrimination legislation (Barnes, 1991) and a series of seminars on researching disability. These seminars brought together disabled people and non-disabled researchers to explore and promote an understanding of the social model of disability. They resulted in guidelines adopted by JRF on how funders should involve disabled people in their activities; a national Conference; and a special issue of *Disability, Handicap and Society* (1992, volume 7, number 2).

The key issue that the Foundation 'stayed with' during the 1990s was that of independent living. Its involvement started with research examining the extent to which community care policies were delivering independent living (Morris, 1993) and included research into the costs and benefits of direct payments, a project that paired a traditional research organisation, the Policy Studies Institute, with the British Council of Organisations of Disabled People (Zarb and Nadash, 1994). Most of the research funded involved organisations or individuals representing research 'subjects' throughout the process. For example, a number of JRF-funded projects carried out by the Norah Fry Research Centre originated from the ideas of people with learning disabilities who were also involved in different aspects of the research (see Ward, 1997); people with learning disabilities from People First were provided with training and support to carry out evaluations of the experiences of people with learning disabilities who moved from institutional care to the community (People First, 1994); and the Social Policy Research Unit at the University of York pioneered involving older people as research advisors (Tozer and Thornton, 1995).

The Foundation tried to ensure that disability organisations had access to research in their campaigning activities and sought directly to influence government itself by, for example, setting up a Task Force on the disincentives to paid employment among disabled people that were created by means-tested charges for community care services. The evidence assembled (Howard, 2001), the involvement in the Task Force of civil servants from the Department of Health and the Treasury and some judicious political lobbying by key disabled individuals persuaded the government in 2001 to discount earned income in the means test for direct payments and community care services. At a time when government's general approach was characterised by increased 'targeting' of resources – that is, means testing – this was an important victory for the universalist principle. Of course, it also created a clear injustice in treating pension income differently from earned income and this injustice strengthens the case against community care charging policies generally. By the time the Prime Minister's Strategy Unit started its work on *Improving the life chances of disabled people* in 2003, there was a body of research and evaluation, informed by the social model of disability, which both put forward a definition of independent living and made the case for policies that would deliver this aim (and which, indeed, had already persuaded the previous

Conservative government to introduce direct payments). Crucially, there was also increasing practical experience of the benefits of giving individuals choice over how their support needs were met. In particular, pilot projects had been set up (as part of the implementation of the national learning disability strategy) using individual budgets. These pilot projects were motivated by a belief that disabled people, including those with the most significant cognitive impairments, should and could have control over their lives and be fully included in society.

Does the emphasis on 'choice' undermine public services?

It is unlikely that a commitment to promote independent living would have been adopted by government without this research and practical evidence. However, it can also be argued that individual budgets are more consistent with a political ideology that prioritises the individual consumer over collective solidarity, and that the notion of 'choice' undermines public services. To examine whether this is a valid concern requires engaging with wider debates on public services, citizenship and social rights.

'Choice' and human rights

The concept of 'choice' is an integral part of current political debates in Britain about citizenship and the role of the state. The Left argues that promotion of choice undermines the relationship between citizens and the state. An ethos of 'customer care', borrowed from the private sector, encourages service users to act solely in their own self-interest and the individual goals of customers undermine the collective goals of public services (Needham, 2004). New Labour's focus on choice in public services is therefore seen as part of the consumerisation of the relationship between government and citizen (Needham, 2003, pp 21-6).

However, this perspective fails to understand the profound importance for disabled people of choice as a means of accessing human rights. For those reliant on others for assistance with personal care, communication or to live an 'ordinary' life, having choice over how that assistance is provided is – disabled people have argued – the only way of protecting fundamental human dignity and of achieving autonomy. This is not to place the provision of personal assistance (or, indeed, other social care services) on a par with consumer services; to depend on others for assistance with intimate tasks is not the same as depending on a mechanic to service a car (Morris, 2001). In both situations the assistance needs to be reliable, competent and provided with respect. However, there are qualitative differences between the two experiences – differences that are rooted in the experience of impairment. Research on older people's experiences of being bathed illustrates this clearly:

> One person, strong and able, stands above and over another who is frail and physically vulnerable, forced to rely on their strength and goodwill. Being naked in the face of someone who is not, contains a powerful dynamic of domination and vulnerability, and it is often used in situations of interrogation and torture as a means of subjugating the individual. (Twigg, 2000, p 21)

Choice and control over how and by whom such assistance is provided is crucial in addressing the vulnerability created by this unequal power relationship.

It has been the lack of choice that consigns people to segregated forms of service provision, which institutionalises disabled and older people within their own homes, leaves them vulnerable to abuse and restricts their ability to participate in family and community life. In contrast, the *Improving the life chances of disabled people* report drew on experiences of tailoring support to meet individuals' needs, experiences which not only increase the quality of their lives and protect them from abuse, but also reflect a more effective use of public resources. This is not an 'empty consumerism'.

Disabled people's support for choice is not, therefore, support for the 'consumerisation' of public services, or an acceptance that we are all 'atomised individuals', or an argument for a minimal state. It is a demand that emerged from collective struggles against a welfare system – designed and run without the input of those using it – which believed, and still believes, that it is acceptable to separate people from their families and communities because it is cheaper to do this than support them to live independently. 'Choice' over how a person's support needs are met is integrally linked to human rights and to the concept of independent living.

'Choice' and independent living

However, 'choice' as commonly used in current debates on public services does not reflect its meaning for those who use social care services. The independent living movement uses the phrase 'choice and control' rather than just 'choice'; having control over the assistance needed is an integral part of the demand for independent living. Although the phrase is associated with disabled people of working age who are involved in the independent living movement, the same words are also used by many older people to define 'independence' (Parry et al, 2004, p 1).

The Disability Rights Commission, which has adopted the entitlement to independent living as one of its policy aims, defines independent living as:

> ... all disabled people having the same choice, control and freedom as any other citizen – at home, at work, and as members of the community. This does not necessarily mean disabled people 'doing everything for themselves', but it does mean that any practical assistance people need should be based on their own choices and aspirations. (Disability Rights Commission, 2002)

There are three elements to this definition. First, an assertion that disabled people should have the same opportunities for choice and control in their lives as non-disabled people; second, a challenge to the usual interpretations of the words 'independent' and 'independence'; and, finally, the aspiration that any assistance required should be under the control of disabled individuals themselves. Independent living is essentially a challenge to the place of disabled people in society: 'Independent living is a philosophy and a movement of people ... who work for self-determination, equal opportunities and self-respect' (Ratzka, no date). 'Choice and control', it is argued, is essential in order to achieve self-determination, while self-determination in its turn is a crucial part of citizenship. This argument addresses the criticism that promoting 'choice' in public services undermines the wider social role of citizenship by instead treating people as individual consumers and that this, in turn, undermines the role of the state in tackling inequalities.

'Choice' and citizenship

Three conditions are crucial to disabled people's access to full citizenship (see Morris, 2005, for a fuller discussion); first, self-determination, which is about making decisions for oneself. 'Put simply, if you have self-determination then this means you are in charge of your own life. If you do not have self-determination then other people are in charge of you' (Duffy, 2003, p 5). Within wider citizenship debates, there is an assumption that individuals have capacity for free choice and, particularly within the liberal tradition, full citizenship involves the exercise of autonomy. Second, the concept of participation is often used by disabled people in debates on social exclusion, in order to argue for the right to be included in family, community and political life. In terms of wider citizenship debates, the concept includes the civic republican concept of political participation and the broader concept of community participation. Third, in making cases for anti-discrimination legislation and the resources required for a reasonable quality of life, disabled people have emphasised the value of their contribution to economic and social life. Such arguments dovetail with the communitarian emphasis on responsibilities and reciprocity, and with debates on the limits to social rights, for example the recent discussions about 'conditionality' and benefits (Stanley and Lohde, 2004; see also Chapter Six for a discussion of these debates in Australia). Arguably, self-determination is the most important of these three elements of citizenship. Without self-determination, people are unable to participate or to make a contribution.

Disabled people's concern with self-determination echoes the concept of autonomy within the literature on citizenship generally – 'the ability to determine the conditions of one's life and to pursue one's life projects' (Lister, 1997, p 16). However, this concept is particularly important in the neoliberal perspective on citizenship, which sees self-determination as the absence of coercion of, or interference with, individual action. The state's role is therefore the limited one of protecting individual freedom. Some analysts of current government policy see the focus on choice and the citizen as consumer as belonging within this neoliberal tradition and, for example, trace Labour's promotion of choice within the health service back to Milton Friedman's promotion of vouchers for public services (Pollard, 2003).

As noted in Chapter Sixteen, it has been argued that the disability movement's successful campaign for direct payments colluded with the neoliberal approach to the state. Indeed, many Labour local authorities and public sector unions saw direct payments as the New Right's Trojan Horse, which would lead to a privatisation of social care services.[2] It would be easy, within this perspective, to see individual budgets in the same light.

In fact, the liberal political tradition of citizenship, particularly its current version adopted by the New Right, poses considerable problems for disabled people. While the New Right defines freedom (self-determination) as the absence of interference with individual action, and the state's role as limited to protecting such freedom, the issue for disabled people is that such negative rights are not sufficient to deliver even simple autonomy. Impairment and disabling barriers impose limits on freedom of action; positive action is therefore required to deliver opportunities for self-determination.

A minimal role for the state means that any additional assistance and resources that disabled people require would only be provided voluntarily. Traditionally that has been the role of charitable organisations. Yet the ideologies and values that underpin charitable activity in Britain (and most western democracies) assume that impairment is a personal tragedy and disabled people are to be looked after; they are the subjects of good deeds and have no contribution to make themselves. None of this is compatible with self-determination. A minimal role for the state also means that it would be left up to individuals as to whether they changed their attitudes towards impairment, old age and mental illness.

For disabled people, therefore, self-determination cannot be achieved without social rights. However, neither can it be achieved if disabled people are merely passive recipients of social rights. The extension of social rights in the development of the post-war welfare state was done in ways that restricted disabled people's autonomy. Unless disabled people and their organisations are key participants in the evolution of social rights it is unlikely that they will achieve self-determination. In this respect, the distinction between hierarchical power (the ability of one group to exert its will over another) and generative power (participation in struggles against inequality) is useful (Giddens, 1991). Disabled people's autonomy has been constrained by the experience of inequality yet struggles against such inequality have been generated by, and have further promoted, self-determination.

The key example of this is to be found in the origins of the independent living movement in Britain. Residents at Le Court residential home, Hampshire, England, were engaged throughout the late 1950s and 1960s in struggles for more autonomy in their lives, campaigning to be represented on the Management Committee in order to counter restrictive rules (Mason, 1990). These struggles became the foundation stones for the redefinition of 'independence' and generated the subsequent campaign by some individuals to move out of the home in the 1970s and 1980s. While self-determination was only realisable once the various authorities concerned were persuaded to redirect their resources to enable people to live independently, the originating force came from disabled people themselves. Self-determination was both a motivating force for, and a product of, the struggle to influence how resources were used.

If disabled people are to claim autonomy in order to assert their rights to citizenship, it is necessary to re-examine the meaning of the word. Doyal and Gough's definition of autonomy is 'to have the ability to make informed choices about what should be done and how to go about doing it' (Doyal and Gough, 1991, p 53). Traditionally, disabled people's autonomy has been seen to be restricted by physical and/or cognitive impairment. In this sense, the disabled people at Le Court did not even have the 'ability' to choose what time to go to bed in the evenings (one of their original campaigning issues). Their lack of control over their lives and exclusion from society led researchers to label them as 'socially dead' (Miller and Gwynne, 1972). Yet out of that experience of powerlessness came an assertion of self-determination that later led to a change in government policy – an example of what Doyal and Gough call 'critical autonomy'. It was the realisation that, just because they needed help with going to bed, this did not mean that they had to be put in their pyjamas at six o'clock in the evening. This is at the heart of the social model of disability; it is not an impairment in itself which restricts what someone can do, but the lack of choice and control over the required assistance. This is not about consumerism, or the application of market forces to undermine public services; instead it is about fundamental rights to self-determination that, if denied, prevent certain groups of people from being fully part of society.

Self-determination, which is key to disabled people's status as full and equal citizens, cannot be achieved without the removal of barriers; the provision of necessary support; and choice and control over that support.

Demands for choice and control are not, therefore, about a minimal role for the state; neither are they intended to undermine public services. On the contrary, collective provision is crucial to disabled people's equal citizenship. Moreover, direct payments – which are very much the forerunner to the current proposal of individual budgets – came about because of collective action by disabled people, and their implementation depends on the support of disabled people's organisations to the individuals using them. Both direct payments and individual budgets are part of the collective provision and redistribution of resources necessary to address inequality and promote social justice. They are the result of positive action by the state.

Are the current proposals sufficient to deliver self-determination for disabled people?

While there is limited understanding of the importance of self-determination for disabled people among critics of 'choice' in public services, the government's proposals themselves do not adequately address what is required for self-determination.

The government's promotion of choice in public services is to a large extent fuelled by the belief that the private and voluntary sectors should play a bigger role in providing publicly funded services. However, the issue for disabled people is not only about service delivery mechanisms but also about whether levels of resources are sufficient to deliver self-determination. For example, vouchers for wheelchairs were introduced some years ago but have not delivered the choice that they were intended to because of their limited value. Too often direct payments are not provided at a level sufficient to deliver full choice and control; and the assistance people need to use cash to purchase the support required is not always available. Giving people 'choice' is therefore not sufficient to enable disabled people to exercise self-determination.

Moreover, the *Improving the life chances of disabled people* report referred to evidence that increased demands on health and social care budgets can result from a failure to provide housing adaptations or equipment, and that more personalised support can increase people's ability to take up paid employment and fulfil family responsibilities. Yet the implications of this have not been followed through. In particular, the opportunity has been missed to take a more holistic and transparent approach to public expenditure. If the cost implications for other budgets of not increasing expenditure on promoting independent living were taken into account, the economic case for such increased expenditure would be obvious.

In addition, self-directed support is necessary to self-determination and this requires a fundamental cultural shift in the provision of social care. There is a danger that the implementation of individual budgets will lose touch with their original aim of changing the organisation of social care 'so that people who need support can take more control over their own lives and fulfil their role as citizens' (see www.in-control.org.uk). *Improving the life chances* envisages both a change in the role of professionals and an increased role for user-led organisations:

> The new system would require a cultural shift so that social
> care professionals are working to promote self-directed

support. Such a shift would be encouraged by closer
working relationships between health and social care
organisations and organisations of disabled people. (Prime
Minister's Strategy Unit, 2005, p 78)

Key to bringing about this cultural shift is the proposal that 'by 2010,
each locality ... should have a user-led organisation modelled on
existing Centres for Independent Living' (Prime Minister's Strategy
Unit, 2005, p 76). However, the subsequent Green Paper on adult
social care makes no such commitment (DH, 2005). This chapter has
argued that social policy developed and delivered without the full
involvement of disabled people and their organisations has led to public
resources being used in ways that disempower people and deny human
rights. These mistakes will be repeated if the involvement of people
who need support to go about their daily lives is not placed at the
heart of the proposed new system.

Finally, none of the proposals will deliver an entitlement to
independent living. When the Prime Minister's Strategy Unit consulted
disabled people and their organisations about what an entitlement to
independent living would look like, the most common response was
that it would involve a right to not be forced to move into residential
care. Such a right is necessary because, while strictly speaking people
cannot be forced into residential care, in reality this happens by default
because local authorities restrict expenditure on support at home to
the costs of residential care. This results in particular discrimination
against older people as they are forced into residential care when the
costs of their care reach a lower ceiling than that applied to people
below retirement age (Morris, 2004). Increasing numbers of young
people with high levels of needs are also at risk of having to move
into residential care as they move into adulthood, because support
services and housing are often not available to meet their needs.

However, the government's commitment to 'choice' does not
apparently extend to giving people a choice about whether they move
into residential care or not. Instead, the Strategy Unit proposed, and
the subsequent adult social care Green Paper implemented, a
consultation on:

> ... the merits of a 'right to request' not to live in a residential
> or nursing care setting, taking full account of the particular
> issues faced by the individual, and considering the financial,
> organisational and legal implications of both the staus quo
> and alternative options. This 'right to request' would require

service providers to make explicit the reasons behind their decision to recommend residential care, including cost considerations. (DH, 2005, p 32)

This is a long way short of the legal protection that disabled and older people require if they are to avoid being forced into residential care.

Conclusion

Since the early 1990s local and national disability organisations have had significant successes in promoting independent living. Research using the social model of disability and involving disabled people and their organisations has played a key role in influencing policy development. The influence of both this research and the disability movement is apparent in the proposals of the *Improving the life chances of disabled people* report and the Green Paper on adult social care.

Nevertheless, there is still limited understanding, across the political spectrum and within the research community, of what independent living means and what is necessary to achieve it. The disability movement is vulnerable to – from the Left – attacks on 'choice' in public services; and – from the Right – attacks on public expenditure. It is important that these debates are informed by an understanding of the importance of choice and control for disabled people, and by research into whether and how expenditure on independent living – for people of all ages – should be seen as a form of social and economic investment.

Notes

[1] This chapter draws on work undertaken by the author as part of the Prime Minister's Strategy Unit team working on the report (Prime Minister's Strategy Unit, 2005) and the associated policy proposals.

[2] In fact, of course, the privatisation of social care services (or the shift from the provider to the commissioner role among local authorities) has proceeded apace uninfluenced by the take-up of direct payments, which account for a very small percentage of expenditure on social care.

EIGHTEEN

Securing the dignity and quality of life of older citizens

Hilary Land

Policy proposals published in England during 2005 emphasise the importance of ensuring that older people and adults needing care achieve 'independence' and are given 'choices' consistent with their own well-being. Indeed, the Green Paper on social care is entitled *Independence, well-being and choice: Our vision for the future of social care for adults in England* (DH, 2005). This chapter will first explore how far the interpretation of the complex and fluid concepts of 'independence' and 'choice' reflected in current policies is adequate 'to secure the dignity and quality of life of older citizens, and to ensure that they receive the support they need in the place, and manner they prefer' (Baldwin, 1995, p 138). This exploration will be placed within the contexts of the growing emphasis on individuals as consumers rather than as citizens; the increasing identification of 'active citizenship' with being in paid employment; and the increasing commodification and marketisation of care services. In particular, current policy developments in domiciliary and residential care services will be examined to illustrate some of the contradictions and dilemmas that arise in these contexts, which are very different from those of the post-war British welfare state.

The 'active' and 'independent' citizen

As Lewis argues in Chapter Two, by the end of the 20th century the solutions to poverty, welfare dependency and the rising costs of pensions being advocated in many advanced industrialised societies were for more adults to become and remain active in the labour market. In 1999, the Organisation for Economic Co-operation and Development (OECD) published a report *A caring world: The new social policy agenda*. As well as advocating the combination of employment-oriented social policies with family-friendly policies so that parents could more easily combine care and employment, the authors of the report argued that countries should develop 'an active ageing policy'. This would include:

> ... expanding and encouraging the capacity of people as they grow older to lead productive lives in the society and economy, through paid work and unpaid activities like voluntarism and family care-giving.... In order to cope with fiscal and other challenges posed by an ageing population it will be necessary to encourage those who are able to work longer to do so. (OECD, 1999, p 146)

The British government's recent commitments to restricting the numbers claiming disability and sickness benefits to those 'who genuinely qualify', removing the possibility of retiring 'early' and considering raising retirement ages beyond 65 years, are all entirely consistent with the recommendations in this report. In these policy debates, those who are retired, irrespective of their state of health, are seen as 'burdens' on society in general and on taxpayers in particular, an assumption questioned by Zsusza Ferge:

> It seems to me that the increasingly loud rhetoric about the unsustainability of the current pensions systems and hence the necessity to lower the collective provisions for the elderly is related to their loss of economic value. The rejection of inter-generational solidarity in the name of individual responsibility is in all likelihood both a cause and a consequence of the devaluation of the ageing population. (Ferge, 1997, pp 30-1)

While voluntary work and care within the family are mentioned in the OECD report and in subsequent British government policy documents, these contributions to society remain undervalued, despite the growing evidence of the scale of these activities. With more sophisticated time-use surveys and the development of Household Satellite Accounts, it is now possible, by using the wage rates of paid childcare workers (nannies) and adult social care workers together with data on the amount of time family and friends spend caring, to place a monetary value on the informal care they provide (see Murgatroyd and Newberger, 1997). This was estimated to be over £800 billion in 2000. A quarter of this was accounted for by childcare and adult care (ONS, 2002). This dwarfs the formal care sectors; for example, the annual cost of public social care services for adults is only about £10 billion (DH, 2005). Half of all family carers of adults are aged between 45 and 64 and a further fifth are over 65 years (Maher and Green, 2002, table 4.6). A third of employed mothers in Britain rely to a greater or lesser extent on informal childcarers, most of whom are grandmothers (DfES, 2004b, p 37). Thus, the older generation is *already* contributing a great deal to the care of both the younger and very older generations.

During 2004, the World Bank and the International Monetary Fund berated European governments that had reduced their standard working hours; in contrast, the UK and the US were commended for their long hours culture (*Financial Times*, 2004). People who had left the formal labour market were represented as a drain on the economy (measured in foregone tax revenue and greater expenditure on benefits). There was no acknowledgement that the generation of older people who have now reached their eighties were encouraged in the 1980s to retire early to make way for growing numbers of young people. This is also the generation that, as young men and women, contributed as civilians or in the armed forces to fighting the Second World War. They then supported the post-war welfare state as both taxpayers and National Insurance contributors, for there was almost full employment for men until the 1970s. In addition, the expansion of health, welfare and education services depended heavily on women, including married women who were employed part time while they had young children. It is perhaps not surprising, therefore, if members of this generation feel cheated when their state National Insurance pension is so low that it has to be topped up with a means-tested benefit: 'I think it's demeaning, after working hard so long and then through no fault of my own I come down to relying on the state which you shouldn't have to' (Parry et al, 2004, p 37). Having experienced *and* understood solidarity between the generations as being very different from the 'targeting' of benefits and free social services on those defined as 'poor', they reject the official perception that they are 'burdens' on the state. Chapter Six also describes the substantial discrepancies between the assumptions of national governments and supranational organisations and those of the general public, that the non-employed should be viewed primarily as an economic burden rather than having a legitimate claim on the welfare state.

The increasing use of 'active' to describe citizens and the privileging of activities in the labour market over those in the family or community, risks devaluing both those who contribute in other no less important ways as well as those whose capacity for action is diminished by old age or disability. In his study of the transformation of welfare states,

Gilbert (2002, p 189; emphasis in original) criticises the opposition of 'active' and 'passive' in policy debates:

> If policy choices are posed, for example, between *active* and *passive* social benefits, there is little doubt that all would prefer an active benefit. The word *active* speaks of life's energy, whereas *passive* suggests a state of mild depression. But if the choice is between *activation*, which presses disabled people, women with young children into the labour force, and *social protection* against the risks of modern capitalism, the tendency to embrace activation would be less compelling. Policies devoted entirely to cultivating independence and private responsibility leave little ground for a life of honourable dependence for those who may be unable to work.

Independence

Martha Nussbaum has drawn attention to the social contract tradition in which the parties, who are imagined as more or less equal, come together to achieve the benefits of cooperation and the impact this has had on how 'the person' is conceptualised. 'Even when people have no awareness of the particular texts of the tradition, the idea of the citizen as an independent bargainer, who pays for the benefits he gets by his own productive contribution, is a daily part of our lives' (Nussbaum, 2004, p 289). (The use of the male pronoun is entirely appropriate in this context.) Nussbaum suggests instead that 'the person' should be seen as *both* capable *and* needy; after all, everyone is 'disabled' in some way with respect to their judgement, understanding, perceptions or bodily functions.

Although policy makers persist in elevating 'independence' to a state to which we should all aspire, in reality it is a complex concept. A recent study of older people funded by the Department for Work and Pensions noted that 'independence is neither a static nor an abstract concept, but a multi-dimensional, fluid entity that was understood by individuals in relation to their particular social context' (Parry et al, 2004, p 37). The researchers found that 'the very subjectivity of the concept, encompassing meanings such as self-esteem, purpose in life and personal continuity, make it possible for pensioners simultaneously to experience high levels of dependence and independence' (Parry et al, 2004, p 111). The ability to reciprocate was also found to be important in another recent study of older people; indeed, those surveyed stressed 'interdependence' rather than 'independence':

> ... formal help was not just to be resorted to in the absence of supportive family and friends: it might indeed be preferable in order not to be perceived as a 'burden' on them ... whilst people identified the need for practical help, they also sought to sustain social engagement and valued social activities, even when they experienced restrictions on account of a disability. (Godfrey et al, 2004, p 222)

Choice

The perception of individuals as rational actors capable of making appropriate choices in their own best interests is also consistent with the greater emphasis on the use of markets to deliver social services. In 2001, the British government established an Office of Public Services Reform to work with central and local government departments 'to improve current structures, systems, incentives and skills to deliver better, more customer-focused public services' (Thomson, 2002, contents page). The four principles on which reform is based are the setting of national standards; devolution and delegation; flexibility; and 'choice for the customer'. The last principle is justified because:

> Giving people a choice about the service they can have and who provides it helps ensure that services are designed around their customers. An element of contestability between alternative suppliers can also drive up standards and empower customers locked into a poor service from their traditional suppliers. (Thomson, 2002, p 10)

Increasing 'choice' has thus become a new and desirable objective of social policies. However, there is little evidence to show that 'choice' is valued above other priorities. On the contrary, although nearly two-thirds of people say that if they had cancer they would want to choose their own treatment, only 12% of people with cancer do actually want to (Schwartz, 2004). 'What patients really seem to want from their doctors ... is competence and kindness. Kindness of course includes respect for autonomy, but it does not treat autonomy as an inviolable end in itself' (Schwartz, 2004, p 32). Instead of emphasising the desirability of maximising 'choice', Schwartz suggests that the focus instead should be on 'satisficing' (a concept developed in the 1950s by the Nobel prize-winning economist and psychologist Herbert Simon):

> To satisfice is to settle for something that is good enough and not worry about the possibility that there might be something better. A satisficer has criteria and standards. She searches until she finds an item that meets those standards, and at that point she stops. (Schwartz, 2004, p 79)

Although Schwartz draws on US research, studies of education and health services in the UK suggest that many people would be satisfied to know that their local school, hospital or doctor's surgery is good enough, even if it is not the very best in the UK. Moreover, proximity to home, family and friends is also valued and important in its own right, particularly among older people (Godfrey et al, 2004).

There are further problems about relying on 'choice' to drive the provision of services for older people. First, research into public attitudes and expectations of services in older age reports that most people say they want to be able to remain in their own homes as long as possible (see, for example, DH, 2006). However, this question is often asked of adults long before they have become frail and possibly suffering from dementia, isolated and living in a house that has become inconvenient and expensive to heat. A more revealing approach might be to follow Rawls' use of the notion of 'a veil of ignorance'. (The central idea is that just arrangements are those that people would agree on if they were ignorant of the position in society they themselves would come to occupy, if they had no vested interests themselves [Rawls, 1971].) People would therefore be asked what services they would want society to provide in their older age if they did not know whether or not they would be poor, chronically sick and confused and with no surviving friends, children or other concerned relatives nearby. Such an approach might focus attention more clearly on what domiciliary services should be provided and what alternatives to living at home should be offered to those who, to use Hirschman's terms, have no 'voice' and are not able to 'exit' from the system if they are dissatisfied (Hirschman, 1970).

Second, research shows that people's understandings of 'independence' change over time:

> A sizeable proportion [of respondents] explained that the meanings they attached to independence changed as they

got older, and that in response they both saw things and acted differently. These shifting perspectives were particularly related to health ... those who displayed the most stable ideas about independence tended to have experienced little recent change, being married or else widowed or divorced some time ago. (Parry et al, 2004, p 2)

Third, there are problems in principle as well as in practice about relying too heavily on individual 'choice' as a rationale for determining the patterns and methods of providing public services. The choice to 'consume' a particular service is not only of interest to the individual and their family but is also of interest to the wider society. In other words, these services are *public* consumption goods. This is not just because these services are funded at least in part by the state, but because the resulting benefit (or harm) does not only accrue to the individual concerned. Social services are best not treated as pure commodities. As Wærness describes in Chapter Three, care is a personal service, making it different from a commodity that can be separated from the person making or delivering it. In other words, caregiving takes place within the context of a *particular* relationship, and this takes time to build and sustain. Carers are not interchangeable in the same way that supermarket checkout operators are. The Audit Commission, in collaboration with the Local Government Association and the Association of Directors of Social Services, recommends 'a holistic approach to the delivery of services for older people, which promotes 'control and interdependence' in contrast to a more market driven emphasis on 'choice and independence'" (Audit Commission, 2004, p 2).

The next section examines the operation of the current private markets for residential and domiciliary care services in England. It illustrates vividly the dominance of the market approach to the provision of care services criticised by Wærness in Chapter Three. It will conclude that, as Titmuss observed of the US private healthcare system 40 years ago, 'I find no support here for the model of choice in the private market; on criteria of efficiency, of efficacy, of quality or of safety' (Titmuss, 1967, p 16).

Residential and domiciliary care markets in England

Government, central or local, no longer needs to provide every public service. Gone are the days when Whitehall or

indeed the town hall always knew best. What counts today
is the quality of the service, not the origin of the provider.
(Secretary of State for Health and Social Services, 2002a,
p 2)

Since 1993, the budget for residential care and domiciliary care,
including what had formerly been a care element of the social security
system, has been managed by local authority social service departments.
Thus, the arrangement that operated during the 1980s, where poorer
older people had an entitlement through the national social security
system to public funding for residential care, was replaced by one
based entirely on local professional social workers' judgements about
levels of need and risk. In addition, the government ensured that
independent (private, non-profit, for-profit and voluntary) providers
of social care services would grow, by requiring local authorities to
spend at least 85% of their social care budget in this sector.

The consequent decrease in the numbers of residential homes
provided directly by local authorities was inevitable and rapid. By the
end of the 1990s, nine out of 10 residential care places were found in
the independent sector (DH, 1999b, table 4), compared with one in
10 in 1988. By 2001, over 80% of residents supported by local authority
funding were in independent sector homes; in many homes these
residents make up at least 70% of all residents. The level of the fee is
set by the local authorities but central government sets their social
care budgets. Local authorities have argued that they are underfunded,
despite the fact that they only have to pay the full fees of those they
sponsor if they have limited assets and savings. Any owner-occupier
who enters residential care under local authority sponsorship must
sell their house and use the capital realised to pay the fees (unless a
spouse or a carer over the age of 65 is living in the house). The private
sector continually presses for higher fees and puts pressure on relatives
to 'top up' inadequate fees paid by local authorities. Recently a private
consultancy firm that works closely with both the private residential
care and childcare sectors estimated a 'fair' fee and calculated that the
private residential care sector 'needed' another £1 billion a year (Laing,
2002).

The community care reforms of the early 1990s also gave the
independent domiciliary care sector a 'kick-start' (Laing and Saper,
1999) and this sector now provides most domiciliary care services,
including help with routine household tasks in and outside the home,
personal care and breaks for family carers. By 2003, staff employed
directly by local authority social service departments provided less

than a third of all home care contact hours, compared with 97% in 1993 (ONS, 2004b, para 8.2). This trend has been accompanied by the more intensive (in this context defined as six or more visits and/ or more than 10 hours of care a week) use of domiciliary services by a decreasing number of households. Thus, the total number of clients fell by 25% between 1992 and 2000, while the total number of contact hours increased by two-thirds. These services are now concentrated on the most dependent older people, who are also likely to be without informal carers.

The growing concentration of intensive home care support on decreasing numbers of households is being driven mainly by priorities within the National Health Service and *not* by the choices of older people or their families. While those who would once have been looked after in hospital for longer periods now need appropriate support when they return to live in their own homes, those requiring less intensive care *also* need services. During the 1980s and 1990s, numbers of long-stay hospital beds declined, as places in private nursing and residential homes increased. Furthermore, hospitals need to get patients back home as quickly as possible if they are to reduce waiting lists and meet national performance targets. In 2002 it was estimated that at any point in time there were 5,000 'bed blockers' (itself a term that is disrespectful of older people) who could have been discharged from hospital with appropriate social services support. Since 2002, social services departments have been fined if they fail to 'unblock' these beds by providing appropriate domiciliary support and an extra £1 billion was allocated 'to stabilise the home care market and to buy more home care' (Secretary of State for Health and Social Services, 2002b, p 1). Current priorities mean that those with carers or fewer needs get no support. The Royal Commission on Long Term Care established in 1997 to consider services for older adults reported in 1999. The Commission recognised the lack of support for family carers and recommended that older people's needs for social care services should be assessed on a 'carer-blind' basis (that is, their needs assessed as if there were no one providing any informal care). The intention was that older people *and* family carers should have a choice about how much to rely on informal care or formal services.

The Commission also proposed that intimate personal care, which has never been free as of right unless it is provided within a hospital, should be free on the same basis as healthcare so that older people would only have to meet their living costs. This was rejected by the English government (Secretary of State for Health, 2000) and initially by the Welsh Assembly (which subsequently, in 2003, agreed to introduce free personal care but has yet to do so). However, the devolved government in Scotland did accept the Royal Commission's recommendation. In contrast the English government has advocated the use of direct payments, whereby older people who are assessed as needing publicly funded social care services can receive a cash payment with which to purchase the help they need, as the main mechanism for increasing choice. However, only in exceptional circumstances can older recipients choose to use direct payments to pay a close, co-resident family member to provide the necessary care. This is a particularly British restriction because similar payments for care in other European Union countries do not exclude relatives (see Chapter Twelve on the scheme in Flanders; also Ungerson, 2004).

Quality of care

In the childcare and adult social care sectors, the pay of carers accounts respectively for two-thirds and three-quarters of the total costs of the service. However, the current wage levels of social care workers put them in the bottom decile of the earnings distribution (Simon and Owen, 2005, p 202). The logic of the private for-profit sector is to constrain the wage bill. However, fewer staff to look after residents or visit older people in their own homes means the standard of care decreases. Training increases the quality but not the quantity of care. If the wages of care workers do not keep pace with rising average earnings, there will be a recruitment crisis unless there is an oversupply of workers willing to work for very low wages. Immigrant workers desperate for work are very attractive in these circumstances and, as Chapter Eleven shows, already provide substantial amounts of care in Austria. The Laing (2002) estimate of a fair fee for residential care cited above assumed care staff wage levels little different from the minimum wage, three days' paid training a year and a 165% return on capital. The private sector is also willing to use its power to resist government policies it judges to be against its interests. In 2002, when the government attempted to impose higher standards on residential homes, representatives of the sector warned that many would close if these were implemented. The government watered down its proposals (see White, 2003; Netten et al, 2005, p 320).

Two-thirds of adult social care workers in the UK are now employed in the private, for-profit and voluntary sectors – mostly in the former (Skills for Care, 2005, p 30). High staff turnover rates lower the quality of care because, as noted above, care takes place in the context of a relationship based on trust and familiarity. The Social Services

Inspectorate compared workers in the public and independent sectors and found turnover rates in the private sector to be double those in the public sector:

> The in-house home care service was long established, usually with a stable workforce in whom there had been investment in training and personal development over a number of years. Private agencies were mostly of more recent origin and were often not funded to provide the kind of terms and conditions, such as mileage and travelling time which in-house staff enjoyed. We came across some examples of agencies retaining staff on zero hours contracts because the business terms of the social services contracts did not offer these agencies sufficient security to employ people on a reasonable level of basic hours. It was difficult to recruit, retain and train good quality staff on these terms. (SSI, 2002, p 38)

For the older people concerned this means that they may be unable to get to know and trust those caring for them and undertaking personal and intimate tasks. For example, higher turnover rates mean they may be helped to bed by a different person each night. With greater pressure on their time because social services are purchasing shorter time 'packages' for each client, the home carer may be so rushed during her 15-minute visit that she does not take her coat off, does not wait to see if the older person drinks the cup of tea or eats the food she has prepared, let alone help the person to do so, and does not engage in conversation so never finds out if there is anything worrying the older person. These practices are not consistent with respecting an older person's dignity because both high staff turnover and insufficient time damage the quality of care provided.

Another consequence of high turnover rates and financial pressures on home care providers is that a growing proportion of home care staff do not stay in the same job long enough to receive the training required to do more skilled tasks or learn to work with people with more complex needs. As a result more experienced and longstanding staff may become demoralised because it is very demanding to be working mainly with the most confused and uncommunicative clients unrelieved by time spent with clients with whom they can more easily enjoy a relationship. As Knijn (2000) found in the Netherlands, the home care sector is in danger of ceasing to be an attractive occupation for working-class women without formal qualifications but with a wealth of experience relevant to providing good care. Over a quarter of social care workers in the UK are over the age of 50. Home helps and home carers have never been well paid, but evidence from the former local authority in-house services shows that they took pride in their work and that most enjoyed a good relationship with their clients and knew that what they did for them was needed and valued. Many did far more than they were paid to do (Hunt, 1970). The market culture does not guarantee to offer good-quality care.

Accountability

The treatment of older people as consumers rather than as citizens involves a significant erosion of their rights to contribute to the debates concerning the services on which they and their families depend. When local authorities were directly responsible for providing services, they could more easily be held to account by their local community. Local councillors were known and could be challenged in public meetings. Now shareholders, perhaps living in another country, make key decisions. Public institutions over the years have had their fair share of scandals but the private sector is not inherently better. For example, the reaction of some private homes to complaints has been unhelpful and there have been reports of residents being asked to leave unless their relatives sign statements saying they would cease making complaints (*The Observer*, 2002). Residents without close relatives or friends and those excluded from local authority funding because of the capital and assets test are particularly vulnerable for they have no advocates.

Purchasing care is not like buying a washing machine that can be returned to the makers if it proves faulty or unsuitable. Those who have been ill-served by health and social services can use the 1998 Human Rights Act, which incorporates the principles embodied in the European Convention on Human Rights, making them directly justiciable in the UK courts. Public authorities have a duty of care towards those who use their services and this Act can be used to hold public authorities to account. However, the legislation cannot be used directly to hold a private for-profit company to account. In a recent case of serious abuse in a private residential home for adults with learning disabilities, it was the local authority responsible for inspecting the home that was held accountable and sued for damages (*The Guardian*, 2003). The Commission for Social Care Inspection is a national body that in 2003 became responsible for the inspection of residential and nursing homes and will shortly be amalgamated with the health services inspectorate (the Commission for Healthcare Audit and Inspection (CHAI)). On the one hand, this makes it more remote from local communities but, on the other, it distances it from local vested interests. While local authorities wield some power over service providers through their purchasing and commissioning powers this varies greatly between areas. The Commission for Social Care Inspection (CSCI, 2005a, p 80) noted with concern that in some areas the balance of power had tipped in favour of the private for-profit providers. Overall there are concerns that central government funding for adult social care is not ring-fenced, the level is inadequate (estimated at £1.8 billion annually [*Financial Times*, 2006]) and that the regulatory bodies cannot overcome all of the problems and uncertainties of providing care through the private market (see Netten et al, 2005). Self-funded residents are particularly vulnerable as in many areas local authorities provide them with little or no advice, let alone support.

On the other hand, as the larger corporations account for a larger share of the market, the ability of providers of care in the private sector to seek protection or redress in the courts is increasing. They are more likely than small providers to have access to the necessary resources and legal expertise. While the domiciliary care market is still small, fragmented and local because it has had less time and encouragement to consolidate in the ways in which the nursing home and (to a lesser extent) the residential care sectors have done, the latter sectors are becoming dominated by the large companies with chains of homes in the UK and in North America. 'Nursing home group is sold for £560 million' was the headline of a report that a US private equity group had purchased 355 homes with more than 17,500 beds from Nursing Home Properties (*The Guardian*, 2004a). Similarly, in 2004 a German insurer bought the Four Seasons care home business for £775 million. 'With the number of elderly people reliant on state funded care homes almost certain to rise steadily, private equity operators have had little trouble raising debt against future revenues' (*The Guardian*, 2004b). In contrast, small homeowners are continuing to leave the sector, some tempted by the rise in property prices, others because regulations concerning width of corridors and so on have been harder for them to implement, particularly where fees have not kept pace with rising costs. Laing (2002) estimated that a home has to have at least 60 residents to be financially viable. Selling may be a sensible business decision, but if it means closing the home, unless the closure and the residents' transfer to another is properly planned with them, a great deal of stress – or worse – can be the result (see Netten et al, 2002). The increasing dominance of the big international companies does not seem to fit easily with the UK government's professed aim to give 'local leaders responsibility and accountability for delivery and the opportunity to design and develop services around the needs of local people' (Thomson, 2002, p 10).

An ethics of care

The feminist concept of an 'ethics of care' is set out in Chapter Three. Fisher and Tronto (1990) conceptualise the caring process in terms of four dimensions: caring about; caring for; taking care of; and care receiving. The values at the core of an ethics of care are attentiveness, responsibility, competence and responsiveness. As Wærness argues in Chapter Three, this means that we need to integrate care into a wide range of social practices in 'a variety of social institutions, like health care, education, city planning, or business management and also family practices' (Sevenhuijsen, 2000, p 29; see also Daly, 2002).

The Audit Commission (2004) has recently drawn attention to the importance of the collective impact of public services in the lives of older people. Nussbaum also notes that how our houses, towns and cities are planned and organised can increase or decrease our dependency. Using Jonathan Swift's hero Gulliver's experience when he visits the land of the giants, she writes:

> But society is typically arranged to cater for the most typical disabilities. Thus we do not find staircases so high that only the giants of Brobdingnag can climb them, nor do our symphony orchestras play at frequencies inaudible to the human ear and only audible to canine ears. When a person is blind, or deaf, or has to go around in a wheelchair, societies are not so well adjusted to making such persons fully mobile, fully able to occupy public space on the basis of equality. What blind Law Professor Jacobus Ten Broek calls 'the right to be in the world' is unevenly extended to its citizens and people who could perfectly well get around if the streets were maintained in a particular way, for example, are put by social contingency in a position of dependency – on a dog, other humans, a network of support. (Nussbaum, 2004, p 276)

Such arguments about the social and environmental factors that create the experience of disability – and the growing acceptance of this explanatory paradigm within mainstream policy and practice – are described in Chapters Four, Sixteen and Seventeen. For example, thanks to campaigning by organisations of disabled people, since the early 1960s, access to public buildings and movement within them has improved. However, this approach remains less clearly articulated in relation to services for older people. Anthea Tinker has suggested that 'If all houses were designed with disability in mind a great deal of trouble could be saved in the future' (Tinker, 1995, p 197).

It may be that the marketisation of services and the growing role of the private sector in providing services for older people create additional barriers – arguably private sector markets may respond both less quickly and consistently than a publicly funded and delivered welfare state. Nevertheless there are ways in which technology could help compensate for the reduction in capacities associated with ageing. If there is sufficient demand, markets will respond. For example, car manufacturers are beginning to wake up to the opportunities the increasing numbers of older drivers could bring them and to think of car design not only in terms of speed and power. However, at the same time, transport and planning policies need to be considered in as broad a context as possible, and be informed by an ethics of care, if older people are not to feel like Gulliver. The Audit Commission recognised this when it reported that older people require 'comfortable, secure homes, safe neighbourhoods, friendships and opportunities for learning and leisure, the ability to get out and about, an adequate income, good, relevant information and the ability to keep active and healthy' (Audit Commission, 2004, p 3). These are the essential ingredients of a dignified old age.

Part Six
Conclusions

NINETEEN

Conclusions

Caroline Glendinning and Peter A. Kemp

The separation between 'cash' and 'care' is deeply rooted in the structure and traditions of the British welfare state. Policies relating to cash have traditionally been concerned primarily with replacing or supplementing income from paid employment; cash payments have been delivered through the social security or income tax systems. Policies relating to care have generally focused on the provision of services, funded by the state and delivered by a range of statutory and voluntary agencies. This traditional division between cash and care was underpinned by assumptions about the responsibilities of families and the different roles of women and men within them; about patterns of authority and deference in relationships between professional providers and lay users of services; and about the underlying divisions of rights and responsibilities between the welfare state and citizens.

As many of the chapters in this book show, this traditional division between cash and care is no longer so marked and is beginning to break down. This is seen particularly clearly with the introduction of cash payments of different kinds as alternatives to the provision of services; and also in the increasing focus in social protection policies on combating social exclusion rather than simply replacing or supplementing a lack of income. To a considerable extent these changes reflect the increasing dominance of market arrangements both within welfare states and in the wider society in general. Moreover, they are not peculiar to Britain, as the contributions from Breda et al (Flanders, Belgium), Kreimer (Austria), Saunders (Australia) and Wærness (Norway) show. Although these countries represent very different traditions and welfare regimes, they have nevertheless experienced many similar trends.

Challenging assumptions about care work

The contributions in Part Two of this volume outlined some of the theoretical perspectives on care work. Feminism has challenged the traditional domestic gender division of labour that assigned primary responsibility for breadwinning to men and for caring and housework to women. As Lewis points out, increased female participation in the labour market, rising rates of divorce and relationship breakdown and the growth in lone parenthood have also all contributed to undermining the gendered assumptions and roles embodied in the traditional married male breadwinner family model of social policy.

More recent feminist scholarship has also challenged traditional assumptions that caregiving is an inherently female activity and one that therefore should be largely the preserve of women. Indeed, the assumption that care is 'naturally' and spontaneously the responsibility of women has arguably helped in the past to create and sustain gendered inequalities in opportunities across the lifecourse. As a result of this feminist critique, caregiving has 'moved from being what the sociologist C. Wright Mills would have termed a private concern to a public issue (Mills 1959). In the process, care has become problematised and opened up to academic as well as more popular and political scrutiny' (Fine, 2004, p 218).

Thus, rather than being a natural female preserve, feminist academics have argued that care is a widespread activity in which we are all implicated (Lloyd, 2000, 2003) and, indeed, is 'imperative to human existence' (Watson et al, 2005, p 333). Caring relationships constitute one of the fundamental underpinnings of social solidarity, social relationships and, hence, of individual identity. From this position has emerged a stream of theoretical and empirical work on the 'ethics of care', which, as Wærness and other contributors to this book describe, argues for greater understanding, value and resources to be assigned to care work, both in the labour market and within the family. These arguments may be reflected in new policies that aim, at least in part, to give societal recognition to the work of families in providing care, as discussed in the contributions by Breda et al, Kreimer, Glendinning, and Skinner and Finch. However, it is questionable how far these new policies embody an ethics of care and how far they reflect other imperatives and processes. As Wærness points out, even in Scandinavian welfare states with traditions of women-friendly policies, the ethics of care has made relatively little impact on the economic rationality that drives much public policy.

Commodifying care work

An important focus of this book is the commodification of caregiving relationships through the introduction of cash payments of different types for work that might otherwise have been performed on an unpaid basis by families (and especially by women) (Ungerson, 1997). The contributions by Skinner and Finch, Kreimer, Breda et al and Glendinning describe the different conditions under which such payments are made. These conditions interact with the nature of caregiving relationships within families; to the extent that they are not compatible with familial obligations and the 'moral reasoning' (Williams, 2004) that creates and sustains these obligations, they may fail to achieve the objectives of supporting family-based care.

The provision of cash payments, allowances or subsidies in respect of caregiving responsibilities is a market-style solution to the 'problem' of care. Although this approach may be compatible with current trends towards individualisation (Ungerson, 2003) and the exercise of choice, it also relocates responsibility for finding acceptable solutions to the private world of the family (and often to women within the family). Marketisation has transformed the provision of formal services as well, in ways that are frequently incompatible with an 'ethics of care'. Wærness and Land both show, albeit from very different perspectives, how this marketisation can have adverse consequences for the quality of formal services, to the extent that these services may be incompatible with the concept and practice of 'care'.

Welfare states and their citizens

The shift from services to cash allowances and budgets with which individuals can purchase their own services is part of a wider transformation of welfare states, from being producer-driven towards a more consumer-focused approach. The assumption underpinning this shift is that market-style mechanisms are the only – or the most effective – method of achieving a transfer of power from producers to consumers. Contributors such as Land call this assumption into question, pointing out that markets and choice may impair dignity and citizenship for at least some groups of people.

Meanwhile, the relationship between welfare states and citizens has also been redefined in respect of the conditions under which individuals receive cash from the social security system to replace or supplement income. Receipt of welfare benefits has been made subject to increasingly specific and extensive expectations or 'responsibilities' (Dwyer, 1998). As with marketisation, this redefinition is associated with the rising ascendancy of neoliberal politics and policies, a process clearly set out by Saunders in relation to Australian developments. In particular, the introduction of new conditions under which income benefits are paid, including 'activation' and welfare-to-work measures, is believed to be necessary to maintain or improve competitiveness in the face of global economic competition.

Thus, receipt of income maintenance benefits is increasingly conditional, as illustrated by the active labour market policies and 'mutual obligation' described in the contributions by Saunders and Millar. Welfare-to-work has also been promoted both specifically as a route out of poverty and as a means of preventing social exclusion more generally. But as the chapters by Ridge and by Skinner and Finch show, combining paid employment with childcare is not unproblematic. Arksey and Kemp also show that the same is true about combining paid work with the provision of substantial amounts of informal support to disabled and older relatives. While welfare states can help to reconcile work and family life, there is some way to go before Britain matches the performance of the Scandinavian welfare states in this respect.

Challenging disability

The transformation of relationships between the welfare state and its subjects has not just been a 'top-down' or one-way process, in which the state imposes ever tighter and more complex conditions on the receipt of welfare, whether in the form of cash or care. On the contrary, new social movements have challenged from the 'bottom up' the traditional structuring of relationships between welfare state institutions, professional providers and the recipients of welfare. A number of contributors to this book – including McLaughlin, Morris, and Postle and Beresford – describe the challenges that have been mounted by disabled people to traditional discourses of disability, care and dependency. These include critiques of the disabling inequalities and indignities created by the receipt of services that are underpinned by traditional assumptions about professional expertise and knowledge and therefore by substantial power inequalities. The disability movement has demanded a greater say for people with impairments over the provision of, and access to, welfare resources and services. It is argued that direct payments and other forms of personal allowances have the potential to provide disabled people with greater choice, control and dignity than is possible through producer-led forms of service delivery or reliance on informal carers.

Thus, the commodification of care – the substitution of cash for care – can be a vehicle for empowering disabled people, enabling them to exercise choice and control through the employment of personal assistants. Indeed, Morris argues that claims for increased choice and control are not simply expressions of a consumerist ethos, but are fundamental to citizenship and human rights. However, there are potential dangers with this shift, not least the fact that it can require disabled people to become employers and take on the 'transaction costs' (in the broadest sense) associated with organising their own support. Many disabled people may argue that these costs are a small price to pay for the significant gains in control and independence.

However, this approach may not be universally acceptable. A number of factors outlined above – the current and projected increases in women's labour market participation, the drive to find sustainable solutions to demographic ageing and pressures of marketisation and consumerism – have also led to the introduction of cash payments and subsidies to support or partially replace family care for children and for older people. However, the levels of these allowances and the conditions under which they are paid have generally not resolved longstanding problems of gender inequality. Moreover, a potential consequence of the cash payment approach is the residualisation of formal welfare services (or the failure to develop these, as Kreimer describes in Austria), with potentially damaging implications for those older or disabled people who continue to depend upon them.

New dilemmas

Changes in the roles of welfare states and actual or assumed changes in the responsibilities of individuals and families have created new tensions in managing the relationships between cash and care, particularly in relation to the double demands of securing an income and providing care. First, the shifting boundaries between state and individual or family responsibilities and the introduction of active responsibilities on the part of welfare recipients have created additional disadvantages. Thus, for several decades after the Second World War, the gendered assumptions underlying the married male breadwinner family model, and the social security system around which it was largely based, meant that lone parents and partners of benefit recipients were not expected to look for work. During the final two decades of the 20th century, in the face of rising numbers of lone parents and benefit recipients, policies for lone parents in the UK were ambivalent about whether the latter should be treated primarily as workers or stay-at-home caregivers (Kiernan et al, 1998). This ambivalence has now apparently been resolved with the clear expectation that lone parents are, and should seek to be, wage earners. However, this creates pressures on their parenting roles and, as Ridge shows, may require their children to contribute their unpaid labour as well in order to help maintain family well-being.

Second, measures that are intended to relieve families of some of their caregiving responsibilities are sometimes neither adequate nor consistent with individuals' own views of what constitutes appropriate or good-quality care. Thus, as Skinner and Finch demonstrate, lone parents may prefer informal to formal childcare arrangements, particularly when their children are young. Despite the availability of formal services and financial subsidies for childcare, this preference reflects the dominance of normative values about care.

Third, the provision of substitute services is often less than the need for them, and the level of care allowances is often relatively low, whether these are intended to provide support for disabled or older relatives or for childcare responsibilities. As Kreimer describes, such inadequacies fail to overcome the disadvantages experienced by women in the labour market.

Fourth, marketised services, whether privately or publicly purchased, create new forms of disadvantage and social exclusion, as Land describes in relation to the support needed by older people. Many of these new inequalities are also intrinsically created by, or linked to, needs for, or the provision of, additional support or care.

Fifth, the tensions involved in managing the dual demands of paid work and care are intensified in the context of consumer societies. Millar's chapter provides qualitative evidence to reinforce and illuminate the findings of quantitative research that paid work can indeed provide an important route out of poverty (Kemp, 2005) and can improve material well-being and access to consumer goods. However, achieving this route depends on a degree of stability in income, expenditure and family routines – these conditions cannot always be met. Moreover, Collard's chapter shows that low-income people continue to experience a particularly acute, but largely hidden, form of social exclusion because of their difficulties in accessing mainstream forms of credit. As a result they are more likely to have to rely on the means-tested, discretionary safety net of the Social Fund or make use of relatively expensive forms of credit.

Finally, Hohnen illustrates some of the day-to-day realities for low-income households living in consumer societies, even in the relatively egalitarian Scandinavian welfare states. Her chapter provides interesting parallels with Ridge's (2002) study of children's perspectives on poverty and social exclusion in Britain. Because televisions and other forms of mass communication are now ubiquitous, people on low incomes are arguably now more exposed to inequalities in consumption than they were in the past. Low-income individuals are also unprotected from inequalities in access to those private resources and services such as credit that underpin consumer society.

Future challenges – research and its contribution to policy

Between them, the contributions to this book raise fundamental questions about the consequences of some of the major trends within welfare states since the 1980s. Two of the central challenges for welfare states – those of inequality and of care – have not yet been satisfactorily resolved. Indeed, some of the recent attempts to resolve them as described in this book have created new insecurities, inequalities and injustices.

Many of the contributions to this book present the latest evidence in long-established histories of research and debate on cash and care. However, regardless of the rigour and quality of research evidence, the relationships between evidence and policy are neither simple nor linear, as Eithne McLaughlin points out – not least because the development and implementation of policy is based on politics and ideology as well as (one hopes) evidence of 'what works'. In this context, the contribution of disabled people and disability research to re-conceptualising the nature of 'disability' and transforming the basis of policy is important, both symbolically and instrumentally. This paradigm shift also reflects the contribution and acceptance of different types of evidence – experiential as well as scientific – as legitimate in changing attitudes and policy. This success should provide optimism that the evidence presented in this volume might make similar contributions to policy and practical measures in relation to gender and material inequalities and to care. Such changes require attention to the complexities of caregiving and care relationships; to continuing gender inequalities in the labour market and the family; to income inequality and social mobility; to the causes as well as the manifestations of social exclusion; to cultural diversity and 'race' equality; and to the conditions under which aspirations for citizenship can be achieved. These are major challenges for market-oriented welfare states of the 21st century.

References

Abel, E. and Nelson, M. (1990) *Circles of care: Work and identity in women's lives*, New York: State University Press.

Abramovici, G. (2003) 'Social protection: cash family benefits in Europe', in *Statistics in Focus*, Theme 3 – 19/2003, Luxembourg: Eurostat.

ABS (Australian Bureau of Statistics) (2000) *Household Expenditure Survey, user guide, 1998-99*, Catalogue No 6527.0, Canberra: ABS.

ABS (2001) *Household Expenditure Survey, Australia, government benefits, taxes and household income, 1998-99*, Catalogue No 6537.0, Canberra: ABS.

ACOSS (Australian Council of Social Service) (2005a) *Ten myths and facts about the Disability Support Pension (DSP)*, Sydney: ACOSS.

ACOSS (2005b) '300,000 Australians worse off if welfare law passed', *ACOSS News*, 25 July, Sydney: ACOSS.

Adelman, L., Middleton, S. and Ashworth, K. (2003) *Britain's poorest children: Severe and persistent poverty and social exclusion*, London: Save the Children.

Alstott, A. (2004) *No exit: What parents owe their children and what society owes parents*, Oxford: Oxford University Press.

Alvsvåg, H. and Gjengedal, E. (eds) (2000) *Omsorgstenkning: En innføring i Kari Martinsens forfatterskap*, Bergen: Fagbokforlaget.

Anderson, R. (2004) 'Working carers in the European Union', in S. Harper (ed) *Families in ageing societies*, Oxford: Oxford University Press, pp 95-113.

Arber, S. and Gilbert, N. (1989) 'Men: the forgotten carers', *Sociology*, vol 23, no 1, pp 111-18.

Arber, S. and Ginn, J. (1995) 'Gender differences in the relationship between paid employment and informal care', *Work, Employment and Society*, vol 9, no 3, pp 445-71.

Arksey, H. (2003) 'People into employment: supporting people with disabilities and carers into work', *Health and Social Care in the Community*, vol 11, no 3, pp 283-92.

Arksey, H., Kemp, P.A., Glendinning, C., Kotchetkova, I. and Tozer, R. (2005) *Carers' aspirations and decisions around work and retirement*, Department for Work and Pensions Research Report No 290, Leeds: Corporate Document Services.

Arnstein, S. (1969) 'A ladder of citizen participation', *Journal of the American Institute of Planners*, vol 35, no 4, pp 216-24.

Arthur, S., Snape, D. and Dench, G. (2003) *The moral economy of grandparenting*, London: National Centre for Social Research.

Askheim, O.P. (2005) 'Personal assistance – direct payments or alternative public service: does it matter for the promotion of user control?', *Disability & Society*, vol 20, no 3, pp 247-60.

Audit Commission (2004) *Older people – independence and well-being: The challenge for public services*, London: Audit Commission.

Badelt, C., Holzmann-Jenkins, A., Matul, C. and Österle, A. (1997) *Analyse der Auswirkungen des Pflegevorsorgesystems*, Forschungsbericht im Auftrag des BMAGS, Vienna: Bundesministerium für Arbeit, Gesundheit und Soziales.

Baldwin, S. (1985) *The costs of caring: Families with disabled children*, London: Routledge and Kegan Paul.

Baldwin, S. (1994) 'The need for care in later life: social protection for older people and family caregivers', in S. Baldwin and J. Falkingham (eds) *Social security and social change*, Hemel Hempstead: Harvester Wheatsheaf, pp 180-95.

Baldwin, S. (1995) 'Love and money: the financial consequences of caring for an older relative', in I. Allen and E. Perkins (eds) *The future of family care for older people*, London: HMSO, pp 119-40.

Baldwin, S. and Twigg, J. (1991) 'Women and community care – reflections on a debate', in M. Maclean and D. Groves (eds) *Women's issues in social policy*, London: Routledge, pp 117-35.

Barnes, C. (1991) *Disabled people in Britain and discrimination: A case for anti-discrimination legislation*, London: Hurst and Company.

Barnes, M. (1997) *Care, communities and citizens*, Harlow: Addison, Wesley and Longman.

Barnes, M., Lyon, N., Morris, S., Robinson, V. and Yau, Y.-W. (2005) *Family life in Britain: Findings from the 2003 Families and Children Study*, Department for Work and Pensions Research Report No 250, Leeds: Corporate Document Services.

Bartlett, W., Le Grand, J. and Roberts, J. (eds) (1998) *A revolution in social policy: Quasi-market reforms in the 1990s*, Bristol: The Policy Press.

Bauman, Z. (1998) *Work, consumerism and the new poor*, Buckingham: Open University Press.

Bauman, Z. (1999) *In search of politics*, Cambridge: Polity.

Beck, U. (1992) *The risk society*, London: Sage Publications.

Beck-Gernsheim, E. (2002) *Reinventing the family: In search of new lifestyles*, Cambridge: Polity.

Becker, S. (2003) "Security for those who cannot': Labour's neglected welfare principle', in J. Millar (ed) *Understanding social security*, Bristol: The Policy Press, pp 103-22.

Becker, S., Aldridge, J. and Dearden, C. (1998) *Young carers and their families*, Oxford: Blackwell Science.

Bell, A., Finch, N., La Valle, I., Sainsbury, R. and Skinner, C. (2005) *A question of balance: Lone parents, childcare and work*, Department for Work and Pensions Research Report No 230, Leeds: Corporate Document Services.

Beresford, B. (1995) *Expert opinions: A national survey of parents caring for a severely disabled child*, Bristol: The Policy Press.

Beresford, P. (2005) "Service user': regressive or liberatory terminology?', *Disability & Society*, vol 20, no 4, pp 469-77.

Beresford, P. and Croft, S. (1996) 'The politics of participation', in D. Taylor (ed) *Critical social policy: A reader*, London: Sage Publications, pp 175-98.

Beresford, P., Shamash, M., Forrest, V., Turner, M. and Branfield, F. (2005) *Start from our experience: Service users' vision for adult social care*, London: Social Care Institute for Excellence.

Berthoud, R., Lakey, J. and McKay, S. (1993) *The economic problems of disabled people*, London: Policy Studies Institute.

Better Government for Older People (2003) (www.bgop.org.uk/index.aspx?primarycat=2&secondarycat=1).

Bettio, F. and Plantenga, J. (2004) 'Comparing care regimes in Europe', *Feminist Economics*, vol 10, no 1, pp 85-113.

Bettio, F. and Prechal, S. (1998) *Care in Europe*, Joint Report of the Gender and Employment and the Gender and Law Groups of Experts, Brussels: European Commission.

Beveridge, W. (1942) *Social insurance and allied services*, London, HMSO.

Bewley, C. and Glendinning, C. (1994) *Involving disabled people in community care planning*, York: Joseph Rowntree Foundation.

Birchall, J. and Simmons, R. (2004) *User power: The participation of users in public services*, London: National Consumer Council.

Blair, T. (1997) 'Welfare reform: giving people the will to win', Speech delivered at the Aylesbury Estate, Southwark, London, 2 June.

Blaug, R. (2002) 'Engineering democracy', *Political Studies*, vol 50, no 1, pp 102-16.

Bleses, P. and Seeleib Kaiser, M. (2004) *The dual transformation of the German welfare state*, London: Palgrave.

Blumberger, W. and Dornmayr, H. (1998) *Dienstleistungen für private Haushalte*, AMS info 18, Vienna: Wissenschaftsverlag.

Blumer, H. (1969) *Symbolic interactionism: Perspective and methods*, Berkeley, CA: University of California Press.

Blunkett, D. (2000) 'Influence or irrelevance: can social science improve government?', Speech at the Economic and Social Research Council Conference, London, 2 February.

BMAGS (Bundesministerium für Arbeit, Gesundheit und Soziales) (ed) (1998) *Bericht zur sozialen Lage*, Vienna: BMAGS.

BMFV (Bundesministerin für Frauenangelegenheiten und Verbraucherschutz) (ed) (1997) *Eigenständige Alterssicherung für Frauen*, Vienna: Schriftenreihe der Bundesministerin für Frauenangelegenheiten und Verbraucherschutz, Band 14.

BMSGK (Bundesministerium für Soziale Sicherheit, Generationen und Konsumentenschutz) (ed) (2003a) *Social protection systems in Austria: A survey*, Vienna: BMSGK (see www.bmsg.gv.at).

BMSGK (ed) (2003b) *Haushaltsführung, Kinderbetreuung, Pflege*, Ergebnisse des Mikrozensus September 2002, Vienna: BMSGK.

BMUJF (Bundesministerium für Umwelt, Jugend und Familie) (ed) (1999) *Familien & Arbeitswelt, 4, Österreichischer Familienbericht*, Vienna: BMUJF.

Boaz, A. and Pawson, R. (2005) 'The perilous road from evidence to policy: five journeys compared', *Journal of Social Policy*, vol 34, no 2, pp 175-94.

Bonoli, G. (2005a) 'Switzerland: negotiating a new welfare state in a fragmented political system', in P. Taylor-Gooby (ed) *New risks, new welfare*, Oxford: Oxford University Press, pp 157-80.

Bonoli, G. (2005b) 'The politics of the new social policies: providing coverage against new social risks in mature welfare states', *Policy & Politics*, vol 33, no 3, pp 431-49.

Booth, T. (1988) *Developing policy research*, Aldershot: Avebury.

Borland, J. and Tseng, Y.-P. (2005) 'Does "work for the dole" work?', mimeo, Department of Economics, University of Melbourne.

Bourdieu, P. (1984) *Distinction: A social critique of the judgement of taste*, London: Routledge and Kegan Paul.

Bourdieu, P. (1999) *The weight of the world: Social suffering in contemporary society*, Cambridge: Polity.

Bradbury, B., Doyle, J. and Whiteford, P. (1990) *Family incomes and economic growth in the 1980s*, Reports and Proceedings No 102, Sydney: Social Policy Research Centre, University of New South Wales.

Bradshaw, J. (1980) *The Family Fund: An initiative in social policy*, London: Routledge and Kegan Paul.

Bradshaw, J., Kennedy, S., Kilkey, M., Hutton, S., Corden, A., Eardley, T., Holmes, H. and Neale, J. (1996) *The employment of lone parents*, London: Family Policy Studies Centre.

Brandth, B. and Kvande, E. (1997) *Masculinity and childcare*, Skriftserie, Center for Women's Research, NTNU, No 6/97, Trondheim: NTNU.

Brannen, J., Heptinstall, E. and Bhopal, K. (2000) *Connecting children: Care and family life in later childhood*, London: Routledge Falmer.

Bray, J.R. (2001) *Hardship in Australia: An analysis of financial stress indicators in the 1998-99 Australian Bureau of Statistics Household Expenditure Survey*, Occasional Paper No 4, Canberra: Department of Family and Community Services.

Braye, S. and Preston-Shoot, M. (1995) *Empowering practice in social care*, Buckingham: Open University Press.

Brewer, M. and Shephard, A. (2004) *Has Labour made work pay?*, York: Joseph Rowntree Foundation.

Brown, M., Conaty, P. and Mayo, E. (2003) *Life saving: Community development credit unions*, London: New Economics Foundation.

CAB (Citizens Advice Bureau) (2005) *Money with your name on it? CAB clients' experience of tax credits*, London: CAB.

Cabinet Office (1999) *Policy making for the 21st century*, London: Cabinet Office.

Cabinet Office (2000) *Adding it up: Improving analysis and modelling in central government*, London: Cabinet Office.

Cai, L. (2003) 'Length of completed spells on the Disability Support Pension (DSP) programme', *Australian Social Policy*, 2002-03, pp 101-20.

Cai, L. and Gregory, R.G. (2003) 'Inflows, outflows and the growth of the Disability Support Pension (DSP) programme', *Australian Social Policy*, 2002-03, pp 121-43.

Cai, L. and Gregory, R.G. (2004) 'Labour market conditions, applications and grants of Disability Support Pension (DSP) in Australia', *Australian Journal of Labour Economics*, vol 7, no 3, pp 375-94.

Campbell, P. (1996) 'The history of the user movement in the United Kingdom', in T. Heller, J. Reynolds, R. Gomm, R. Muston and S. Pattison (eds) *Mental health matters: A reader*, London: Macmillan, pp 218-25.

Caplovitz, D. (1963) *The poor pay more*, New York, NY: Free Press.

CARC (Community Affairs References Committee) (2004) *A hand up not a hand out: Renewing the fight against poverty: Report on poverty and financial hardship*, Canberra: The Senate, Parliament House.

Carers National Association (1999) *Welfare to work: Carers and employment project evaluation report*, London: Carers National Association.

Carmichael, F. and Charles, S. (2003) 'The opportunity costs of informal care: does gender matter?', *Journal of Health Economics*, vol 22, no 5, pp 781–803.

Carr, S. (2004) *Has service user participation made a difference to social care services?*, Position Paper No 3, London: Social Care Institute for Excellence.

Carrier, J. and Heyman, J. (1997) 'Consumption and political economy', *The Journal of the Royal Anthropological Institute*, vol 3, no 2, pp 355–73.

Carter, T. and Beresford, P. (2000) *Age and change: Models of involvement for older people*, York: York Publishing Services in association with Joseph Rowntree Foundation.

CDFA (Community Development Finance Association) (2004) *Inside out: The state of community development finance 2003*, available at: www.cdfa.org.uk.

CEC (Commission of the European Communities) (2005) *Green Paper: Confronting demographic change: A new solidarity between generations*, Brussels: European Commission.

Chin, E. (2001) *Purchasing power: Black kids and American consumer culture*, Minneapolis, IL, and London: University of Minnesota Press.

Christensen, K. (1998) *Omsorg og arbejd: En sociologisk studie av ændringer i den hjemmebaserede omsorg*, Bergen: Sosiologisk Institutt, University of Bergen.

Christensen, P. and James, A. (2000) 'Introduction: researching children and childhood: cultures of communication', in P. Christensen and A. James (eds) *Research with children: Perspectives and practices*, London: Routledge Falmer, pp 1–9.

Collard, S. and Kempson, E. (2003) *Pawnbrokers and their customers*, London: National Pawnbrokers Association.

Collard, S. and Kempson, E. (2005) *Affordable credit: The way forward*, Bristol: The Policy Press.

Commission of Inquiry into Poverty (1975) *First main report: Poverty in Australia*, Canberra: AGPS.

Commission on Social Justice (1994) *Social justice: Strategies for national renewal*, London: Vintage Press.

Commonwealth of Australia (2002) *Building a simpler system to help jobless families and individuals*, Canberra: Department of Family and Community Services.

Contandriopoulos, D. (2004) 'A sociological perspective on public participation in health care', *Social Science & Medicine*, vol 58, no 2, pp 321-30.

Coote, A. (2004) 'What works in social policy', *The Guardian*, 24 November.

Coote, A., Allen, J. and Woodhead, D. (2004) *Finding out what works*, London: King's Fund.

Council of the European Union (2000) *Lisbon European Council of 23 and 24 March 2000: Conclusions of the Presidency*, Luxembourg: Office for Official Publications of the European Communities.

CPAG (Child Poverty Action Group) (2004) *Welfare benefits and tax credits handbook*, London: CPAG.

Crompton, R. (2002) 'Employment, flexible working and the family', *British Journal of Sociology*, vol 53, no 4, pp 537-58.

Crouch, C. (1999) *Social change in western Europe*, Oxford: Oxford University Press.

CSCI (Commission for Social Care Inspection) (2005a) *The state of social care in England 2004-05*, Leeds: CSCI.

CSCI (2005b) *Social care performance 2004-05*, London: CSCI (available at: www.csci.org.uk/PDF/dis_report_2004-05.pdf),

CYPU (Children and Young People's Unit) (2002) *Young people and politics: A report on the YVote?/YNot? Project by the Children and Young People's Unit*, available at: www.cypu.gov.uk.

Dahl, H.M. and Eriksen, T. (eds) (2005) *Dilemmas of care in the Nordic welfare state: Continuity and change*, Aldershot: Ashgate.

Daly, M. (1997) 'Welfare states under pressure: cash benefits in European welfare states over the last ten years', *Journal of European Social Policy*, vol 7, no 2, pp 129-46.

Daly, M. (2002) 'Care as a good for social policy', *Journal of Social Policy*, vol 31, no 2, pp 251-70.

Datamonitor (2004) *UK non-standard and sub-prime lending 2004*, London: Datamonitor.

Davies, H., Nutley, S. and Smith, P. (eds) (2000) *What works? Evidence-based policy and practice in public services*, Bristol: The Policy Press.

Davies, H., Nutley, S. and Smith, P. (eds) (2002) *Evidence-based policy: Rhetoric and reality*, Bristol: The Policy Press.

Davies, V., Taylor, J., Hartfree, Y. and Kellard, K. (2004) *Delivering the Jobcentre Plus vision: Qualitative research with staff and customers (phase 3)*, Department for Work and Pensions Research Report No 222, Leeds: Corporate Document Services.

Davis, J. and Ridge, T. (1997) *Same scenery, different lifestyle: Rural children on a low income*, London: The Children's Society.

Dawson, T., Dickens, S. and Finer, S. (2000) *New Deal for Lone Parents: Report on qualitative interviews with individuals*, Research and Development Report ESR55, Sheffield: Employment Service.

Daycare Trust (2003) *Informal care: Bridging the childcare gap for families*, London: Daycare Trust.

Daycare Trust (2004) *Childcare costs survey*, available at: www.daycaretrust.org.uk.

Dejong, G., Batavia, A.I. and McKnew, L. (1992) 'The independent living model of personal assistance in national long-term care policy', *Generations*, vol 16, no 1, pp 89-96.

Department of FaCS (Family and Community Services) (2004) *Characteristics of disability support pensioners, June 2004*, Canberra: FaCS.

DfEE (Department for Education and Employment) (2000) *Work–life balance: Changing patterns in a changing world*, London: DfEE.

DfES (Department for Education and Skills) (2004a) *Childcare: Extending protection and broadening support*, Nottingham: DfES.

DfES (2004b) *Five year strategy for children and learners*, London: DfES.

DH (Department of Health) (1990) *Handbook of research and development*, London: DH.

DH (1999a) *Caring about carers: A national strategy for carers*, London: DH.

DH (1999b) *Community care statistics 1998*, London: DH.

DH (2001) *Practitioner's guide to carers' assessments under the Carers and Disabled Children Act 2000*, London: DH.

DH (2002) *Requirements for social work training* (vol 2004), General Social Care Council, available at: www.dh.gov.uk/assetRoot/04/06/02/62/04060262.pdf, accessed 6 February 2005.

DH (2005) *Independence, well-being and choice: Our vision for the future of social care for adults in England*, London: The Stationery Office.

DH (2006) *Your health, your care, your say: Research report on the views of the people who took part in the listening exercise*, London: DH.

DHSS (Department of Health and Social Security) (1974) *Social security provision for chronically sick and disabled people*, London: HMSO.

Dilnot, A., Kay, J. and Morris, C. (1984) *The reform of social security*, Oxford: Oxford University Press.

Disability Rights Commission (2002) *Policy statement on social care and independent living*, available at: www.drc-gb.org/publicationsandreports/, accessed March 2005.

Dixon, J., Carrier, K. and Dogan, R. (2005) 'On investigating the 'underclass': contending philosophical perspectives', *Social Policy and Society*, vol 4, no 1, pp 21-30.

Dobson, B. and Middleton, S. (1998) *Paying to care: The cost of childhood disability*, York: Joseph Rowntree Foundation.

Dobson, B., Middleton, S. and Beardsworth, A. (2001) *The impact of childhood disability on family life*, York: Joseph Rowntree Foundation.

Dominy, D. and Kempson, E. (2003) *Pay day advances: The companies and their customers*, London: British Cheque Cashers' Association.

Dörfler, S. (2004) *Das recht auf teilzeit der eltern: Top oder flop?*, Working Paper 38–2004, Vienna: Austrian Institute for Family Studies.

Douglas, M. and Isherwood, B. (1996) *The world of goods: Towards an anthropology of consumption*, London: Routledge.

Doyal, L. and Gough, I. (1991) *A theory of human need*, Basingstoke: Macmillan.

DSS (Department of Social Security) (1998) *New ambitions for our country: A new contract for welfare*, Cm 3805, London: The Stationery Office.

DSS (1999) *Opportunity for all: Tackling poverty and social exclusion*, Cm 4445, London: The Stationery Office.

Duffy, S. (2003) *Keys to citizenship*, Birkenhead: Paradigm.

Duncan, S. (1995) 'Theorizing European gender systems', *Journal of European Social Policy*, vol 5, no 4, pp 263-84.

Duncan, S. (2003) *Mothers, care and employment: Values and theories*, Care, Values and the Future of Welfare (CAVA) Working Paper, Bradford: University of Bradford.

Duncan, S. and Edwards, R. (1999) *Lone mothers, paid work and gendered moral rationalities*, London: Macmillan Press.

Dutton, P. (2005) 'Disability and work: inclusion or coercion', Paper presented to the Australian Social Policy Conference, University of New South Wales, 21 July.

DWP (Department for Work and Pensions) (2004) *Annual report by the Secretary of State for Work and Pensions on the Social Fund 2003/2004*, London: The Stationery Office.

DWP (2005a) *Households below average income: An analysis of the income distribution 1994/5-2003/04*, Leeds: Corporate Document Services.

DWP (2005b) *Five year strategy: Opportunity and security throughout life*, Cm 6447, London: The Stationery Office.

DWP (2005c) *Employment opportunity for all: DWP five year strategy*, London: DWP.

Dwyer, P. (1998) 'Conditional citizens? Welfare rights and responsibilities in the late 1990s', *Critical Social Policy*, vol 18, no 4, pp 493-517.

Eardley, T., Saunders, P. and Evans, C. (2001) 'Community attitudes towards unemployment, activity testing and mutual obligation', *Australian Bulletin of Labour*, vol 26, no 3, pp 211-35.

EC (European Commission) (2000) *Social policy agenda*, COM (2000) 379 Final, Brussels: Commission of the European Communities.

EC (2002) *Increasing labour force participation and promoting active ageing*, COM (2002) 9 Final, Brussels: Commission of the European Communities.

EC (2003) *Scoreboard on implementing the social policy agenda*, COM (2003) 57 Final, Brussels: Commission of the European Communities.

EC and Council of the European Union (2002) *Joint report on employment*, available at: www.europa.eu.int/comm/employment_social/employment_strategy/report_2002/jer2002_final_en.pdf, accessed 20 March 2003.

Edgell, S. and Hetherington, K. (1996) 'Introduction', in S. Edgell, K. Hetherington and A. Warde (eds) *Consumption matters*, Oxford: Blackwell Publishers, pp 1-8.

Edvardsen, D., Førsund, F. and Aas, E. (2000) *Effektivitet i pleie- og omsorgssektoren*, Rapport 2/2000, Stiftelsen Frischsenteret for samfunnsøkonomisk forskning, Oslo: University of Oslo.

Eliasson, R. (1987) *Forskningsetik och perspektivval*, Stockholm: Studentlitteratur, pp 231-45.

Eliasson, R. (1996) 'Efterord', in R. Eliasson (ed) *Omsorgens skiftninger*, Lund: Studentlitteratur.

Eliasson-Lappalainen, R. (1999) 'Etik och moral i äldreomsorgens vardag', in K. Christensen and L.J. Syltevik (eds) *Omsorgens forvitring? Antologi om velferdspolitiske utfordringer*, Bergen: Fagbokforlaget, pp 229-40.

Equal Opportunities Commission (2003) *Response to HM Treasury and DTI document – balancing work and family life: Enhancing choice and support for parents*, London: Equal Opportunities Commission.

Ermisch, J. and Francesconi, M. (2001) *The effects of parents' employment on children's lives*, London: Family Policy Studies Centre for the Joseph Rowntree Foundation.

Esping-Andersen, G. (1996) 'Welfare states without work: the impasse of labour shedding and familialism in continental European social policy', in G. Esping-Andersen (ed) *Welfare states in transition: National adaptions in global economies*, London: Sage Publications, pp 66-87.

Esping-Andersen, G. (1999) *Social foundations of post-industrial economies*, New York, NY, and Oxford: Oxford University Press.

Esping-Andersen, G. (2002) *Why we need a new welfare state*, Oxford: Oxford University Press.

Esping-Andersen, G., Gallie, D., Hemerijck, A. and Myles, J. (2001) *A new welfare architecture for Europe? Report to the Belgian Presidency of the EU*, Brussels: Commission of the European Communities.

Esping-Andersen, G., Gallie, D., Hemerijck, A. and Myles, J. (2002) *Why we need a new welfare state*, Oxford: Oxford University Press.

European Foundation for the Improvement of Living and Working Conditions (2000) *Employment and working time in Europe*, Dublin: European Foundation for the Improvement of Living and Working Conditions.

European Foundation for the Improvement of Living and Working Conditions (2003) *Flexibility and social protection*, Luxembourg: Office for Official Publications of the European Communities.

Evandrou, M. (1995) 'Employment and care, paid and unpaid work: the socio-economic position of informal carers in Britain', in J.E. Phillips (ed) *Working carers: International perspectives on working and caring for older people*, Aldershot: Avebury, pp 20-41.

Evandrou, M. and Glaser, K. (2003) 'Combining work and family life: the pension penalty of caring', *Ageing and Society*, vol 23, no 5, pp 583-602.

Evandrou, M. and Winter, D. (1993) *Informal carers and the labour market in Britain*, London: Suntory and Toyota International Centre for Economics and Related Disciplines, London School of Economics and Political Science.

Evans, M., Harkness, S. and Ortiz, R. (2004) *Lone parents: Cycling in and out of work and benefit*, Department for Work and Pensions Research Report No 217, Leeds: Corporate Document Services.

Faris, N. and McLaughlin, E. (2004) *Report of the independent element of the operational review of the statutory equality duty in Northern Ireland*, London and Belfast: Northern Ireland Office and Office of the First Minister and Deputy First Minister.

Farrell, C. and O'Connor, W. (2003) *Low-income families and household spending*, Department for Work and Pensions Research Report No 192, Leeds: Corporate Document Services.

Ferge, Z. (1997) 'The changed welfare paradigm: the individualisation of the social', *Social Policy and Administration*, vol 31, no 1, pp 20-44.

Ferrera, M., Hemerijck, A. and Rhodes, M. (2000) *The future of social Europe: Recasting work and welfare in the new economy*, Report for the Portuguese Presidency of the European Union, Pavia: University of Pavia; Milan: Bocconi University; Leiden: Department of Public Administration, Leiden; Florence: Department of Social and Political Studies, European University Institute.

Financial Times (2004) 'Middle East and Europe: the IMF calls for longer working hours in Eurozone', 4 August.

Financial Times (2006) 'Gaps in social services funding 'will put NHS targets at risk'', 16 March.

Finch, H., O'Connor, W. with Millar, J., Hales, J., Shaw, A. and Roth, W. (1999) *New Deal for Lone Parents: Learning from the prototype areas*, Department of Social Security Research Report No 92, Leeds: Corporate Document Services.

Finch, J. and Groves, D. (eds) (1983) *A labour of love: Women, work and caring*, London: Routledge and Kegan Paul.

Finch, J. and Mason, J. (1993) *Negotiating family responsibilities*, London and New York, NY: Tavistock/Routledge.

Finch, N. and Kemp, P.A. (2004) *The use of the Social Fund by families with children*, London: Department for Work and Pensions.

Fine, M. (2004) 'Renewing the social vision of care', *Australian Journal of Social Issues*, vol 39, no 3, pp 217-32.

Finn, D. (2003) 'Employment policy', in N. Ellison and C. Pierson (eds) *Developments in British social policy 2*, Basingstoke: Palgrave, pp 111-28.

Fisher, B. and Tronto, J. (1990) 'Towards a feminist theory of caring', in E. Able and M. Nelson (eds) *Circles of care, work and identity in women's lives*, New York, NY: State University of New York Press.

Folbre, N. (1994) *Who pays for the kids? Gender and the structures of constraint*, London: Routledge.

Folbre, N. (1995) 'Holding hands at midnight: the paradox of caring labor', *Feminist Economics*, vol 1, no 1, pp 73-92.

Folbre, N. (2004a) 'A theory of the misallocation of time', in N. Folbre and M. Bittman (eds) *Family time: The social organisation of care*, London: Routledge, pp 7-24.

Folbre, N. (2004b) 'Questioning care economics', in K. Wærness (ed) *Dialogue on care* (volume 16), Bergen: Centre for Women's and Gender Research, University of Bergen, Skriftserien, pp 11-14.

Folbre, N. and Nelson, J.A. (2000) 'For love or money – or both?', *Journal of Economic Perspectives*, vol 14, no 4, pp 123-40.

Foucault, M. (1973) *The birth of the clinic: An archaeology of medical perception*, London: Tavistock Publications.

Foucault, M. (1988) 'Technologies of the self', in L.H. Martin, H. Gutman and P.H. Hutton (eds) *Technologies of the self*, Amherst, MA: University of Massachusetts Press, pp 16-49.

Foucault, M. (1991) 'Governmentality', in G. Burchell, C. Gordon and P. Miller (eds) *The Foucault effect: Studies in governmentality: With two lectures by and an interview with Michel Foucault*, Chicago, IL: University of Chicago Press, pp 87–104.

Fox, N. (2003) 'Practice-based evidence: towards collaborative and transgressive research', *Sociology*, vol 37, no 1, pp 81–102.

Frankfurt, H. (2005) *On bullshit*, Oxford: Princeton University Press.

Fraser, N. (1994) 'After the family wage: gender equity and the welfare state', *Political Theory*, vol 22, no 4, pp 591–618.

Fraser, N. (1997) *Justice interrupts: Critical reflections on the 'post-socialist' condition*, London: Routledge.

Fung, A. and Wright, E. (2001) 'Deepening democracy: innovations in empowered participatory governance', *Politics and Society*, vol 29, no 1, pp 5–41.

Galinsky, E. (1999) *Ask the children: What America's children really think about working parents*, New York, NY: William Morrow.

Gautier, J. and Gazier, B. (2003) 'Equipping markets for people: transitional labour markets as the central part of a new social model', Paper presented at the SASE conference, Aix en Provence, 18 June.

Gershuny, J. (2000) *Changing times: Work and leisure in post-industrial society*, Oxford: Oxford University Press.

Giddens, A. (1991) *Modernity and self-identity*, Cambridge: Polity.

Gilbert, N. (2002) *The transformation of the welfare state: The silent surrender of public responsibility*, Oxford: Oxford University Press.

Ginn, J. (2003) *Gender, pensions and the lifecourse: How pensions need to adapt to changing family forms*, Bristol: The Policy Press.

Glasby, J. and Littlechild, R. (2002) *Social work and direct payments*, Bristol: The Policy Press.

Gleeson, B. (1998) 'Disability and poverty', in R. Fincher and J. Niewenhuysen (eds) *Australian poverty: Then and now*, Melbourne: Melbourne University Press, pp 314–33.

Glendinning, C. (1990) 'Dependency and interdependency – the incomes of informal carers and the impact of social security', *Journal of Social Policy*, vol 19, no 4, pp 469–97.

Glendinning, C. (1992) *The costs of informal care: Looking inside the household*, London: HMSO.

Glendinning, C. and Igl, G. (2006: forthcoming) 'Long term care', in G. Naegele and A. Walker (eds) *Social policy in ageing societies: Britain and Germany compared*, Basingstoke: Palgrave Macmillan.

Glendinning, C. and McLaughlin, E. (1993) *Paying for care: Lessons from Europe*, Social Security Advisory Committee Research Paper No 5, London: HMSO.

Glendinning, C., Schunk, M. and McLaughlin, E. (1997) 'Paying for long term domiciliary care: a comparative perspective', *Ageing & Society*, vol 17, no 2, pp 123-40.

Godfrey, M., Townsend, J. and Denby, T. (2004) *Building a good life for older people in local communities*, York: Joseph Rowntree Foundation.

Goode, J., Callender, C. and Lister, R. (1998) *Purse or wallet? Gender inequalities and income distribution among families on benefits*, London: Policy Studies Institute.

Gordon, D. (2000) 'The scientific measurement of poverty: recent theoretical advances', in J. Bradshaw and R. Sainsbury (eds) *Researching poverty*, Aldershot: Ashgate, pp 37-58.

Gordon, D., Adelman, L., Ashworth, K., Bradshaw, J., Levitas, R., Middleton, S., Pantazis, C., Patsios, D., Payne, S., Townsend, P. and Williams, J. (2000) *Poverty and social exclusion in Britain*, York: Joseph Rowntree Foundation.

Gorman, H. and Postle, K. (2003) *Transforming community care: A distorted vision?*, Birmingham: Venture Press.

Gornick, J. and Meyers, M. (2003) *Families that work: Policies for reconciling parenthood and employment*, New York: Russell Sage.

Gornick, J.C., Meyers, M.K. and Ross, K.E. (1997) 'Supporting the employment of mothers: policy variation across fourteen welfare states', *Journal of European Social Policy*, vol 7, no 1, pp 45-70.

Gough, R. (1987) *Hemhjälp till gamla*, Stockholm: Arbetslivcentrum.

Gough, R. (1996) *Personlig assistans: En social bemästringsstrategi*, Göteborg: GIL förlaget.

Graham, H. (2002) 'Building an inter-disciplinary science of health inequalities: the example of lifecourse research', *Social Science & Medicine*, vol 55, no 11, pp 2005-16.

Graham, J., Tennant, R., Huxley, M. and O'Connor, W. (2005) *The role of work in low-income families with children – a longitudinal qualitative study*, Department for Work and Pensions Research Report No 245, Leeds: Corporate Document Services.

Gregg, P. and Washbrook, E. (2003) *The effects of early maternal employment on child development in the UK*, Working Paper 03/070, Bristol: Centre for Market and Public Organisation.

Griffiths, R. (1988) *Community care: Agenda for action*, The Griffiths Report, London: HMSO.

Hadley, R. and Hatch, S. (1981) *Social welfare and the failure of the state: Centralised social services and participatory alternatives*, London: George Allen and Unwin.

Hammer, E. and Österle, A. (2001a) 'Neoliberale gouvernementalität im österreichischen wohlfahrtsstaat: von der reform der pflegevorsorge 1993 zum kinderbetreuungsgeld 2002', *Kurswechsel*, no 4, pp 60-9.

Hammer, E. and Österle, A. (2001b) *Welfare state policy and informal long-term-caregiving in Austria: Old gender divisions and new stratification processes among women*, Working Paper No 7, Vienna: Department of Social Policy, Vienna University of Economics and Business Administration.

Hammersley, M. (2001) 'On 'systematic reviews' of research literatures: a 'narrative' response to Evans & Benefield', *British Educational Research Journal*, vol 27, no 5, pp 543-54.

Hancock, R. and Jarvis, C. (1994) *The long term effects of being a carer*, London: HMSO.

Harding, A. (1996) 'Recent trends in income inequality in Australia', in P. Sheehan, B. Grewal and M. Kumnick (eds) *Dialogues on Australia's future: In honour of the late Professor Ronald Henderson*, Melbourne: Centre for Strategic Economic Studies, Victoria University, pp 281-305.

Hargreaves, D. (1996) *Teaching as a research-based profession: Possibilities and prospects*, Teacher Training Agency Annual Lecture, London: Teacher Training Agency.

Harries, T. and Woodfield, K. (2002) *Easing the transition into work*, Department for Work and Pensions Research Report No 175, Leeds: Corporate Document Services.

Hasler, F. (2004) 'Direct payments', in J. Swain, S. French, C. Barnes and C. Thomas (eds) *Disabling barriers: Enabling environments* (2nd edn), London: Sage Publications, pp 219-25.

Hasler, F., Campbell, J. and Zarb, G. (1999) *Direct routes to independence*, London: Policy Studies Institute.

Hawkins, S. (1991) 'Child Benefit: what now?', *Benefits*, no 1, pp 37-8.

Heitmueller, A. and Inglis, K. (2004) *Carefree? Participation and pay differentials for informal carers in Britain*, IZA Discussion Paper No 1273, Bonn: Institute for the Study of Labor (IZA).

Heitzmann, K. and Schmidt, A. (eds) (2004) *Wege aus der frauenarmut*, Band 14 der Schriftenreihe 'Frauen, Forschung, Wirtschaft', Frankfurt: Peter Lang.

Henry, K. (2003) 'Address to the Melbourne Institute's 40th anniversary dinner', Melbourne Institute of Applied Economic and Social Research, University of Melbourne, 7 February.

Herbert, A. and Kempson, E. (1996) *Credit use and ethnic minorities*, London: Policy Studies Institute.

Herz, N. (2001) 'Democracy in crisis: why we stayed away', *The Observer*, 21 May.

Hetherington, P. (2002) 'Phone voting 'will entice' young', *The Guardian*, 10 April, p 7.

Hewitt, M. (1999) 'New Labour and social security', in M. Powell (ed) *New Labour, new welfare state?*, Bristol: The Policy Press, pp 149-70.

Heyman, J. (2000) *The widening gap: Why America's working families are in jeopardy and what can be done about it*, New York, NY: Basic Books.

Hills, J. (2004) *Inequality and the state*, Oxford: Oxford University Press.

Himmelweit, S. and Sigala, M. (2004) 'Choice and the relationship between identities and behaviour for mothers with pre-school children: some implications for policy from a UK study', *Journal of Social Policy*, vol 33, no 3, pp 455-78.

Hirschman, D. (1970) *Exit, voice and loyalty*, Cambridge, MA: Harvard University Press.

Hirst, M. (2001) 'Trends in informal care in Britain', *Health and Social Care in the Community*, vol 9, no 6, pp 348-57.

Hirst, M. (2002) 'Transitions to informal care in Great Britain during the 1990s', *Journal of Epidemiology and Community Health*, vol 56, no 8, pp 579-87.

Hjort, T. (2002) *Konsumtionsvillkår för hushåll med knapp ekonomi – et svagt utvecklat kunskapsfält*, Working Paper 1:2 2002, Copenhagen: The Danish National Institute of Social Research (Socialforskningsinstituttet).

Hjort, T. (2004) *Nödvändighetens pris: Konsumtion och knapphet bland barnfamiljer*, Lund Dissertations in Social Work No 20, Lund: Lund University.

HMRC (HM Revenue & Customs) (2005) *Child and working tax credits statistics, April 2005*, London: National Statistics.

HM Treasury (2004a) *Promoting financial inclusion*, London: HM Treasury.

HM Treasury (2004b) *The child poverty review*, Norwich: HMSO.

HM Treasury (2004c) *Choice for parents, the best start for children: A ten year strategy for childcare*, Norwich: HMSO.

HM Treasury (2005a) *Britain meeting the global challenge: Enterprise, fairness and responsibility*, Pre-Budget Report 2005, Cm 6701, London: The Stationery Office.

HM Treasury (2005b) *Budget 2005: Investing for our future: Fairness and opportunity for Britain's hard working families*, London: The Stationery Office.

Hochschild, A.R. (1975) 'The sociology of feeling and emotion: selected possibilities', in M. Millman and R.M. Kanter (eds) *Another voice*, New York, NY: Anchor Books, pp 280-307.

Hochschild, A.R. (1995) 'The culture of politics: traditional, postmodern, cold-modern and warm-modern ideals of care', *Social Politics: International Studies in Gender, State and Society*, vol 2, no 3, pp 331-46.

Howard, M. (2001) *Not just the job: Report of a working group on disabled people using personal assistance and work incentives*, York: Joseph Rowntree Foundation.

Huber, J. and Skidmore, P. (2003) *The new old: Why baby boomers won't be pensioned off*, London: DEMOS.

Hudson, J. and Lowe, S. (2004) *Understanding the policy process: Analysing welfare policy and practice*, Bristol: The Policy Press.

Hunt, A. (1970) *The home help service in England and Wales*, Government Social Survey, London: HMSO.

Huxley, P. (1993) 'Case management and care management in community care', *British Journal of Social Work*, vol 23, no 4, pp 365-81.

Hyde, A., Lohan, M. and McDonnell, O. (2004) *Sociology for health professionals in Ireland*, Dublin: Institute of Public Administration.

James, A. and Prout, A. (1997) 'A new paradigm for the sociology of childhood? Provenance, promise and problems', in A. James and A. Prout (eds) *Construction and reconstructing childhood* (2nd edn), London: Falmer, pp 7-33.

Jenkins, S. and Rigg, J. (2001) *The dynamics of poverty in Britain*, Department for Work and Pensions Research Report No 157, Leeds: Corporate Document Services.

Jensen, J. and Jacobzone, S. (2000) *Care allowances for the frail elderly and their impact on women care givers*, Labour Market and Social Policy Occasional Paper 41, Paris: Organisation for Economic Co-operation and Development.

Jenson, J. and Sineau, M. (eds) (2001) *Women's work, childcare, and welfare state redesign*, Toronto: University of Toronto Press.

Jochimsen, M.A. (2003) *Careful economics: Integrating caring activities and economic science*, Boston, MA: Kluwer Academic Publishers.

Jones, P. (2002) *Access to credit on a low income*, Manchester: The Cooperative Bank.

Joshi, H. and Verropoulou, G. (2000) *Maternal employment and child outcomes: Analysis of two birth cohort studies*, London: The Smith Institute.

Kagan, C., Lewis, S. and Heaton, P. (1998) *Caring to work: Accounts of working parents of disabled children*, London: Family Policy Studies Centre.

Kasparova, D., Marsh, A., Vegeris, S. and Perry, J. (2003) *Families and children 2001: Work and childcare*, Department for Work and Pensions Research Report No 191, Leeds: Corporate Document Services.

Kaufman, F.-X., Kuijsten, A., Schulze, H.J. and Strohmeier, K.P. (eds) (2002) *Family life and family policies in Europe* (volume 2), Oxford: Oxford University Press.

Keefe, J., Fancey, P. and Glendinning, C. (forthcoming) 'Financial support for informal carers: policy approaches and debates', in A. Martin-Matthews and J. Phillips (eds) *Blurring the boundaries: Ageing at the intersection of work and home life*, Mahwah, NJ: Lawrence Erlbaum Associates.

Kelly, G. and Muers, S. (2002) *Creating public value: An analytical framework for public service reform*, London: Strategy Unit.

Kemp, P.A. (2005) 'Routes out of poverty', *Benefits*, vol 13, no 3, pp 173-78.

Kempson, E. (1996) *Life on a low income*, York: York Publishing Services for Joseph Rowntree Foundation.

Kempson, E. (2002) *Over-indebtedness in Britain*, London: Department of Trade and Industry.

Kempson, E. and Whyley, C. (1999) *Kept out or opted out? Understanding and combating financial exclusion*, Bristol: The Policy Press.

Kempson, E., Bryson, A. and Rowlingson, K. (1994) *Hard times? How poor families make ends meet*, London: Policy Studies Institute.

Kiernan, K., Land, H. and Lewis, J. (1998) *Lone motherhood in twentieth century Britain*, Oxford: Oxford University Press.

King, A. (1998) 'Income poverty since the 1970s', in R. Fincher and J. Niewenhuysen (eds) *Australian poverty: Then and now*, Melbourne: Melbourne University Press, pp 71-102.

Kirkevoll, M. (2000) 'Utviklingstrekk i Kari Martinsens forfatterskap', in H. Alvsvåg and E. Gjengedal (eds) *Omsorgstenkning: En innføring i Kari Martinsens forfatterskap*, Bergen: Fagbokforlaget, pp 193-208.

Knijn, T. (2000) 'Marketisation and the struggling logics of (home) care in the Netherlands', in M. Harrington (ed) *Care work, gender, labor and the welfare state*, London and New York, NY: Routledge, pp 232-48.

Knijn, T. (2001) 'Care work: innovations in the Netherlands', in M. Daly (ed) *Care work: The quest for security*, Geneva: International Labour Office, pp 159-74.

Knijn, T. (2004) 'Challenges and risks of individualisation in The Netherlands', *Social Policy and Society*, vol 3, no 1, pp 57-65.

Knijn, T. and Kremer, M. (1997) 'Gender and the caring dimension of welfare states: towards inclusive citizenship', *Social Politics*, vol 4, no 3, pp 328-61.

Kochuyt, T. (2004) 'Giving away one's poverty: on the consumption of scarce resources within the family', *The Sociological Review*, vol 52, no 2, pp 139-61.

Kreimer, M. (2003) 'Wahlfreiheit und chancengleichheit: frauenpolitik zwischen familie und beruf', *Kurswechsel*, 2002-03, pp 27-36.

Kreimer, M. and Schiffbänker, H. (2005) 'The Austrian care arrangement and the role of informal care for social integration', in B. Pfau-Effinger and B. Geissler (eds) *Care and social integration in European societies*, Bristol: The Policy Press, pp 173-91.

Kröger, T., Anttonen, A. and Sipilä, J. (2003) 'Social care in Finland: stronger and weaker forms of universalism', in A. Antonnen, J. Baldock and J. Sipilä (eds) *The young, the old and the state: Social care systems in five industrial countries*, Cheltenham: Edward Elgar, pp 25-54.

Kuhn, T. (1962) *The structure of scientific revolutions*, Chicago, IL: University of Chicago Press.

La Tour, B. (1993) *We have never been modern*, Hemel Hempstead: Harvester Wheatsheaf.

La Valle, I., Finch, S., Nove, A. and Lewin, C. (2000) *Parents' demand for childcare*, Department for Education and Employment Research Report No 176, Nottingham: Department for Education and Employment.

Laing, W. (2002) *Calculating a fair price for care: A toolkit for residential and nursing care costs*, Bristol: The Policy Press.

Laing, W. and Saper, P. (1999) 'Promoting the development of a flourishing independent sector alongside good quality public services', in Royal Commission on Long Term Care *With respect to old age: Long term care – rights and responsibilities*, Research Volume 3, Cm 4192-II/3, London: The Stationery Office, pp 87-102.

Land, H. (1983) 'Who still cares for the family?', in J. Lewis (ed) *Women's welfare: Women's rights*, London: Croom Helm, pp 64-85.

Land, H. (1994) 'The demise of the male breadwinner – in practice but not in theory: a challenge for social security systems' in S. Baldwin and J. Falkingham (eds) *Social security and social change*, Hemel Hempstead: Harvester Wheatsheaf, pp 100-15.

Land, H. (2002) 'Spheres of care in the UK: separate and unequal', *Critical Social Policy*, vol 22, no 1, pp 13-32.

Laurie, H. and Gershuny, J. (2000) 'Couples, work and money', in R. Berthoud and J. Gershuny (eds) *Seven years in the lives of British families*, Bristol: The Policy Press, pp 45-72.

Leder, D. (1990) *The absent body*, Chicago, IL: Aldine.

Leece, J. and Bornat, J. (2006) *Developments in direct payments*, Bristol: The Policy Press.

Leitner, S. (2003) 'Varieties of familialism: the caring function of the family in comparative perspective', *European Societies*, vol 5, no 4, pp 353-75.

Lewis, J. (1992) 'Gender and the development of welfare regimes', *Journal of European Social Policy*, vol 2, no 3, pp 159-73.

Lewis, J. (2001) 'The decline of the male breadwinner model: the implications for work and care', *Social Politics*, vol 8, no 2, pp 152-70.

Lewis, J. (2002) 'Gender and welfare state change', *European Societies*, vol 4, no 4, pp 331-57.

Lewis, J. (2003) 'Developing early years childcare in England, 1997-2002', *Social Policy and Administration*, vol 37, no 3, pp 219-38.

Lewis, J. and Giullari, S. (2005) 'The adult worker model family, gender equality and care: the search for new policy principles and the possibilities and problems of a capabilities approach', *Economy and Society*, vol 34, no 1, pp 76-104.

Lewis, J. and Glennerster, H. (1996) *Implementing the new community care*, Buckingham: Open University Press.

Lewis, J. and Hobson, B. (1997) 'Introduction', in J. Lewis (ed) *Lone mothers in European welfare regimes: Shifting policy logics*, London/Philadelphia, PA: Jessica Kingsley Publishers, pp 1-20.

Lewis, J. and Meredith, B. (1987) *Daughters who care*, London: Routledge.

Lewis, J. and Ostner, I. (1994) *Gender and the evolution of European social policies*, Working Paper No 4/94, Bremen: Centre for Social Policy Research, University of Bremen.

Lewis, J., Mitchell, L., Sanderson, T., O'Connor, W. and Clayden, M. (2000) *Lone parents and personal advisers: Roles and relationships*, Department of Social Security Research Report No 122, Leeds: Corporate Document Services.

Lewis, V. (2001) *Family and work: The family perspective*, Melbourne: Australian Institute for Family Studies.

Lindblom, C. (1979) 'Still muddling, not yet through', *Public Administration Review*, vol 39, no 6, pp 517-26.

Lister, R. (1994a) "She has other duties' – women, citizenship and social security', in S. Baldwin and J. Falkingham (eds) *Social security and social change*, Hemel Hempstead: Harvester Wheatsheaf, pp 31-44.

Lister, R. (1994b) 'Dilemmas in engendering citizenship', Paper presented at a 'Panel on social citizenship: the dilemmas of gender', at the 'Crossing Borders' conference, Stockholm, 27-29 May.

Lister, R. (1997) *Citizenship: Feminist perspectives*, Basingstoke: Macmillan.

Lister, R. (2000) 'Strategies for social inclusion: promoting social cohesion or social justice', in P. Askonas and A. Stewart (eds) *Social inclusion: Possibilities and tensions*, Basingstoke: Palgrave, pp 37-54.

Lister, R. (2002) 'The dilemmas of pendulum politics: balancing paid work, care and citizenship', *Economy and Society*, vol 31, no 4, pp 520-32.

Lister, R. (2003) *Citizenship: Feminist perspectives*, Basingstoke: Macmillan.

Lister, R. (2004) *Poverty*, Cambridge: Polity.

Lloyd, L. (2000) 'Caring about carers – only half the picture?', *Critical Social Policy*, vol 20, no 1, pp 136-50.

Lloyd, L. (2003) 'Caring relationships: looking beyond welfare categories of 'carers' and 'service users'', in K. Stalker (ed) *Reconceptualising work with 'carers': New directions for policy and practice*, Research Highlights in Social Work 43, London: Jessica Kingsley Publishers, pp 37-55.

Lødemel, I. and Trickey, H. (eds) (2001) *'An offer you can't refuse':Workfare in international perspective*, Bristol: The Policy Press.

Lodziak, C. (2002) *The myth of consumerism*, London: Pluto Press.

Löfgren, O. (1996) 'Konsumption som vardaglig praktik och ideologiskt slagfält', *Socialventenskaplig tidskrift*, nos 1-2, pp 116-27.

Lohan, M. and Coleman, C. (2005) 'Explaining the absence of the lay voice in sexual health through sociological theories of healthcare', *Social Theory and Health*, vol 3, no 2, pp 83-104.

London Edinburgh Weekend Return Group (1979) *In and against the state*, London: Pluto.

Lundsgaard, J. (2005) *Consumer direction and choice in long term care for older persons, including payments for informal care: How can it help improve care outcomes, employment and sustainability?*, Paris: Organisation for Economic Co-operation and Development.

Lutz, H. (2003) 'Auswirkungen der kindergeldregelung auf die beschäftigung von frauen mit kleinkindern', *Wifo-Monatsberichte*, vol 76, no 3, pp 213-27.

Lutz, H. (2004) *Wiedereinstieg und beschäftigung von frauen mit kleinkindern*, Wifo–Monographien 3/2004, Vienna: Österreichisches Institut für Wirtschaftsforschung.

McColl, R., Pietsch, L. and Gatenby, J. (2001) 'Household income, living standards and financial stress', *Australian Economic Indicators: June 2001*, Catalogue No 1350.0, Canberra: Australian Bureau of Statistics, pp 13-32.

McKay, S. and Rowlingson, K. (1999) *Social security in Britain*, Basingstoke: Macmillan.

McLaughlin, E. (1991) *Social security and community care: The case of the Invalid Care Allowance*, Department of Social Security Research Report No 4, London: HMSO.

McLaughlin, E. (1992) 'Mixed blessings? The Invalid Care Allowance and carers' income needs', *Benefits*, no 3, pp 8-11.

McLaughlin, E. (1993) 'Paying for care in Europe: carers' income needs and the Invalid Care Allowance in Britain', in J. Twigg (ed) *Informal care in Europe*, York: Social Policy Research Unit, University of York, pp 191-214.

McLaughlin, E. and Byrne, B. (2005) *Equality and disability – themes of sameness and difference*, Equality and Social Inclusion in Ireland Project Working Paper No 9, Belfast: Queen's University of Belfast.

McLaughlin, E., Millar, J. and Cooke, K. (1989) *Work and welfare benefits*, Aldershot: Avebury.

Madden, D. and Walker, I. (1999) *Labour supply, health and caring: Evidence from the UK*, Dublin: University College Dublin.

Maher, J. and Green, H. (2002) *Carers 2000*, London: The Stationery Office.

Mairhuber, I. (2000) *Die regulierung des geschlechterverhältnisses im Sozialstaat Österreich: Traditionen, wandel und feministisches umbauoptionen*, Frankfurt: Peter Lang.

Marmot, M. (2004) 'Evidence based policy or policy based evidence', *British Medical Journal*, vol 328, no 7445, pp 906-7.

Marsh, A. and Vegeris, S. (2004) *The British lone parent cohort and their children 1991–2001*, Department for Work and Pensions Research Report No 209, Leeds: Corporate Document Services.

Martimo, K. (1998) 'Community care for frail older people in Finland', in C. Glendinning (ed) *Rights and realities: Comparing new developments in long-term care for older people*, Bristol: The Policy Press, pp 67-82.

Martinsen, K. (1989) *Omsorg, sykepleie og medisin*, Bergen: TANO.

Martinsen, K. (1993) *Fra Marx til Løgstrup: Om moral, samfunnskritikk og sanselighet i Sykepleien*, Oslo: TANO.

Martinsen, K. (1996) *Fenomenologi og omsorg: Tre dialoger med etterord av Katie Eriksson*, Oslo: Tano Aschehoug.

Martinsen, K. (2000) *Øyet og kallet: Sykepleiefilosofiske betraktninger*, Bergen: Fagbokforlaget.

Mason, P. (1990) 'The place of Le Court residents in the history of the disability movement', Unpublished paper on The Disability Archive UK website: www.leeds.ac.uk/disability-studies/archiveuk/titles.html, accessed March 2005.

Means, R. and Smith, R. (1998) *Community care: Policy and practice* (2nd edn), Basingstoke: Macmillan.

Means, R., Morbey, H. and Smith, R. (2002) *From community care to market care? The development of welfare services for older people*, Bristol: The Policy Press.

Medwar, P. (1984) *The limits of science*, Oxford: Oxford University Press.

Metlife Mature Market Institute (1997) *The Metlife study of employer costs for working caregivers*, New York: Metropolitan Life Insurance Company (www.metlife.com).

Middleton, S., Ashworth, K. and Braithwaite, I. (1997) *Small fortunes*, York: Joseph Rowntree Foundation.

Middleton, S., Ashworth, K. and Walker, R. (1994) *Family fortunes*, London: Child Poverty Action Group.

Millar, J. (2005) 'Work as welfare? Lone mothers, social security and employment', in P. Saunders (ed) *Welfare to work in practice: Social security and participation in economic and social life*, Aldershot: Ashgate, pp 23-42.

Millar, J. and Ridge, T. (2001) *Families, poverty, work and care: A review of the literature on lone parents and low-income couple families with children*, Department for Work and Pensions Research Report No 153, Leeds: Corporate Document Services.

Millar, J. and Warman, A. (1995) *Family obligations in Europe*, London: Family Policy Studies Centre.

Miller, E.J. and Gwynne, G.V. (1972) *A life apart*, London: Tavistock.

Milne, A. (2001) *Caring in later life: Reviewing the role of older carers*, London: Help the Aged.

Mizen, P., Pole, C. and Bolton, A. (2001) 'Why be a school age worker?', in P. Mizen, C. Pole and A. Bolton (eds) *Hidden hands: International perspectives on children's work and labour*, London: Routledge Falmer, pp 37-54.

Molloy, D. and Snape, D. (1999) *Low income households: Financial organisation and financial exclusion*, London: Department of Social Security.

Mooney, A., Statham, J. and Simon, A. (2002) *The pivot generation: Informal care and work after fifty*, Bristol: The Policy Press.

Morgan, K. and Zippel, K. (2003) 'Paid to care: the origins and effects of care leave policies in western Europe', *Social Politics*, vol 10, no 1, pp 45-85.

Morris, A. and Abello, D. (2004) *Disability Support Pension new customer focus groups*, Report prepared for the Department of Family and Community Services, Sydney: Social Policy Research Centre, University of New South Wales.

Morris, J. (1991) *Pride against prejudice*, London: The Women's Press.

Morris, J. (1993) *Independent lives? Disabled people and community care*, Basingstoke: Macmillan Press.

Morris, J. (2001) 'Impairment and disability: constructing an ethics of care that promotes human rights', *Hypatia*, vol 16, no 4, pp 1-16.

Morris, J. (2004) 'Independent living and community care: a disempowering framework', *Disability and Society*, vol 19, no 5, pp 427-42.

Morris, J. (2005) 'Citizenship and disabled people', Paper commissioned by the Disability Rights Commission, available at: www.drc.gov.uk/disabilitydebate/uploads/Citizenship_and_disabled_people_final.doc, accessed September 2005.

Morrison, J. and Newman, D. (2001) 'On-line citizenship: consultation and participation in New Labour's Britain and beyond', *International Review of Law, Computers and Technology*, vol 15, no 2, pp 171-94.

Moss, P. and Deven, F. (1999) *Parental leave: Progress or pitfall? Research and policy issues in Europe*, Brussels: NIDI/CBGS Publications.

Mühlberger, U. (2000) *Neue formen der beschäftigung: Arbeitsflexibilisierung durch atypische beschäftigung in Österreich*, Vienna: Braumüller.

Murgatroyd, L. and Newberger, H. (1997) 'Household satellite account for the UK', *Economic Trends*, no 527, October.

National Audit Office (2004) *Early years: Progress in developing high quality childcare and early education accessible to all*, Report by the Comptroller and Auditor General, HC 268 Session 2003-2004, London: The Stationery Office.

National Audit Office (2005) *Inland Revenue: Standard report 2003-2004: Child and working tax credits and stamp duty land tax*, London: National Audit Office.

National Centre for Social Research (2000) *Political interest and engagement among young people*, York: Joseph Rowntree Foundation, available at: www.jrf.org.uk/knowledge/findings/socialpolicy/pdf/520.pdf.

National Consumer Council and Policis (2005) *Affordable credit: A model that recognises real needs* (Factsheet), London: National Consumer Council (available at: www.ncc.org.uk).

NAVF (Norges Almenvitenskapelige Forskningsråd) (1979) *Lønnet og ulønnet omsorg*, Arbeidsnotat 5/79, Oslo: Norges Almenvitenskapelige Forskningsråd, Sekretariat for Kvinneforskning.

Needham, C. (2003) *Citizen-consumers: New Labour's marketplace democracy*, London: Catalyst.

Needham, C. (2004) 'Customer care and the public service ethos', Paper presented at the Political Studies Association conference, Lincoln, 6–8 April.

Nelson, E.A. (2003) 'Once more, with feeling: feminist economics and the ontological question', *Feminist Economics*, vol 9, no 1, pp 109–18.

NESC (National Economic and Social Council) (2005) *The developmental welfare state*, Report 113, Dublin: NESC.

Netten, A., Darton, R. and Williams, J. (2002) *The rate, causes and consequences of home closures*, Discussion Paper 1741/2, Canterbury: Personal Social Services Research Unit, University of Kent.

Netten, A., Williams, J. and Darton, R. (2005) 'Care-home closures in England: causes and implications', *Ageing & Society*, vol 25, no 3, pp 319–38.

Neyer, G., Buber, I., Horvath, T., Oberdammer, P. and Streissler, A. (1999) *Karenzurlaub*, Vienna: Unveröffentlichte Studie im Auftrag des AMS.

NOU (Norges offentlige utredninger) (1976) *Levekårsundersøkelsen*, Sluttrapport, Oslo: Norges offentlige utredninger, Universitetsforlaget.

Nussbaum, M. (1999) *Sex and social justice*, Oxford: Oxford University Press.

Nussbaum, M. (2003) 'Capabilities as fundamental entitlements: Sen and social justice', *Feminist Economics*, vol 9, no 2–3, pp 33–59.

Nussbaum, M. (2004) 'Care, dependency and social justice: a challenge to conventional ideas of the social contract', in P. Lloyd-Sherlock (ed) *Living longer*, London and New York, NY: Zed Books, pp 275–99.

Nussbaum, M.C. (1998) 'Public philosophy and international feminism', *Ethics*, vol 108, no 4, pp 762–97.

O'Brien, J. and Tyne, A. (1981) *The principles of normalisation: A foundation for effective services*, London: Values Into Action.

OECD (Organisation for Economic Co-operation and Development) (1999) *A caring world: The new social policy agenda*, Paris: OECD.

OECD (2003a) *Transforming disability into ability: Policies to promote work and income security for disabled people*, Paris: OECD.

OECD (2003b) *Babies and bosses: Reconciling work and family life, volume 2, Austria, Ireland and Japan*, Paris: OECD.

Oliver, M. (1996) *Understanding disability: From theory to practice*, Basingstoke: Macmillan.

Oliver, M. (1997) 'Emancipatory research: realistic goal or impossible dream?', in C. Barnes and G. Mercer (eds) *Doing disability research*, Leeds: The Disability Press, pp 15-31.

ONS (Office for National Statistics) (2002) *Household satellite account methodology*, London: The Stationery Office.

ONS (2004a) *First release: 2004 annual survey of hours and earnings*, London: National Statistics.

ONS (2004b) *Social Trends 34*, London: The Stationery Office.

Orloff, A. (1993) 'Gender and the social rights of citizenship: state policies and gender relations in comparative research', *American Sociological Review*, vol 58, no 3, pp 303-28.

Österle, A., Hammer, E. and Haidinger, B. (2001) *The Austrian long-term care allowance in the context of welfare, care and work, National Report – Austria*, Vienna: Department of Social Policy, Vienna University of Economics and Business Administration.

Østerud, Ø., Engelstad, F. and Selle, P. (2003) *Makten og demokratiet: En sluttbok fra Makt- og demokratiutredningen*, Oslo: Gyldendal.

Overbye, E. (2005) 'Dilemmas in disability activation and how Scandinavians try to live with them', in P. Saunders (ed) *Welfare to work in practice: Social security and participation in economic and social life*, Aldershot: Ashgate, pp 155-71.

Pahl, J. (1980) 'Patterns of money management within marriage', *Journal of Social Policy*, vol 9, no 3, pp 313-35.

Pahl, J. (1989) *Money and marriage*, Basingstoke: Macmillan.

Pahl, J. (1995) 'His money, her money: recent research on financial organisation in marriage', *Journal of Economic Psychology*, vol 16, no 3, pp 361-76.

Pahl, J. (2005) 'Individualisation in couple finances: who pays for the children', *Social Policy and Society*, vol 4, no 4, pp 381-91.

Pahl, J. and Quine, L. (1987) 'Families with mentally handicapped children', in J. Orford (ed) *Coping with disorder in the family*, London: Croom Helm, pp 39-61.

Park, A., Philips, M. and Johnson, M. (2004) *Young people in Britain: The attitudes and experiences of 12 to 19 year olds*, London: National Centre for Social Research for Department for Education and Skills, available at: www.dfes.gov.uk/research/data/uploadfiles/RR564.pdf.

Parker, G. (1990) *With due care and attention: A review of research on informal care*, London: Family Policy Studies Centre.

Parker, G. (1993) 'Informal care of older people in Great Britain: the 1985 General Household Survey', in J. Twigg (ed) *Informal care in Europe*, York: Social Policy Research Unit, University of York, pp 151-69.

Parker, G. and Clarke, H. (2002) 'Making the ends meet: do carers and disabled people have a common agenda?', *Policy & Politics*, vol 30, no 3, pp 347-59.

Parker, G. and Lawton, D. (1994) *Different types of care, different types of carer: Evidence from the General Household Survey*, London: HMSO.

Parliamentary and Health Service Ombudsman (2005) *Tax credits: Putting things right*, Third Report, 2005-2006, HC 124, London: The Stationery Office.

Parry, J., Vegeris, S., Hudson, M., Barnes, H. and Taylor, R. (2004) *Independent living in later life*, Department for Work and Pensions Research Report No 216, London: Department for Work and Pensions.

Pawson, R. and Tilley, N. (1997) *Realistic evaluation*, London: Sage Publications.

People First (1994) *Outside but not inside ... yet! Leaving hospital and living in the community: An evaluation by people with learning difficulties*, London: People First.

Phillips, J., Bernard, M. and Chittenden, M. (2002) *Juggling work and care: The experiences of working carers of older adults*, Bristol: The Policy Press.

Pickard, L. (2001) 'Carer break or carer blind? Policies for informal carers in the UK', *Social Policy and Administration*, vol 35, no 4, pp 441-58.

Pickard, L. (2004) *The effectiveness and cost effectiveness of support and services to informal carers of older people*, London: Audit Commission.

Pijl, M. (2000) 'Home care allowances: good for many but not for all', *Practice*, vol 12, no 2, pp 55-65.

Plantenga, J. (2001) 'Combining work and care in the polder model: an assessment of the Dutch part-time strategy', Paper prepared for the CAVA International Seminar 1: 'New Divisions of Labour', University of Leeds, 19-21 January.

Pollard, S. (2003) 'The genie of choice: has it been let loose in Britain?', *National Review*, 30 June.

Postle, K. and Beresford, P. (2005) 'Capacity building and the reconception of political participation: a role for social care workers?', *British Journal of Social Work* (doi:10.1093/bjsw/bch330).

Postle, K., Wright, P. and Beresford, P. (2005) 'Older people's participation in political activity – making their voices heard: a potential support role for welfare professionals in countering ageism and social exclusion' (doi:10.1093/bjsw/bch330).

Preston, G. (2005) *Helter skelter: Families, disabled children and the benefit system*, London: Centre for the Analysis of Social Exclusion, London School of Economics and Political Science.

Priestley, M. (2003) *Disability: A life course approach*, Cambridge: Polity.

Prime Minister's Strategy Unit (2004) *Improving the life chances of disabled people: Analytical report*, London: Strategy Unit.

Prime Minister's Strategy Unit (2005) *Improving the life chances of disabled people: Final report*, London: Strategy Unit.

Prior, D., Stewart, J. and Walsh, K. (1995) *Citizenship, rights, community and participation*, London: Pitman Publishing.

Prior, L. (2003) 'Belief, knowledge and expertise: the emergence of the lay expert in medical sociology', *Sociology of Health and Illness*, vol 25, no 3, pp 41-57.

Quine, L. and Pahl, J. (1989) *Stress and coping in families caring for a child with severe mental handicap*, Canterbury: Centre for Health Services Studies, University of Kent.

Ratzka, A. (no date) *What is independent living – a personal definition*, available at: www.mosilc.org/cilmanual/WhatIL.htm, accessed March 2005.

Rawls, J. (1971) *A theory of justice*, Cambridge, MA: Harvard University Press.

RGWR (Reference Group on Welfare Reform) (2000) *Participation support for a more equitable society: Full report*, Canberra: Department of Family and Community Services.

Ridge, T. (2002) *Childhood poverty and social exclusion: From a child's perspective*, Bristol: The Policy Press.

Riedel, B. (1999) 'Dienstleistungen für pflegebedürftige Menschen und Pflegende', in Bundesministerium für Umwelt, Jugend und Familie (ed) *Familien & Arbeitswelt, 4, Österreichischer Familienbericht*, Band 2, Vienna: BMUJF, pp 102-15.

Roker, D. (1998) *Worth more than this: Young people growing up in family poverty*, London: The Children's Society.

Rønning, R. (2004) *Omsorg som vare? Kampen om omsorgens sjel i norske kommuner*, Oslo: Gyldendal Akademiske.

Rose, N. (1990) *Governing the soul: The shaping of the private self*, London: Routledge.

Rowlingson, K. (1994) *Moneylenders and their customers*, London: Policy Studies Institute.

Royal Commission on Long Term Care (1999) *With respect to old age: Long term care – rights and responsibilities*, Cm 4192-I, London: The Stationery Office.

Russell, A., Fieldhouse, E., Purdam, K. and Kalra, V. (2002) *The Electoral Commission research report: Voter engagement and young people*, The Electoral Commission (available at: www.electoralcommission.gov.uk).

Saunders, P. (2002) *The ends and means of welfare: Coping with economic and social change in Australia*, Melbourne: Cambridge University Press.

Saunders, P. (2003) *The meaning and measurement of poverty: Towards an agenda for action*, Submission to the Senate Community Affairs References Committee Inquiry into Poverty and Financial Hardship, Sydney: Social Policy Research Centre, University of New South Wales.

Saunders, P. (2005) *The poverty wars: Reconnecting research with reality*, Sydney: UNSW Press.

Saunders, P. and Adelman, L. (2004) 'Income poverty, deprivation and exclusion: a comparative study of Australia and Britain', Paper presented to the 28th General Conference of The International Association for Research in Income and Wealth (IARIW), Cork, Ireland, 22-28 August.

Saunders, P., Norris, K. and Brown, J. (2004) *Exploring the determinants and impact of participation among FaCS customers: Draft stage II report*, Prepared for the Department of Family and Community Services, Canberra, Sydney: Social Policy Research Centre, University of New South Wales.

Schmid, G. (2000) 'Transitional labour markets', in B. Marin, D. Meulders and D.J. Snower (eds) *Innovative employment initiatives*, Aldershot: Ashgate, pp 223-54.

Schwartz, B. (2004) *The paradox of choice*, New York, NY: HarperCollins.

Secretary of State for Health (2000) *The NHS plan: A plan for investment, a plan for reform*, London: The Stationery Office.

Secretary of State for Health and Social Services (2002a) 'Time to break up old, monolithic social services', Speech to the National Social Services Conference, Cardiff, 16 October.

Secretary of State for Health and Social Services (2002b) 'Expanded services and increased choices for older people', Department of Health press release, 23 July.

Seddon, D., Robinson, C. and Jones, K. (2004) *Carers in employment: Towards an integrated system of support*, Final report to the Wales Office of Research and Development for Health and Social Care, Bangor: Centre for Social Policy Research and Development, University of Wales.

Sen, A.K. (1999) *Development as freedom*, New York, NY: Anchor Books.

Sestoft, C. (2002) *Med hensyn til den politiske forbruger*, København: Akademisk Forlag.

Sevenhuijsen, S. (2000) 'Caring in the third way', *Critical Social Policy*, vol 20, no 1, pp 5-37.

Sevenhuijsen, S.L. (2002) 'A third way? Moralities, ethics and families: an approach through the ethic of care', in A. Carling, S. Duncan and R. Edwards (eds) *Analysing families: Morality and rationality in policy and practice*, London: Routledge, pp 129-44.

Seymour, W. (1989) *Bodily alterations: An introduction to a sociology of the body for health workers*, Sydney: Allen & Unwin.

Shakespeare, T. (2000) *Help*, Birmingham: Venture Press.

Shearn, J. and Todd, S. (2000) 'Maternal employment and family responsibilities: the perspectives of mothers of children with intellectual disabilities', *Journal of Applied Research in Intellectual Disabilities*, vol 13, no 3, pp 109-31.

Simon, A. and Owen, C. (2005) 'Using the Labour Force Survey to map the care workforce', *Labour Market Trends*, vol 113, no 5, pp 201-8.

Skills for Care (2005) *Skills research and intelligence annual report No 2*, Leeds: Commission for Social Care Inspection.

Skinner, C. (2003) *Running around in circles: Coordinating childcare, education and work*, Bristol: The Policy Press.

Skinner, C. (2005) 'Co-ordination points: a hidden factor in reconciling work and family life', *Journal of Social Policy*, vol 34, no 1, pp 99-119.

Slagsvold, B. (1995) *Mål eller mening*, Rapport nr. 1, PhD thesis, Oslo: Norsk Gerontologisk Institutt.

Smale, G., Tuson, G. and Statham, D. (2000) *Social work and social problems: Working towards social inclusion and social change*, Basingstoke: Macmillan.

Smart, C., Neale, B. and Wade, A. (2001) *The changing experience of childhood: Families and divorce*, Cambridge: Polity.

Smyth, M. and Robus, N. (1989) *The financial circumstances of families with disabled children living in private households*, OPCS Report 5, London: HMSO.

Snape, D., Molloy, D. and Kumar, M. (1999) *Relying on the state, relying on each other*, Research Report 103, London: Department of Social Security.

Speak, S. and Graham, S. (2000) *Service not included: Social implications of private sector service restructuring in marginalized neighbourhoods*, Bristol: The Policy Press.

SSI (Social Services Inspectorate) (1996) *Carers (Recognition and Services) Act 1995: Practice guide*, London: Department of Health.

SSI (2002) *The state of social care in England 2001*, London: Department of Health.

Städtner, K. (2002) *Arbeitsmarktrelevante konsequenzen der inanspruchnahme von Elternkarenz*, Working Paper 25 – 2002, Vienna: Austrian Institute for Family Studies.

Stainton, T. and Boyce, S. (2004) "I have got my life back': users' experience of direct payments', *Disability & Society*, vol 19, no 5, pp 443-54.

Stanley, K. and Lohde, L.A. (2004) *Sanctions and sweeteners: Rights and responsibilities in the benefits system*, London: Institute for Public Policy Research.

Statistik Austria (2003a) *Statistisches jahrbuch 2003*, Vienna: Statistik Austria.

Statistik Austria (2003b) *Kindertagesheimstatistik*, Vienna: Statistik Austria.

Stelzer-Orthofer, C. (2001) 'Auf dem weg zu einem schlanken sozialstaat? Zur privatisierung sozialer risken im österreichischen sozialen sicherungssystem', *Kurswechsel*, no 4, pp 51-59.

Stevens, A. (2004) 'Survival of the ideas that fit: towards a selection bias framework for the use of evidence in policy', Paper submitted to *Evidence & Policy*, University of Kent.

Strell, M. and Duncan, S. (2001) 'Lone motherhood, ideal type care regimes and the case of Austria', *Journal of European Social Policy*, vol 11, no 2, pp 149-64.

Such, E. and Walker, R. (2004) 'Being responsible and responsible beings: children's understanding of responsibility', *Children & Society*, vol 18, no 3, pp 231-42.

Sutherland, A., Beresford, P. and Shamash, M. (2005) *The barriers experienced by disabled people*, London: Disability Rights Commission.

Szebehely, M. (1995) *Vardagens organisering: Om vårdbiträden och gamla i hemtjänsten*, Lund: Arkiv Forlag.

Tálos, E. (1999) 'Atypische beschäftigung in Österreich', in E. Tálos (ed) *Atpypische beschäftigung: Internationale trends und sozialstaatliche regelungen: Europa, USA*, Vienna: Manz, pp 252-84.

Taylor, C. (1971) 'Interpretation and the sciences of man', *Review of Metaphysics*, vol 25, no 1, pp 3-51.

Taylor-Gooby, P. (2004) 'The work-centred welfare state', in A. Park, J. Curtice, K. Thomson, C. Bromley and M. Phillips (eds) *British social attitudes: The 21st report*, London: National Centre for Social Research, pp 1-22.

Taylor-Gooby, P. (ed) (2005) *New risks, new welfare*, Oxford: Oxford University Press.

The Guardian (2003) 'The price of failure', 22 October.

The Guardian (2004a) 'Nursing home group is sold for £560 million', 30 November.

The Guardian (2004b) 'Six poised to buy 3i nursing homes', 14 October.

The Observer (2002) 'A home unfit for heroes', 9 June.

Thomas, P. (1985) *The aims and outcomes of social policy research*, London: Croom Helm.

Thomson, P. (2002) *Reforming our public services*, London: Office of Public Services Reform.

Thornton, P. and Corden, A. (2005) 'Personalised employment services for disability benefits recipients: are comparisons useful?', in P. Saunders (ed) *Welfare to work in practice: Social security and participation in economic and social life*, Aldershot: Ashgate, pp 173-85.

Thorsen, K. and Wærness, K. (eds) (1999) *Blir omsorgen borte? Eldreomsorgens hverdag i den senmoderne velferdsstaten*, Oslo/Bergen: Ad Notam Gyldendal, pp 11-24.

Timmermans, J.M. (2003) *Mantelzorg: Over de hulp van en aan mantelzorgers*, The Hague: Sociaal en Cultureel Planbureau, p 254.

Tinker, A. (1995) 'Housing and older people', in I. Allen and E. Perkins (eds) *The future of family care for older people*, London: HMSO, pp 181-200.

Titmuss, R. (1967) *Choice and the welfare state*, Fabian Tract 370, London: Fabian Society.

Todd, M. and Taylor, M. (2004) 'Introduction', in M. Todd and M. Taylor (eds) *Democracy and participation: Popular protest and new social movements*, London: The Merlin Press, pp 1-28.

Togeby, L., Andersen, J.G., Christiansen, P.M., Jørgensen, T.B. and Vallgårda, S. (2003) *Magt og demokrati i Danmark: Hovedresultater fra Magtudredningen*, Århus: Aarhus Universitetsforlag.

Tozer, R. and Thornton, P. (1995) *A meeting of minds: Older people as research advisers*, York: Social Policy Research Unit, University of York.

Travers, P. and Robertson, F. (1996) *Relative deprivation among DSS clients: Results of a pilot survey*, Monograph No 2, Adelaide: National Institute of Labour Studies, Flinders University.

Turner, M., Brough, P. and Williams-Findlay, R. (2003) *Our voice in our future: Service users debate the future of the welfare state*, York: Joseph Rowntree Foundation.

Twigg, J. (2000) *Bathing: The body and community care*, London: Routledge.

Twigg, J. and Atkin, K. (1994) *Carers perceived: Policy and practice in informal care*, Buckingham: Open University Press.

Ungerson, C. (1987) *Policy is personal*, London: Tavistock.

Ungerson, C. (1997) 'Social politics and commodification of care', *Social Politics*, vol 4, no 3, pp 362-81.

Ungerson, C. (1999) 'Personal assistants and disabled people: an examination of a hybrid form of work and care', *Work, Employment & Society*, vol 13, no 4, pp 583-600.

Ungerson, C. (2000) *Care work: Gender, labor and the welfare state*, London: Routledge.

Ungerson, C. (2003) 'Commodified care work in European labour markets', *European Societies*, vol 5, no 4, pp 377-96.

Ungerson, C. (2004) 'Whose empowerment and independence? A cross-national perspective on 'cash for care' schemes', *Ageing & Society*, vol 24, no 2, pp 189-212.

van Staveren, I. (2001) *The values of economics: An Aristotelian perspective*, London and New York, NY: Routledge.

Vegeris, S. and Perry, J. (2001) *Families and children 2001: Living standards and the children*, Department for Work and Pensions Research Report No 190, Leeds: Corporate Document Services.

Wærness, K. (1975) 'Kvinners omsorgsarbeid i den ulønnede produksjon', Arbeidsnotat nr 80, Levekårsundersøkelsen, published in English: Wærness, K. (1978) 'The invisible welfare state: women's work at home', *Acta Sociologica*, vol 21 supplement, Special Congress Issue: The Nordic Welfare States, pp 193-208.

Wærness, K. (1982) *Kvinneperspektiver på sosialpolitikken*, Bergen: Universitetsforlaget.

Wærness, K. (1984) 'The rationality of caring', in M. Söder (ed) *Economic and industrial democracy*, London: Sage Publications, pp 185-212.

Wærness, K. (1999) 'Hva er hensikten med sammenliknende studier av effektiviteten i pleie-og omsorgssektoren i norske kommuner?', *Sosialøkonomen*, no 1/99, pp 12-14.

Walker, A. (1997) 'Community care policy: from consensus to conflict', in J. Bornat, J. Johnson, C. Pereira, D. Pilgrim and F. Williams (eds) *Community care: A reader* (2nd edn), Basingstoke: Macmillan, in association with the Open University, pp 196-220.

Walker, D. (2001) 'The party's over', *The Guardian*, 16 January, available at: www.guardian.co.uk/analysis/story/0,3604,422763,00.html.

Walsh, A. and Lister, R. (1985) *Mother's life-line: A survey of how women use and value Child Benefit*, London: Child Poverty Action Group.

Walter, I., Nutley, S. and Davies, H. (2003) *Research impact: A cross-sector literature review*, St Andrews: Research Unit for Research Utilisation, Department of Management, St Andrew's University.

Ward, L. (1997) 'Funding for change: translating emancipatory disability research from theory to practice', in C. Barnes and G. Mercer (eds) *Doing disability research*, Leeds: The Disability Press, pp 32-49.

Ward, S. (2002) *Politicians must exploit internet to win 'apathetic' young voters – study*, ESRC press release (available at: www.esrcsocietytoday.ac.uk/ ESRCInfoCentre/PO/releases/2002/september/ politicians.aspx?ComponentId=2168&SourcePageId=1403).

Warde, A. (1996) 'Afterword: the future of the sociology of consumption', in S. Edgell, K. Hetherington and A. Warde (eds) *Consumption matters*, Oxford: Blackwell Publishers, pp 302-12.

Waterplas, L. and Samoy, E. (2001) 'Attribution d'un budget personnalisé: nouvelle panacée ou cheval de troie dans les dispositifs de services aux personnes handicapées?', *Handicap – revue de sciences humaines et sociales*, no 90, pp 1-27.

Watson, N., McKie, L., Hughes, B., Hopkins, B. and Gregory, S. (2005) '(Inter)dependence, needs and care', *Sociology*, vol 38, no 2, pp 331-50.

Weiss, C. (1986) 'Research and policy-making: a limited partnership', in F. Heller (ed) *The use and abuse of social science*, London: Sage Publications, pp 214-35.

Weiss, C.H. and Bucuvalas, M.J. (1980) *Social science research and decision making*, New York, NY: Columbia University Press.

Wendell, S. (1996) *The rejected body: Feminist philosophical reflections on disability*, London: Routledge.

White, M. (2003) 'Held to ransom', *CareandHealth Magazine*, no 44, 8 October.

Whiteford, P. (2000) *The Australian system of social protection – an overview*, Policy Research Paper No 1, Canberra: Department of Family and Community Services.

Whyley, C. and Brooker, S. (2004) *Home credit: An investigation into the UK home credit market*, London: National Consumer Council.

Whyley, C., Collard, S. and Kempson, E. (2000) *Saving and borrowing*, Department of Social Security Research Report No 125, Leeds: Corporate Document Services.

Wiener, J. (2003) 'The role of informal support in long term care', in J. Brodsky, J. Habib and M. Hirschfeld (eds) *Key policy issues in long term care*, Geneva: World Health Organization, pp 3-24.

Wiener, J., Tilly, J. and Cuellar, A.E. (2003) *Consumer directed home care in the Netherlands, England and Germany*, Washington: AARP Public Policy Institute.

Williams, F. (1999) 'Good enough principles for welfare', *Journal of Social Policy*, vol 28, no 4, pp 667-87.

Williams, F. (2004) *Rethinking families*, London: Calouste Gulbenkian Foundation.

Wintour, P. (2001) 'Hi-tech voting aims to raise turnout', *The Guardian*, 23 November, p 10.

Woodland, S., Mandy, W. and Miller, M. (2003) *Easing the transition into work (part 2 – client survey)*, Department for Work and Pensions Research Report No 186, Leeds: Corporate Document Services.

Woodland, S., Miller, M. and Tipping, S. (2002) *Repeat study of parents' demand for childcare*, Department for Education and Skills Research Report No 348, Nottingham: Department for Education and Skills.

Woolley, M. (2004) *Income and expenditure of families with a severely disabled child*, York: Family Fund.

Wörister, K. (2001) 'Eigenständige absicherung von frauen, Entwicklungen in Österreich und aktuelle Reformvorschläge', *Soziale Sicherheit*, vol 53, no 3, pp 269-82.

Work and Pensions Committee (2003) *Childcare for working parents: Fifth report of session 2002-03: Volume 1*, HC 564-I, London: The Stationery Office.

Wright, P. and Treacher, A. (1982) *The problem of medical knowledge: Examining the social construction of medicine*, Edinburgh: Edinburgh University Press.

Young, I.M. (1990) *Justice and the politics of difference*, Oxford: Princeton University Press.

Young, K., Ashby, D., Boaz, A. and Grayson, L. (2002) 'Social science and the evidence based policy movement', *Social Policy and Society*, vol 1, no 3, pp 215-24.

Zaidi, A. and Burchardt, T. (2003) *Comparing incomes when needs differ: Equivalisation for the extra costs of disability in the UK*, CASE Paper No 64, London: Centre for the Analysis of Social Exclusion, London School of Economics and Political Science.

Zarb, G. and Nadash, P. (1994) *Cashing in on independence*, Derby: British Council of Organisations of Disabled People.

Zelizer, V. (1997) *The social meaning of money: Pin money, paychecks, poor relief, and other currencies*, Princeton, NJ: Princeton University Press.

Index

Page references for tables are in *italics*; those for notes are followed by *n*.